CW01464214

EYEWITN

The Great Northern Coalfield

EYEWITNESS:

The Great Northern Coalfield

Edited by Mike Kirkup

TUPS Books

© Mike Kirkup 1999

Published by TUPS Books
30 Lime Street, Newcastle upon Tyne NE1 2PQ

Typeset by Sumner Type, London SE22
Printed by Trade Union Printing Services, Newcastle
upon Tyne

A C.I.P. catalogue record for this book is available
from the British Library

ISBN: 1 901237 10 9

CONTENTS AND SOURCES

Benwell, Walbottle, Wylam,
Jarrow, Hebburn, St Hilda's,
Friar's Goose, Team, Ellison Main,
Brandling, Garesfield, Walridge, Pelton,
Hartley, Sunderland, Pemberton Main,
South Hetton, Letch, Broomside,
Whitwell, Beamish, St Helen's Auckland
Old Etherley, Middlesbro' Drops,
Whitworth Park, Port Clarence.

ACKNOWLEDGEMENTS

Thanks to descendants of Chester Armstrong and Methuen publishers for permission to print extracts from *Pilgrimage from Nenthead*; to Denise Robertson and Constable publishers for permission to use extracts from *A Year of Winter*; to the executors of Jack Davison's estate for permission to use extracts from *History of Northumberland Miners 1929–39*; to George Hetherington for his 1980 president's address to the North of England branch of the Institute of Mechanical Engineers; to Woodhorn Colliery Museum for a copy of the 1916 Woodhorn disaster inquest; to Keith Armstrong of Northern Voices for permission to include the Spennymoor Settlement extracts from *Homespun*, published in 1992; and to all other copyright holders whom we have tried but failed to contact. The 'Pitmen's Derby' extract was first published by MidNAG in 1990; Sir John Hall's memories of North Seaton were first published in *Was there ever Railway Row?* (Woodhorn Press, 1996).

Thanks also to the following for the use of personal photos: Michael Beattie, Frank Ramsay, Nancy James, Gladys Mitchell, Foster Proudlock, Ian S. Carr. And for photo reproduction to Jack Wallace, Reuben Daglish, and Jim Brooks.

THE GREAT NORTHERN COALFIELD
William Fordyce, 1860

The lineal boundaries assume the form of an irregular triangle. To follow the line, leave the Tees near to Port Clarence where the boundary line on the south proceeds by the coast to Hartlepool, thence it follows by the old Hartlepool Dock and Railway line, passing through Monk Hesleton Dean, near to Castle Eden, south of Hutton Henry.

To make a straight line of boundary, we may, perhaps, go not so far south as Wynyard, or Newton Parks, thence on by Sherraton, Chilton, the Clarence Railway, to Middridge, East Thickley, Brusselton, south of Witton Park Iron Works, Evenwood, Norwood, Cowden, Cockfield Fell, Butter Knowle, and Copley Bent, in the parishes of Langsack-cum-Softley, where it joins the extreme boundary.

The country beyond that point is mountainous and destitute of workable Coal seams. After forming an angle at Copley Bent, the boundary line proceeds in a northerly direction, with a slight inclination towards the east, in nearly a straight course to the Derwent, near to Hamsterley Hall, before which it crosses the river Wear below Wolsingham, thence towards Towlaw, Thornley Colliery, and Hedley Hope, and then to Consett, near Shotley Bridge, on the Derwent.

The Coal seams 'crop' out at Newland, and many places along the hill towards the Derwent, putting in again near to the more elevated crown woods at Chopwell, Garesfield, Hedley, Stella, Townley, and Mickley; and again cropping out west in the lowlands near the Tyne, at Horsley Wood, near Wylam, and westward at Bywell. Thence the course of the boundary is over Prestwick Carr, past Mitford near Morpeth, towards the harbour of Amble on the Sea near Warkworth.

The Coal-measures slope or dip from the outcrop towards the sea, from Widdrington Castle on the north coast to Castle Eden near Hartlepool, in a south-easterly direction. On the west and north-west they are bounded by the out-cropping of the underlying millstone grit and mountain limestone, which, in some cases, causes the Coal to be found in patches, as at Shilbottle, Scremerston, Newton-on-the-Moor, and other places, such as North Tyne, Acomb, and Stublick.

The lowest working seams of Coal are at Monkwearmouth Pit, under the limestone, where the shaft, which is about one mile distant from the 100 feet above the level of the sea, has been sunk to the depth of nearly 1,700 feet to the Hutton seam, below which, as usual, will be found the Beaumont, Harvey or Townley, Five-Quarter, Stone Coal, Three-Quarter and Brockwell seams.

1

IMAGINE LIFE WITHOUT COAL

If all the mines of precious metals were closed at once, and if gold and silver were no longer obtained for our use, society would, after certain evolutions and adjustments in adopting other representatives of value, go on as before. But let civilised communities be deprived of their Coal, and it is difficult to see how they could hold together as before.

There can be no denying that when this statement was made at the beginning of the 19th century by Dr Buckland in his Bridgewater Treatise, the true source of Britain's wealth lay in thick, vigorous coal seams, running many fathoms below the surface. The annual production in 1840 of all the gold and silver mines of North and South America, as it was then, was estimated at a little over £9 million. British coal brought in revenue of £16 million at the pit head, and £30 million at its place of consumption. As the learned Dr Buckland noted, we could all get along quite well without the glitter of gold and silver, but deprive the nation of its coal, and Britain at that time would have faced financial ruin. In the early 1800s, coal was not only used as a means of warmth for rich and poor alike, but it fuelled the Industrial Revolution which turned Britain into the factory of the world, supplying the needs of those in remote regions of the globe. Imagine life without coal at the height of the manufacturing boom: James Watt staring at a clay-cold kettle; functionless forges and foundries; Stephenson's Rocket anchored to the buffers; a non-gyrating spinning jenny; and, with Bessemer deprived of coal, the vital ingredient for his steel-making process, we would still be using the crude implements of savages as cutlery. Without coal, Britain would have been one of the lesser players in the game of high finance as it literally ran out of steam with factories closed; railways left to rust; steamships dismantled and decaying in dock; manufacturing returned to its original cottage industry.

Yes, indeed, this nation owes a lot to coal and to its miners. It was because of the rape of another of Britain's natural resources, timber, that coal began to be used in quantity for domestic purposes towards the end of the 13th century. Indiscriminate felling of trees led to a shortage and householders began to burn coal. Immediately the new fuel was looked upon with suspicion. Parliament petitioned Edward I on the subject and he prohibited the burning of 'Sea-coale' in London and the suburbs 'to avoid the sulpherous smoke and savour of the firing'. The king also commanded everyone to burn only wood on their fires; the only exceptions being black-smiths. From Stowe's *Chronicles* comes the news that 'Within thirty years last, the nice dames of London would not come into any house or roome where Sea-coales were burned, nor willingly eat of the meat that was either sod or roasted with Sea-coale'. It was not long, however, before even the king succumbed to the delights of a coal fire, and it was reported that less than twenty years after his initial proclamation, Edward was burning coal in the grate of the royal palace. A periodical published in 1649 by W. Blithe stated: 'It was not many years since the famous city of London petitioned the Parliament of England against two nuisances; and these were Newcastle Coals, in regard of their stench etc; and Hops, in regard they would spoil the taste of drink and endanger the people.' In that same year it was reported that 'many thousand people are employed in this trade of coals, many live by conveying them in waggons and wains to the river Tine and many are employed in conveying the coals in keels from the staiths aboard the ship'.

As trade increased, so there came an increase in the number of men employed in coal-winning, and it is estimated that by the early 1800s the Newcastle coal trade employed something like 6,530 pitmen, whilst the total number of pitmen employed in the sea-exporting collieries at Blyth, Hartley, Newcastle and Sunderland, amounted to 9,700.

Soon distinguished writers began extolling the virtues of coal. In the mid-19th century, Leigh Hunt observed:

I am one of those who delight in a fireside, and can enjoy it even without the help of a cat or tea-kettle, My fire is left quite to itself; it has full room to breathe and blaze, and I can poke it as I please! What recollections does that idea excite! Poke it as I please. Think, benevolent reader, think of the pride and pleasure of having in your hands that awful, but at the same time artless weapon, a poker; of putting it into the proper bar— gently levering up the Coals, and seeing the instant and bustling flame above.

To what can I compare that moment? That sudden empyreal enthusiasm? That fiery expression of vivification? That ardent acknow-ledgement, as it were, of the care and kindliness of the operator?

At night, the window which presents a large face of watery grey intersected by strong lines, is imperceptibly becoming darker; and as that becomes darker, the fire assumes a more glowing presence. The contemplatist keeps his easy posture, absorbed in his fancies; and everything around him is still and serene. This is the only time, perhaps, at which sheer idleness is salutary and refreshing.

How observed with the smallest effort is every trick and aspect of the fire. A Coal falling in; a fluttering flame; a miniature mockery of a flash of lightning—nothing escapes the eye and the imagination. Sometimes a little flame appears at the corner of the grate like a quivering spangle; sometimes it swells out at top into a restless and brief lambency.

Soon it is seen only by a light beneath the grate, or it curls around one of the bars like a tongue, or darts out with a spiral thinness and a sulphureous and continued puffing as from a reed.

The glowing Coals meantime exhibit the shifting forms of hills and vales and gulfs; of fiery Alps, whose heat is inhabitable even by spirits, or of black precipices, from which swart fairies seem about to swing away on sable wings; then heat and fire are forgotten, and walled towns appear, and figures of unknown animals, and far distant countries scarcely to be reached by human journey; then coaches, and camels, and barking dogs as large as either, and forms that combine every shape and suggest every fancy; till at last the ragged Coals tumbling together, reduce the vision to chaos, and the huge profile of a gaunt and grinning face seems to make jest of all that has passed.

During these creations of the eye, the thought roves about into a hundred abstractions, some of them suggested by the fire, some of them arising from the general sensation of comfort and composure.

When left alone, there is sometimes a charm in watching out the decaying fire, in getting closer and closer to it with tilted chair and knees against the bars, and letting the whole multitude of fancies that work in the night silence, come whispering about the yielding faculties. The world around is silent; and for a moment the very cares of day seem to have gone with it to sleep, leaving you to snatch a waking sense of disenthral-ment, and to commune with a thousand airy visitants that come to play with innocent thoughts.

But earth recalls us again—the last flame is out. The fading embers tinkle with a dreariness; and the chill reminds us where we should be. Another gaze on the hearth that has cheered us, and the last lingering action is to wind up the watch for the next day.

Romans burned coal on Hadrian's Wall

The first written record of the existence of coal is the description of a fossil given by Theophrastus, a pupil of Aristotle, although the use of the word 'coal' in the Scriptures could have meant the burning of wood. The early Chinese were also said to have burned coal, and even as late as the mid-19th century numerous mines were worked in China; these were of the most rudimentary kind, without shafts or machinery at all. A flint axe found in a vein of coal at Craig Y Parc, Monmouthshire in Wales, is proof that the use of coal was known to the Ancient Britons; and ashes discovered along the Roman Wall at Lanchester and Ebchester show that coal was being burned by Roman legions as they set about building and defending Hadrian's Wall.

One of the earliest documents in which coal is mentioned is the

Bolden Book (1180) of Bishop Pudsey; this detailed record contained the services on all the demesne lands and possessions of the
Bishopric of Durham. In this document, though the term
'woodlades' frequently occurs, it refers to coal at Escomb, near
Bishop Auckland, where 'a collier holds a toft and a croft, and four
acres, providing Coals for the cart-smith of Coundon'. At
Bishopwearmouth, 'the smith has twelve acres for the ironwork of
the carts, and finds his own Coals'. And at Sedgefield the smith had
one oxgang with similar conditions. During this time the coal was to
be found as an outcrop into a field. Later delving led to
perpendicular boring, resulting in a drift-mine which in turn led to
horizontal working, away from the original pit mouth. The people
who worked in the coalmines 600 or 700 years ago were unwilling
workers who had been employed on the land. Scottish miners were
often chained to the mine to stop them absconding. In some
European countries during the same period, the mines were worked
entirely by slaves and criminals.

Early coalmining activities in the North-East

The following is taken from Fynes, *History of Northumberland and
Durham Miners* (1873), and W. Fordyce's *History of Coal, Coke,
and Coalfields in Northern England* (1860).

1239   A special charter by Henry III granted 'to the good men of
       Newcastle licence to dig coals in the common soil of the
       ground, without the walls thereof, in the place called Castle
       Field and the Forth, and from thence to draw and convert
       them to their own profit in aid of their fee-farm rent of £100
       per annum'.

1280   The revenue raised from coals in Newcastle amounted to
       £200.

1330   The Priory of Tynemouth leased a colliery called Heygrove
       at 'Elstewyke' (Elswick) for £5, and other collieries nearby
       for a similar sum. Edward III granted further licences to

Newcastle for work in the Castle Field and Castle Moor. He also issued orders that coals won in the Gateshead coalfield be taken across the Tyne in boats to Newcastle on condition that they paid the usual port fees. The coals were then dispatched to any part of Britain. Foreign exporting was not allowed, unless it was to Calais. Coalfields opened at Collierly, near Lanchester.

1343   Similar collieries began at Merrington and Ferryhill.

1367   More pits were worked at Winlaton, and 676 chauldrons were purchased from here, consigned for the Clerk of Works at Windsor Castle.

1500   Collieries worked at Gateshead, Whickham, and Tynemouth

1530   Mines now let for £20 a year, with a condition that not more than twenty chauldrons be drawn in a single day.

1538   Tynemouth Priory let a further two mines at a yearly rent of £50.

1554   Queen Mary granted a lease of 21 years on the mines 'within the fields and and bounds at Elstwick'.

1582   Queen Elizabeth I obtained a 99-year lease of the manors of Gateshead and Whickham for £90 per annum. This 'Grand Lease', as it was called, caused a rapid increase in trade. The lease was eventually handed over to Sir William Riddell for the use of the Mayor and Burgesses of Newcastle in consideration of a fee of £12,000. From the outset of this period of the 'Grand Lease' coal prices fluctuated enormously, rising from six shillings a chauldron to nine shillings. Hackles rose in London, whose Lord Mayor complained to his Lord Treasurer against what he considered the exorbitant prices being charged by the Newcastle hostmen (coalowners).

1601   Sunderland was beginning to come to the fore as a coal exporter—so much so that the Newcastle hostmen tried to shackle them with a duty of one shilling a chauldron (53 cwt).

1602   The number of hostmen who sold coal from Newcastle was set at a maximum of twenty-eight, who were limited to winning precisely 9,080 tons of coal a year and providing 85 keel boats for their coastal transport.

1606 Mr Bowes, after whom the Bowes Museum is named, died, but not before writing: 'There is coles gotten in five several places of the Biddick estates, the furthest place thereof is not 3 miles from the house; and I have sonke a shaft within the domaine, having only bestowed £4 charges, and have already gotten some coles, which if the seame of coles prove to be 3 quarters of a yard thick, the same with £200 stock will yeald clear profit.'

1615 The number of vessels rose to 400, half of which supplied London, and the other half the rest of England. The French also traded with Newcastle during this period, often sending as many as 50 sailing ships in a combined fleet to carry the Newcastle coals to Picardy, Normandy, Bretagne and other ports.

1616 The quantity of coals coming out of Newcastle mines and shipped from the port was 13,675 tons.

1625 A patent was granted by James VI of Scotland to Mr David Ramsey for the discovery of an engine for raising water from coal mines. Various other methods were modified from this invention.

1632 The first railways with wooden rails and sleepers were introduced into the North-East coalfields. The cost of the wooden rails, known in other parts of the country as Newcastle Roads, was approximately £600 per mile (T. J. Taylor). Mr Grey, in his book *Chorographia,* stated:

Some south gentlemen upon hope of benefit came into the county of Durham to hazard their monies in Coal mines; Mr Beaumont, a gentleman of great ingenuity and rare parts, adventured into our mines with his £30,000, who brought many rare engines not known in these parts, as the art to bore with rods to try the deepness and thickness of the Coal—rare engines to draw water out of the pits—waggons with one horse to draw coals from the pits to the staiths and to the river. Within a few years he consumed all his money, and rode home upon a light horse.

The waggons introduced by Beaumont revolutionised the conveyance of coal.

1635 The Jury of Bedlington, in a list of the Bishop's rights, say: 'There is one pit wherein coals are wrought and two other pits sunk, but no coal received as yet. Rent received for the colliery, £2.'

1640 Trade in coals, as in all other commodities in and around Newcastle, slumped when the town fell into the hands of the Covenanters and found itself in a state of siege. From being the main employers of some 10,000 men and boys, the coal bosses found that barely a tenth of that number were fit for any kind of strenuous work. Scores of people fled from the area, thinking the marauding Scots would show them no mercy. More than 100 London ships arriving off Tynemouth Bar the day after the battle and, hearing of the possession of the town by the Scots, returned to the Thames with empty holds. Even after the kilted warriors had quit the town, the canny folks of Newcastle found their misfortune continuing.

1642 In January, an Act of Parliament prohibited ships from carrying coals or salt from 'Newcastle, Sunderland, or Blithe'. Further restrictions on local trade conspired to make coal so expensive that a chauldron in London, which only a few years before had cost a few shillings, rose in price to an incredible £4.

1643 The Parliamentarians were made to see sense on 12 May, when it was ordained

that there be a free and open trade in the port of Sunderland in the County of Durham and Blithe in the County of Northumberland, to relieve the poor inhabitants thereabouts by reasons of rapines and spoyls those enemies of Newcastle have brought upon them in these two Counties, they all being in great want and extremety.

1655 About 320 keels were now being used to carry coal on the Tyne.

1673 A treatise called *The Grand Concern of England* suggested that the coal trade should in future be managed by Commissioners empowered to supply all ports of the nation with coals at a uniform rate, saying: 'We need not declare how the subjects are abused in the price of coals; how many poor have been starved for want of fewel by reason of the horrid prices put upon them, especially in time of War, either by the Merchants, or the Woodmonger, or between them both.' The reopening of the coal-trade ports and the removal of all restrictions saw trade booming.

1676 Railways of a kind were now in use and were looked upon as a great novelty. Newcastle's Lord Keeper Guildford described the early form of transport in these words:

The manner of carriage of coals is by laying rails of timber from the colliery down to the river, exactly straight and parallel: and bulky carts are made with four rowlers fitting these rails whereby the carriage is so easy that one horse will down four or five chauldrons of coal, and is an immense benefit to the coal merchants.'

Sir Thomas Liddell, of Ravensworth Castle, is said to have laid the first waggonway down from the Teams Colliery to the staiths on the Tyne, near to Derwenthaugh.

1677 Lumley and Hetton collieries in county Durham, and the mine at Jesmond near Newcastle, had chain pumps worked by water wheels to extract excess water from the mine.

1693 Lease granted to Edward Arden, Esq. 'of the coal mines opened, and to be opened, within the lordship of Bedlington with wayleave for 21 years at 40s.[£2] per annum'.

1699 It was reported that no fewer than 14,000 ships were now engaged in the coal-carrying trade from Newcastle. With the continued demand, more and more new collieries were being opened in the North-East. New methods of raising coal were introduced, wooden rails were laid, and waggons to carry each chauldron were brought into use. Before the introduction of waggons and waggonways, coal had to be transported either in keels or in carts. It was recorded by one of Newcastle's hostmen: 'From time out of mynd it hath been accustomed that all cole waynes did usuallie cary and bring eight bouls of coles to all the staithes upon the River Tine, but of late years severall hath brought only or scarce seven bouls.' Before rails were laid some coals were carried to the staithes in panniers on horseback.

1700   Newcomen's application of the steam-engine to drain water was raised by engines worked by horses.

1705   On 25 April the Hon. Charles Montague sank the West Pit at Benwell.

1708   Windmills were erected to work pumps in several collieries, but were ineffectual in calm weather.

1709   The common depth of a mine in and around Newcastle was from 20 to 30 fathoms (a fathom being 6 ft), but some were as deep as 60 fathoms. The expense of sinking a shaft was about £55, and the cost of drawing the coals to the surface, using a horse-gin, was £28.

1710   At Bensham Colliery the first attempt was made to reach the Low Main seam in the neighbourhood of Newcastle. The colliery exploded, with the loss of 80 lives.

1714   A steam-engine was used at Byker for the first time, although similar engines were already in use at Oxclose, near Washington, and Norwood, near Ravensworth.

1771   On 17 November Wylam Colliery was inundated by the flood which destroyed the Tyne Bridge.

1777   The invention of cast-iron tramways by Curr of Sheffield became known as the plate rail. Curr also adopted the method of bringing coals to the surface from the coal-face in the same carriage (later called a tub), which was guided up the shaft by conductors. Some keel boats were later fitted with these tubs, holding coals which until then had been dumped in a heap on the bottom of the boat.

1790   Towards the end of the 18th century the wooden rails gave way to iron ones, and wherever there was an inclined plane horses were replaced by a large coiling drum. By this means light waggons were drawn up the bank by the weight of full ones on the way down. A rope was attached to each set of waggons as well as to the drum, which was fixed at the top of the hill. This latter invention was the work of a Mr Barnes, who first used it at Benwell Colliery. With the increase in knowledge concerning transport it was little wonder that a further boost was given to coal production in and around Newcastle. By now, 500,000 chauldrons were being exported from the Tyne.

1792   Hebburn Colliery, which began in this year, used steam power to draw 30,000 gallons per minute out of the pit. At the Murton winning of the South Hetton Colliery, the water feeders were estimated at 8,000 gallons per minute. Water coming out of a coal-mine was much purer than might be imagined. Many coal villages, such as Ashington, relied on pit water for domestic use. Some of the water, however, contained more salt than that found in the sea.

1794   Malleable iron rails partially laid down at Walbottle Colliery. Thirty persons killed at Picktree Colliery, 27 of whom were buried in one grave at Chester-le-Street.

1808   Iron rails now used in the Earl of Carlisle's Colliery, at Tindale Fell. Explosion at Harraton killed four men and 21 horses; when the pit was reopened four months later, a pit pony was found alive and well.

1809   Sunderland port now exporting over 300,000 chauldrons annually and Newcastle 500,000.

1810   Coal shipped from Blyth and Hartley for the last ten years amounted to 390,000 chauldrons. The staiths at Blyth were once regarded as a branch of Newcastle, and, as such, one shilling (5p.) duty per chauldron was imposed on all coal exported from the town. A petition representing Blyth and Hartley was presented to the House of Commons, and the duty was ordered 'to be laid down and no more taken up'.

1814   George Stephenson's steam-engine was constructed for the Killingworth Colliery Railway. With Stephenson's original Wylam engine, this constituted the start of the modern railway system, which was developed throughout the country and, in turn, the entire world.Ten years later the railway system, using malleable rails, was extensively used on the Stockton and Darlington Railway.

Carrying coals to Newcastle

As reported in the Portland manuscripts, 1725:

From Chester[-le-Street] we go about half a mile to the left where is a very large fire engine for draining the coal pits there. In the same place are two other engines for draining, called Bob-gins, and are moved by water turning a wheel.

Coming from this engine towards Newcastle we pass over two way-leaves which cross the great road. These way-leaves are an artificial road for the conveyance of coal from the pit to the steaths on the riverside; whereby one horse shall carry a greater burden than a whole team on a common way, and as they generally pass through the grounds of several proprietors, are very expensive to the coal owners who pay very high prices for their trespass on that occasion. The nearest to Chester is a single one and belongs to Mr Allan's colliery, the other about half a mile further is a double one, and belongs to Dean Headworth.

The loaded cart goes upon one, and the empty one returns upon the other. The whole length of these two way-leaves from the coal pits to the place from whence the coals are loaded into the lighters or keels at Sunderland, is five miles.

Several steaths, being the places where coals are brought to in order to be shipped from the coal pits, are on each side of the river, close upon the banks; those that are covered with timber work are called trunks. From these steaths or trunks, the fillers take it off in lighters (here called keels) and carry it down to the ships which lie chiefly about Shields. There were many of these keels dispersed on the river, but few or no ships at this time. Each keel contains eight chauldrons, which is equal to sixteen of the London chauldrons. There are just 800 of them in all upon the river, and every keel employs four men.

Fraujus de Saint-Froid, in his *Journey through England*, gave this impression of Tyneside in 1784:

Vessels loaded with coal, for London and different parts of Europe, sail daily from this port, and, so to say, every hour of the day. Besides this commerce, the navigation which results from working these mines, gives an incalculable advantage to the navy, by forming a great nursery of seamen. In times of war, more than a thousand coal vessels can be armed, and do considerable injury to the enemy's commerce.

The first mine I visited belongs to a private individual; it is situated about two miles from Newcastle, and requires one hundred men to work it; thirty of them work above ground, and seventy in the pit; twenty horses live in this abyss, and drag coal through the subterranean passages to the pit bottom; four horses outside work the machine which raises the coal, and some more are employed in auxiliary labours.

The mine has a large steam-engine for pumping out water, and at the same time working a ventilator to purify the air. The winding machine which raises the coal from the pit is convenient, and easily worked by two stout horses.

The buckets in which the coal is brought up, are not of wood, but of osier, strongly made, and having an iron handle. They contain at least 1,200 lbs of coal each; and as the one ascends as the other descends, one of these baskets arrives at the mouth of the pit every four minutes. It is received by a single man who, while it is yet suspended, places it upon a truck drawn by one horse. He then unhooks the basket, puts an empty one in its place, and pushes the truck to a place somewhat raised at a short distance, where he empties the basket on the latticed roof of a kind of shed; the dust passes through the open spaces and falls below, while the large pieces of coal rolling down the inclined plane, fall upon the ground in heaps on the outside of the shed.

This falling-down in a heap led to the term 'heapstead' being used later to describe the workings immediately above and around the shaft on the pit's surface. As the coal sited by a river and extracted by means of outcrop became exhausted, so the need arose to move further inland. Somehow the coal had to be moved quickly and cheaply to the rivers. The same author describes the progress made for conveying the coal in 1784:

Roads which have an almost insensible inclination are formed with the greatest care, and prolonged to the place where the vessels are loaded.

The first operation being finished, two parallel lines are traced along the road, at the exact distance which separates the wheels of the wagons. Logs of hard wood are then laid along these two parallel lines, and firmly fixed in the earth with pins.

The upper surface of these logs is carefully cut into a kind of moulding, which is well rounded, and projects upwards. The thickness of this elevated ledge must correspond with the width of the groove in the wagon-wheels, which are made of cast iron, and hollowed in the manner of a metal pulley.

These wheels are completely cast in one piece, in a mould from which the rims come out hollowed. The large groove is several inches deep, and of a proportional width; so that the wheel exactly encases the projecting part of the log, from which it cannot slide in any direction. As the moulding is well greased and is also polished by continual friction, four-wheeled wagons, containing eight thousand weight of coal each, move along the inclined plane, by the laws of gravity, and proceed as it were by magic one after another, until they reach the Tyne.

Arrived there, a strongly and artistically made wooden frame prolongs the road for several fathoms at such a height above the water as to permit vessels to to pass below it on lowering their masts. A man stationed on the platform .below opens a hatch, whence a large wooden hopper descends towards the vessel, the hatches of which are open. When the wagon comes to the trap in the platform it stops, its conical bottom open, and all the coal runs in a moment through the hopper into the vessel. The wagon being emptied, returns by a second road parallel to the first.

Where local circumstances have permitted, the weight of the load, and of the accelerated movement have been combined in such a manner, that files of loaded wagons run down the inclined plane and at the same time cause empty wagons to re-ascend with the assistance of horses, along another road parallel to the first.

John Buddle, quite famous in his time as a colliery viewer—the Wallsend Buddle Centre is named after him—gave the following evidence in 1829 to Parliament on 'The State of the Coal Trade':

The deepest pit I am acquainted with is 180 fathoms of shaft, but they frequently go deeper by inclined places under ground; the shallowest pit that I know is 23 fathoms, and of very inferior coal.

With regards to expense, I have known, in several cases, it is upwards of £30,000; that includes the machinery requisite for sinking that pit, that is, the steam engine and all its apparatus; that is merely getting to the coal, and it might be called more properly a winning charge than a working charge.

I should think the aggregate capital employed by coal owners on the river Tyne amounts to £1,500,000, exclusive of the craft on the river. Some are owners of the craft; many of them hire keels or barges. On the river Wear I estimate that capital invested is £700,000.

As to the number of men and ships employed on the two rivers, my figures are based on official documents from the Tyne, but for the Wear it is by approximate calculation. The number of persons employed under ground on the Tyne are, men 4,937, boys 3,554, together 8,491; while above ground, men 2,745, boys 718, making 3,463; the whole total being 11,954. For the Wear, I conceive that there are 9,000 employed, making 21,000 employed in digging the coal and delivering it to the ships on the two rivers.

Averaging the coastal vessels, that carry coals to the size of 220 London chauldrons each vessel, there would be 1,400 vessels employed, which would require 15,000 seamen and boys.

The Pitman's Bond of 1767 was the coalowner's safeguard against his workers leaving and taking their labour elsewhere. The owners tried to bind the worker under a long-period contract. Although the Pitman's Bond was usually for a period of one year, the coalowners agreed among themselves that no employer should take on any man who was unable to produce a certificate of leave from his previous employer. This was one reason for the trouble which arose in 1765, as reported in that year's *Annual Register*:

About this time last year, a gentlemen or two upon the river in the neighbourhood of Newcastle, being in great want of pitmen, endeavoured to obtain these useful men by tempting them with extraordinary binding money for one year, as far as two, three, or four guineas [a guinea was £1 1s., or £1.05] , instead of one shilling [5p.], which was heretofore all they used to get.

This encouragement made the men in the other collieries work with great reluctance all the year, and, as the time was approaching when the above-mentioned gentlemen would be again in want, it was natural for the several coal owners on the Tyne and Weare to consider of some method to prevent such proceedings in the future. They had a meeting at which it was agreed that no coal owner should hire another's men unless they produced a certificate of leave from their last master; and as no coal owner would grant such a certificate, it was by the pitmen called a binding during the will of the master; and was, consequently, a species of slavery not to be endured in a free country.

This notion spread like wild fire, on or about the 14th of August last [1764]. All the pitmen on the two rivers left off work, and have continued so ever since, nothwithstanding the coal owners have repeatedly declared they had no intention of hindering them from hiring with whom they pleased, and earnestly exhorted them to return to their work till expiration of their bonds, at which time they would have a regular discharge in writing, if required.

It seems the coal owners have made a custom to bind but 11 months and 15 days to prevent their obtaining a settlement, though this year they attempted to keep them at work for 14 months.

The pitmen on the Tyne and the Weare burnt and otherwise destroyed the utensils of many coal-pits, set fire to the coals both above and below the ground, and broke up the coalways, in spite of the vigilance of the soldiers placed there to prevent them; in consequence of which the wagons were stopt, the keels laid by, upwards of 600 ships kept idle at Newcastle and Sunderland, and 100,000 men out of bread in Newcastle, Sunderland, and London, from near the middle of August last to the end of this month.

The unrest of 1765, and the miners' solidarity in the face of what they considered barbaric treatment, were among the earliest signs of a miners' union taking shape. But it was not until 1810 that the owners agreed to acknowledge delegates from each colliery in order to enter into any kind of negotiation. The following is taken from the Journal of Matthias Dunn, a Durham colliery viewer in 1832:

April 5th [1810] – During the agitation that has been passing at Hetton and neighbouring collieries between the owners and their men, nothing vindictive nor coercive has been done here, but it being now high time that some steps were taken I specially required the presence of Colonel Mills and Colonel Grey here this day when I required the deputation to proceed to explain their demands to the Gentlemen in my presence.

May 5th – Grand coal meeting at Newcastle when it was determined to bind no man who did not abandon the Pitmen's Union. Upwards of 20 special police sworn in for North Hetton preparatory to the miners being turned out of their houses.

May 7th – Colonel Mills and Taylor attended when we turned out 80 families. A subaltern's party of military will now be stationed at Colliery offices, besides 30 police armed with pistols and swords.

May 8th – Remainder of people ejected from their houses. Handbills printed for lead miners and every exertion now to be tried to supply the place of these foolish men. Events will prove that the men of this colliery will be more humiliated by the introduction of strangers than any other as the work is so extremely simple and comfortable.

Durham: 'little more than one huge colliery'

So riddled with coalmines was the North East that, on 5 October 1850, the county of Durham was put under close scrutiny by the editor of *The Times*:

It is very little more than one huge colliery, the prosperity of which rises and falls every day with that of commerce and manufactures of the world. Every fresh steamer on the German Ocean, the Thames, the Mediter-ranean, or even the Red Sea; every street added to this metropolis

[London], or any other town in the eastern and southern counties; every factory built either here or on the neighbouring shores, every new railway, in a great part of this island, is a fresh customer to Durham, to South Shields, to Sunderland, to Monkwearmouth, to Gateshead, to Darlington, and half a dozen other populous centres and ports of the Coal trade.

The cities, the villages, the noblity, the clergy, the tradesmen, the labourers, and we must add, the farmers in the county of Durham, all derive their wealth or their competence from Coal. But for that Coal, one-half of them would never have been there, and the indigenous inhabitants would by this time have been almost reduced to eat one another. They know their own interests, and it is as much their choice as it is their destiny that their fortunes are linked with those of the world at large. It is all the same to them whether they feed the furnace for a British, a French, or a Belgian mill. It is the crop below ground, not above, that they depend upon; and if there is plenty of work below, there will be plenty of cheer above.

William Howitt, an astute observer in the mid-19th century, described Durham like this:

When you get into the Bishopric of Durham, going northward to Newcastle, you begin to see tall engine-houses, and vastly tall chimneys, breathing into the sky long black clouds of smoke. You hear groans and whistlings, and numerous unearthly sounds around you. These engine-houses contain those great steam engines that work the Coal mines; and these noises proceed from pulley and gins, and railways, and other industrious intruments for raising and conveying away the Coal.

As you get into the country nearer Newcastle, all these operations—these gruntings and wailings—these smokes and fires—increase upon you. Here you pass one of those tall engine-houses that you saw in the distance, with its still taller chimney hoisting into the sky its slanting column of turbid smoke.

You now see a huge beam, protruding itself from the upper part of the engine-house, like a giant's arm, alternately lifting itself up, and then falling again. To this beam is attached the rod and bucket of a pump, which probably at some hundred yards deep is lifting out the water from the mine, and enabling the miners to work there otherwise it would be all drowned in subterranean floods.

Or you see a great beam suspended from its centre, and elevated aloft on a proper support, wagging its ends alternately up and down, and up and down, with that busy and whimsical air which has obtained for it the name whimsy. This is performing a similar operation by a different contrivance.

Then, again, these huge engines are at work whirling buckets down into the deep shafts for Coal, or whirling the colliers themselves down to get the Coal. For two or three hundred yards down a hideous gulf into the bowels of the earth are they sent, with a rapidity which to a stranger is frightful, to their labour, and pulled up again, after its performance, to daylight as fast.

All this time these great engines, of perhaps 200 horse power, are groaning and crying over their toils like condemned Titans; and the wheels and pulleys that they put in motion are singing and whistling lamentably, like so many lesser spirits doomed to attend their labours.

Then you see buckets of Coal emerge from the mouth of the pit, and immediately by self-agency run away, empty themslves into a waggon or boat, and come back empty and ready for a fresh exploit. Then, as you advance over the plain, you see a whole train of waggons loaded with Coal, careering by themselves, without horse, without steam engine, without man, except that there sits one behind, who, instead of endeavouring to propel these mad waggons on their way, seems labouring hopelessly by his weight to detain them.

It is obvious that what passed as home and work to the miner caused great amazement and excitement to the passing observer. Just as he accepted the squalor of his surroundings, the pitman had no qualms whatever about entering the mine. The witty playwright Sheridan had this to say on the subject to his son:

'What in the name of nonsense, Tom, can induce you to take the trouble to go down into a Coal-pit?'

'Why, father, I want to go merely for the sake of saying I've been in one.'

'Oh, there can be no objection to your saying you have been in a Coal-pit . . . but why not say so at once!'
Charles Dickens, writing about the celebrated clown Grimaldi who was playing at a Newcastle theatre in 1818, described the clown's antics on entering a local pit:

> Grimaldi was induced by glowing descriptions of the theatre manager to go into a Coal mine. He descended some two hundred feet in a basket, and was met by a guide at the bottom of the shaft. The guide had not conducted him far when a piece of Coal weighing about three tons fell with a large noise upon a spot which they had just passed. 'Hollo,' exclaimed Grimaldi, greatly terrified, 'what was that?' 'Hoots,' said the guide, 'it's on'y a wee bit of Coal faw'n doon. We hae that twe or three times a day.' 'Have you?' replied Grimaldi, running back to the shaft, 'then I'll thank you to ring for my basket, or call out for it, for I'll stop here no longer.'

Two years earlier Grand Duke Nicholas visited the North-East, taking letters to Mr Buddle, the eminent Wallsend engineer. The royal visitor donned some pit gear with the intention of going down Wallsend Colliery with Mr Buddle. On reaching the pit mouth, however, the future Emperor of all the Russias started back from the shaft, protesting: 'Ah! My God, it is the mouth of Hell! None but a madman would enter into it.'
To a pitman, going down the mine was as ordinary an event as one might nowadays take the lift into the bargain basement at one of Newcastle's sumptuous department stores. But William Howitt ventured down Monkwearmouth Pit, near Sunderland. He related:

> It is a hot and fatiguing pit, but on account of its great depth, it is the marvel of the district. That man at the pit's mouth is called a banksman, that is a kind of foreman of the labourers at the surface. He takes under his charge, as his special vocation, the dismissing down and receiving up of all who descend and ascend the shaft.
> Presently he will call down the shaft that gentlemen are coming down,

and you'll hear such a peculiar ringing drawl: 'Ho, ho, hoh, clear away, a-w-a-y there! viewer and gen'lemen a'coming. Hoh, hoh.'

While they are clearing away, we stand on the pit-heap, having been provided with pit dresses, and look round on some scores of active boys, busily employed in wheeling the Coal baskets or tubs from the banksman, who has landed them from the shaft, to the screens, which are ranged in long upright rows.

And against their sounding wires you now hear the volleys of Coal rattling every minute. Now, before descending, just think what is before you, and beneath you, and only listen to the various discordant sounds. You look round for refuge, and your eyes are filled with Coal dust; you would lay hold of a post to keep up your courage, but there is not one; you look down to the ground to avoid ugly objects, and lo! the pit mouth yawns beneath your feet; you sigh for a few friendly greetings, and you hear in hollow tones, the doubtfully welcome words from the banksman: 'Now gen'lemen, the tub is ready—step in, if you please.'

Come, my friend, here is Mr Elliott, the intelligent viewer who has arranged to accompany us; Elliott and I will get into this tub first, then you come after. Now, this said tub is a large iron bucket, capable of holding all the lords of the admiralty, and it is no pleasant thing to have to step into it from the edge of terra firma, whilst it is swinging over a black depth of 1,800 feet, with nothing between its bottom and the bottom of the shaft. However, get in you must—give me your hand— how you shake—don't be so nervous—you are safe enough.

Stand away there ... off! Now you are descending. People who go up in balloons affirm that they have no feeling of motion, but that the earth seems to be flying away from them, while they are sitting still and resting. Much the same may be said, in reverse, of descending a Coal-shaft. You have no sense of descent; but the little round hole of light seems to be flying faster and faster over your head upward, as if it were going to the skies; and at length—in a couple of minutes, perhaps—the orifice of the shaft has apparently turned itself into a day-star, which shines far, far above the firmament.

The first occurrence that brings you to a consciousness of your own rapid descent is, if it so happens, the up-coming of another load, and the passage of that load by you; including, as it does, if a load of live human stock, someone with a candle. And now, before you can have thought of it, you come close to the bottom. You have been about four minutes in descending. Now you feel a full stop, which convinces you that you have previously been in rapid motion. A kind of hollow clanking strikes upon your ears; a damp archway is above your head, a feeble oil lamp hangs up in a corner, half a dozen whity-black beings are grouped around you. Elliott jumps out first, I get out after him, and we touch the bottom.

I have omitted one peculiar misery of this very shaft, because I did not want to smother you with smoke too soon; but the fact is, this same shaft is nothing less than a wonderful chimney of eighteen hundred feet depth! It is an upcast shaft, and the ventilating furnace is at the bottom. All the 'return air' charged with various impurities, and all the furnace smoke (and an immense fire is kept roaring in that furnace), ascend through this shaft which you have been descending. Well, it is no trifle to go down an upcast of this enormous depth, and every moment getting nearer and nearer to the roaring furnace, a glimpse of whose glowing brightness you get on one side as you pass by.

Going up in a balloon is nothing to going down this shaft; for in the balloon you rise continually into purer air—in the Coal-shaft you sink continually into fouler gloom and more fiery darkness. To the Bensham seam is 265 fathoms, and 15 fathoms lower to a reservoir of water; that is, in feet, 1,680 in all. The ordinary time in going down or coming up the shaft, is from two to three minutes respectively. Men and visitors are let down more slowly. The tub in which we travel is seven feet high, and holds 30 cwt. of Coal. The ropes which bear and bring this tub are, themselves, objects of curiosity. A pair of ropes is used together. The load of Coal and carriage upon them averages 36 cwt. at a time; and the weight of the pair of ropes is no less than 6 tons. The shaft is divided or bratticed into two compartments, in the other one of which the pumps and their apparatus are placed. The engineers also descend that compartment.

After all, the descent of this shaft (the shaft alone) is not so much more terrible than that of any of the deeper upcasts in the district. All upcasts are unpleasant, and peculiarly so to strangers. But the romance or novelty connected with it would have carried me double the length, if possible. Few visitors to the mines go down this pit; and perhaps not one would desire to descend it, if they were to see the whole length of it drawn out visibly upon the surface, or if they were to stand under St Paul's [London] first, and to multiply its height by four, or under the Monument, and multiply its height by eight, by way of gaining some idea of their projected trip.

At first you can see little or nothing, and it seems as if you were in total darkness. Then, in a minute or two, you distinguish the men at the shaft bottom, and the sluggish oil lamp, and the little lads coming up with their train of Coal-waggons; then the horses or ponies, being unfastened from one load and conveyed inwards to draw another. Now you can see the remarkable smoothness of the horses' coats, and the sleekness of the ponies' appearance. The horse gets fat, the men lean, the ponies well-conditioned, and the lads ill-conditioned. The horses and ponies are conveyed down the pit in large nets; of course, they seldom get up again, but live night and day in their underground stalls.

But we must proceed on our subterranean journey. The man at the bottom has put a piece of clay into each visitor's hand, between the first and second finger, and inserted a pit candle in the clay, and away we go, carrying our lights with us. While we pass along the main passages the march is not unpleasant, as we are able to walk erect, in a tolerable underground street. A fair current of air passes with us, and we breathe comfortably.

The first signs of pit labour are the passage of numerous trains of Coal waggons, small in size, but long in their trains; and these convey the produce of the interior workings of the mine to the bottom of the shaft. You see, sitting in the foremost, a lad, who is the driver of the horse or ponies that draw the whole. Iron railways or tramplates are laid along the mainways, and the little driver has to act as train-engineer:

Leaving the driver, we now come to a door, shut, and hindering our progress into the interior of this strange country. What can be the use of a solid, heavy door down here? Why, this is the first of the ventilating doors, put up to regulate the current of ventilating air, and these doors perform a most important part of this work; and the little mite of a boy, sitting behind this door is the trapper boy, the youngest piece of humanity employed in the mines; his duty is to pull open the door with this cord, whenever he hears the drivers or trains of Coal waggons coming on one side or the other. The door must only remain open long enough for the passage of the trains, and must then be closed again immediately, or the current of the air would be diverted in its course.

Passing from the little trapper boy, we enter into the lower galleries. The mainways through which we have come, vary in height from seven feet to five feet eight inches. The bords in which we now stand are about five feet eight inches high, that being the thickness of the Coal seam. The lowest working place in this pit is three feet six inches high. Into such places as these last, the best method of entering is by lying flat on a rolley and then being wheeled in by an experienced pitman. The air is now becoming hot and oppressive; so soon as you perspire you feel easy, and can breathe easily.

Here we come to a new set and sort of lads and boys, who may be generally called putters. This term implies the lads who push, or put, the trains of Coal from the places where the hewers fill them to the crane where they are hoisted upon the rolleys, or waggons for transporting the Coals from the crane to the shaft.

A rolley holds two or three tubs, and is ten feet long. The roads along which these rolleys are driven, when loaded by the drivers, are the principal horse roads, extending into distant parts of the mine; and they are made sufficiently high for an ordinary horse by cutting away the roof or the floor. Some of the rolley-ways are two miles long.

We have now passed the end of one, and have arrived at the crane whereby the loads are hoisted. Leaving the cranemen, we are amidst a rough and roystering race of lads and boys who seem but half civilized— they are the putters. Next to the hewers, they are the hardest labourers in the pit; and in some few places their labour is even harder. The term 'putter' includes the specific distinction of the headsman, the half-marrow, and the foal. Where full tubs or baskets are to be pushed along the rails from the hewers to the crane and the drivers, the headsman takes the chief part; a half-marrow goes at each end of the train alternately with another half-marrow, while a foal always precedes the train. All these lads come into the pit an hour or so after the hewers, and then find baskets of Coal ready filled for them. Putting is very exhausting in this pit; the heat of the unbroken mine averages about 78° F; the extreme heat has been known to reach 89° F. The putters are very subject to boils; when a fresh man enters a mine to work he generally suffers from them; and the hewers are generally afflicted with boils or carbuncles for the first month or two. The hewers are the key of the pit, the centre of the mining system; all arrangements below ground are made to suit them. The pick and the spade are the hewer's only tools. You see one kneeling, another sitting, another stooping or bending double, and you may sometimes (especially in thin seams) see them lying on one side, or on their backs, hammering at the Coal before them or above them with their short heavy picks. To hew Coal well is a peculiar and difficult work. The men have been brought up to it, or brought into it, through the successive grades of trapping, teaming, and putting. The best hewers have learned to do their work in quick time, and it is curious to watch them shifting their postures, and strangely adapting themselves to the exact form or figure required to bring down the Coal with advantage and speed. Close behind them stand the tubs or baskets to be filled with Coal. Each miner has, say, six picks, which the smith of the mine keeps in repair at his expense.

The pit dress is made entirely of coarse flannel, and consists of a short jacket with large side pockets, a waistcoat, a flannel shirt, and a pair of stout trousers worn over them. Add to these a pair of hoggers or footless worsted stockings, a tight-fitting round leather cap, and you have the hewer ready for the pit. A pit suit costs about twenty-shillings [£1] if purchased at the slop shop; but on Sunday the hewer is seen dressed in a suit of fine black cloth.

But now it is time to wend our way back to the shaft. We had better not delay any longer for this pit is exhausting. To go back does not seem so long as coming in did. Here we are at last at the bottom of the shaft. We enter the tub, encounter cooler air, and in a trice find ourselves safe at bank.

It should be noted that, though the above was written around 1860, many modern-day miners would find that little had changed from the above description even after more than 100 years.

2

'MINERS—REFUSE TO BOW QUIETLY DOWN'

Richard Fynes described in 1873 the reasons why the early miners needed to unite to better their conditions:

It may readily be imagined that in 1800 an educated pitman was the exception. All learning was positively discouraged amongst the lower ranks of society, and if any person who had received a scanty stock of learning got into trouble, the 'pastors and masters' shook their heads ruefully and declared the misfortune was the result of an impertinent curiosity to know as much as his or her betters.

Previous to the introduction of the steam winding engine, gins were used for handling the corves to bank, and whenever any dispute took place, it was a favourable practice of the men where a strike had originated to visit the neighbouring collieries, and, by pulling down the gins, and destroying the property, prevent the working of the colliery.

Such was the most common method resorted to, to get redress of their grievances, and though they frequently met together in large numbers for various purposes connected with their work, there is no evidence of any organisation of a permanent and stable character occurring amongst the miners till 1809.

At the yearly binding of the collieries, which at this time took place in October, the owners by a preconcerted arrangement amongst themselves, but in which the men were not allowed to have any part, decided that the men should be engaged for a quarter, or a year and a quarter, in order to bring the binding time to the latter end of December.

To this the men at first agreed; but upon mature deliberation they found that they had done wrong, and accordingly on October 16th, 1810, a meeting of delegates was held at Long Benton, when it was resolved to resist the alteration, and that a strike should take place unless the owners would agree to continue the binding time from October 18th, as usual.

The coal owners refused to listen to the men; and the latter struck after the binding day. The delegates from different collieries held frequent meetings, both in the counties of Northumberland and Durham, for the purpose of keeping the men united, but they were hunted about from place to place by the owners and magistrates, assisted by the military, and committed to prison in such large numbers, till the prisons would hold no more. To such an extent was the old Gaol and House of Correction of Durham filled, that, for fear of infection, several were removed to the stables and the stable yard of the Bishop of Durham, where they were guarded by the Durham Volunteers, and special constables, and afterwards by the Royal Carmarthenshire Militia. Fresh seizures continued to be made, day by day, until finally the number imprisoned in the Bishop's stables numbered three hundred.

The men were now awakening to a sense of serfdom in which their forefathers had too long existed, and their employers knew this, and were anxious to stifle their desire for freedom in its birth. It was preposterous that men who had all along been in the habit of looking up with awe and reverence to their employers—men who had shown no disposition hitherto to do anything beyond living and dying on this earth as brute creatures—it was perfectly intolerable that these men should refuse to bow quietly down to imperious requests of their lords and masters. It was thought an outrageous proposition, and such a piece of impertinence and presumption that these men should dare to take the liberty of thinking for themselves, that the united powers of the Church, of the Law, and of the Army, must forthwith be launched to keep them in subjection, and prevent their aspirations for freedom from becoming infectious.

No doubt the Right Reverend Lord Bishop of Durham slept a peaceful sleep in the calm consciousness of having served the cause of law and order by yielding up his stables for a prison-house, and probably he would not inquire too curiously as to whether such conduct as stifling a number of human beings in a horse stable was altogether and entirely consistent with Christian charity.

In the course of this strike which lasted for seven weeks, several other questions were brought forward, particularly the fines for deficient measure, and foul coals. A magistrate, the Rev. Mr Nesfield, having pledged himself that these things should be rectified after the pits had again commenced working, and before the binding took place, by advertisement, called a meeting of the trade, to be held at Chester-le-Street on the morning of December 20th. This was objected to by Mr Martindale, the clerk of trade of the river Wear, 'lest such meeting should hazard a recurrence of the late disturbances,' and because 'the river Wear did not in itself constitute the coal trade, but that the river Tyne, Hartley, Blyth, and Cowpen, formed also a principal part thereof'. A second advertisement called for a meeting of the above coal owners on January 3rd, 1811. This meeting took place, and to it were submitted 'proposals for regulating the contracts between the coal owners and their miners on the rivers Tyne and Wear, and of Hartley, Blyth, and Cowpen, by the Rev W. Nesfield, one of His Majesty's Justices of the Peace for the county of Durham.'

These proposals, which were agreed by the coal owners, have been the basis of the agreement of the employers with the miners ever since. By the words 'binding time' is meant the day from which the contract is made in one year until the same day in the next, when the year of service expires.

Previous to 1810, when there was a great scarcity of miners, a bounty, called 'binding money' was given, which, at some collieries, was as high as 20 guineas [£21] a man. Instead of taking advantage of this scarcity of labour, and its great demand, the poor pitmen eagerly took the proffered guineas and returned to their drudgery, too often after having squandered their bounty in the public-house, and lost their opportunity of asserting their values and their independence.

A poet of the time, by name of Wilson, refers to binding time in the following lines of *The Pitman's Pay*:

Just like wor maisters when wor bun,
If men and lads be varry scant,
They wheedle us wi' yel and fun,
And coax us into what they want.
But myek yor mark, then snuffs and sneers
Siun stop yor gob and lay yor braggin;
When yence yor feet are i' the geers,
Maw soul, they keep yor paunches waggin.

Richard Fynes continues:

From the settlement of the strike about 'binding time' things went peaceably till the year 1825 when there was an attempt made to carry out great social reform. Boys at this time used to be eighteen hours a day in the mine. Allowed to go down at the early, and almost infantile age of six years, the whole of their youthful days were spent in the dismal mine till they became 21 years of age; and during the whole of this long period they hardly ever saw the happy, health-giving, daylight and sunshine, except at short intervals. There were no schools and no time to attend them.

There appears to have been no organisation of any kind amongst the miners till the year 1830, when the two counties joined together in one large Union, which was called Hebburn's Union. Tommy Hebburn, who gave his name to this compact, was a man of intelligence, tact, perserverance, and honest of purpose, and one who was calculated to do, as he did, a great amount of good work amongst the miners.

About this time there were signs of intelligence beginning to spread amongst the miners. They began to understand the great value of public sympathy, and to lay their grievances before the public, and to agitate through the two counties for the establishment of a union of the miners of Northumberland and Durham. It was only at this time that the public became aware by means of this agitation, that the miners as a class, were so barbarously treated, by their requests for protection being refused, and by their being kept in the mines for so many hours in their youth.

Having formed a strong union—the first that had as yet been formed amongst them—the men began to feel their strength, and in the year 1831, the whole of the miners in Northumberland and Durham came out on strike, for the general advance of wages, and shorter hours.

On March 12th, 1831, an immense number of pitmen from the collieries of Tyne and Wear assembled together on the Black Fell, near Eighton Banks in the county of Durham, for the purpose of adopting certain resolutions, and considering the best means of obtaining from their employers an increase in wages.

Again, on the 21st of the same month, another large meeting of the miners of the two counties, was held on the Town Moor, Newcastle, for the same purpose. During the forenoon, great numbers passed through the town in procession; apparently without exciting the least uneasiness or alarm amongst the inhabitants; and it was calculated that nearly 20,000 persons had assembled by one o'clock at the place of the meeting.

Several speakers addressed the meeting, and detailed in homely but energetic language the grievances under which they considered themselves to labour. One source of complaint was the subjection of the men to the caprice of the viewers, not only for continuance of work, but even for shelter for their wives and families, as they were liable to be turned out of their houses.

In the course of the meeting it was resolved to petition Parliament, and subscribe sixpence each to send deputies to London with the petitions; to continue to work, unbound, after their period of service had expired, if the owners would allow them, otherwise to cease working, and claim parish relief until their remonstrances were attended to; and further, that no man should in future buy meat, drink, or candles from anyone connected with the collieries. This last resolution was intended to put a stop to the existence of

'Tommy Shops,' a system by which a miner and his family was placed competely at the mercy of the colliery owners. These shops were generally kept by a relative of the viewer of the colliery, and the pitman was compelled to purchase his provisions there, and his wages were confiscated at the pay day to settle any balance there might be due.

While the meeting was in progress, Mr Archibald Reed, the Mayor of Newcastle, appeared in the midst of the assembly for a few minutes, and advised the leaders to inculcate order and peace as the surest means of obtaining justice. He was thanked for his friendly advice.

The resolutions were put and passed with a show of hands, which, from the immense number held up, had a very great effect. The whole proceedings were conducted without the least disturbance, and the miners returned to their homes in the afternoon in good order, and so ended the first great demonstration of miners in Newcastle.

The great strike of 1831

The first major strike by North-East miners took place in 1831. This is how Richard Fynes reported the incidents during the stoppage and the harrowing scenes which took place when striking miners and their families were evicted:

The year for which the men at the various collieries on the Tyne and Wear had bound themselves having expired on April 5th, 1831, the whole of them refused to enter into fresh engagements with their employers until the differences between them were adjusted. The employers had agreed that boys should in future work only twelve hours a day, and that the workmen should be paid their wages in money, and be at liberty to buy goods where they chose.

On Wednesday, April 6th, the day following the binding day, a great number of miners met on Black Fell with the hope that some further arrangements would be proposed by the coal owners; but no proposition was forthcoming, and the men dispersed with a resolution not to return to their work on the former terms.

Some of the collieries resumed work with a number of men who went back on the old terms, and were accordingly regarded as blacklegs by their companions who remained out to fight the battle to its end. On April 18th, 1,500 miners visited collieries in the neighbourhood of Blyth and Bedlington, and there laid the pits off work by various destructive devices, and threatened to set fire to them if their demands were not complied with. At Bedlington Glebe Pit, they tore the corves to pieces, threw them into the shaft, and did considerable damage to the machinery.

From Bedlington they marched towards Netherton, but a strong opposition having been gathered there against them, they retreated. On their return they entered the house of the resident viewer at Cowpen Colliery, who was not at all a favourite with the men. They broke open the cellar, and took everything out that they could eat or drink, but did no damage to the furniture, nor yet hurt any of the family in the house. On leaving the house they gave a promise that they would visit him again, if he attempted to get the pits to work before they got their terms conceded.

Shortly after their visit an anonymous miner scrawled the following letter and sent it to the viewer:

'I was at yor hoose last neet, and myed mysel very comfortable. Ye hev nee family, and yor just won man on the colliery, I see ye hev a greet lot of rooms, and big cellars, and plenty wine and beer in them, which I got my share on. Noo I naw some at wor colliery that hes three or fower lads and lasses, and they live in won room not half as guid as yor cellar. I divvent pretend to naw very much, but I naw there shudent be that much difference. The only place we can gan to o the week ends is the yel hoose and hev a pint. I dinna pretend to be a profit, but I naw this, and a lot o ma marras na's tee, that wer not tret as we owt to be, and a great filosopher says, to get noledge is to naw wer ignerent. But we've just begun to to find that oot, and ye maisters and owners may luk oot, for yor not gan to get see much o yor awn way, and wer gan to hev some o wors noo. I divvent tell y ma nyem, but I wes won o yor unwelcome visitors last neet.'

Machinery thrown down the pit

On the following morning a large number of men went to Jesmond Dene Colliery, belonging to Mr R. B. Sanderson, and did considerable damage to the machinery, throwing it down the pit and endangering the lives of some workmen who were in the mine.

The whole of the mining districts were in a terribly disturbed state. Large bodies of violent and lawless men traversed the country doing much silly and altogether unjustifiable mischief. On the Wear they were especially violent; at one colliery they even went to the length of threatening to murder the horsekeepers if they went down to feed the poor horses.

A great number of special constables were at once sworn in to protect property, and the Deputy Lieutenant of the County issued an order for calling out the Northumberland and Newcastle Yeomanry. Part of the 82nd Regiment of Foot, then stationed at Sunderland Barracks, marched from thence to the neighbourhood of Hetton, where they were ordered to remain during the unsettled state of the workmen belonging to the collieries in that district. A detachment of eighty Marines and three subalterns under the command of Major Mitchell, sailed from Portsmouth for the Tyne on account of the disturbances among the collieries, and so serious was the case regarded by the authorities, that the vessel sailed in less than an hour after sailing orders were issued.

Marquess of Londonderry addresses men

On April 21st, 1831, a large meeting was held at Jarrow, each colliery bearing a banner, with the name of the colliery and various mottoes. Another on May 5th took place at Black Fell where the miners were met by coal owner, the Marquess of Londonderry, accompanied by military escort. His Lordship addressed the men, requesting them to disperse, and promising to meet their delegates in the Coal Trade Office, Newcastle. Another meeting was held the next day but the men still held out against the terms offered them by the owners; and the whole of the collieries, with the exception of two or three, which had been partially at work for a few days under the protection of the military, were laid completely idle.

From the long strike of the miners the want of coals was at this time severely felt by manufacturers and inhabitants of different towns. For some time detachments of the regular troops, horse and foot, assisted by parties of Colonel Bell's Cavalry and Foot Yeomanry, were stationed at Wallsend; sentries constantly patrolled the immediate locality of certain pits for the protection of the engines and premises, and the men who were at work.

The idle men were showing a very turbulent disposition; and rather than accede to the terms offered, many of them, with wives and families, were wandering about Northumberland and Durham.

On May 16th, a number of men on strike attempted to prevent several bound men from going to their work at South Shields Colliery. There was every prospect of a serious riot resulting, when Mr Fairless, a magistrate, appeared on the scene with a party of marines, and the men on strike at once prudently left the field in the possession of the workmen. The next morning an immense number of men congregated at Hebburn Colliery, and threw down the shaft all the corves, rolleys, and loose materials they could lay their hands upon, to the great terror of the men below. The men were proceeding to commit other acts of violence, when they were prevented by the timely arrival of the military.

About the middle of June, the men were victorious, the masters finding it impossible to hold out against them any longer. The men were very jubilant about their victory, the first unmistakable victory they had ever yet achieved over their hard taskmasters. One of the results of the strike was the establishment of a 12-hour working day for boys, instead of one of almost without limit.

This strike, like all movements of a similar nature amongst all classes of men, called forth the worst passions of both men and masters. The latter displayed their ill-feeling and hatred of the men, by using their influence and wealth to bring a large number of mercenaries into the counties to hunt their men from place to place like beasts of the chase, and the men resorted to all manner of brutal and lawless reprisals.

Miners thank his Majesty

On August 13th, 1831, the miners of Northumberland and Durham met on Boldon Fell, between Gateshead and Sunderland. During the forenoon, the roads in the vicinity of the meeting place presented an unusual bustle, the men walking in procession from the different collieries, bearing flags and banners, and accompanied by bands of music. The banners were numerous, and of the gayest description, nearly all being embellished with a painted design and a motto connected with the recent struggle between the miners and their employers. The object of this meeting was to vote an address to His Majesty, thanking him for his beneficent attention to the wants of his people in having assented to the Reform Bill, and for the support he had given to his ministers.

About twelve o'clock the speakers, who consisted of a few of the delegates from each colliery, mounted a cart and proceeded to the business of the day. Mr Hebburn first presented himself, and recommended order, sobriety, and attention to their religious duties, as the best means they could adopt to preserve the advantages they had gained, and to keep in the public mind that favourable feeling which had been exhibited during the strike.

Seven miners charged

On December 24th, upwards of 1,000 men assembled together at Walridge Colliery, near Chester-le-Street, and while 30 men were at work in the mine, they there stopped the engine kept for pumping water, and then threw large iron tubs, wooden cisterns, corves and other articles, down the shaft, by which workmen below were placed in the utmost danger. For the purpose of securing the apprehension and conviction of the persons concerned in these outrages His Majesty's government offered a reward of 250 guineas [£262.50], and a free pardon to accomplices; whilst the owners of the colliery also offered a reward of 250 guineas to any but the real actors in this outrage. At the Durham Spring Assizes, held on March 2nd, 1832, seven men named: James Becketts, Cuthbert Turnbull, John Rippon, Samuel Brown, Middleton, David Kelly and Thomas

Moore, were put upon their trial for these outrages, and after a patient investigation the jury retired for ten minutes and returned with a verdict which found the first six men named as guilty, but found Thomas Moore not guilty. Sentences ranged from six to fifteen months imprisonment

It appeared upon the trial, that the miners employed at this colliery had refused to work and in consequence the owners had employed some lead miners, who were down the mine at the time of the outrage. Mr Hebburn deprecated in strong terms this misconduct, and added: 'Unfortunately, the innocent are suffering for the guilty, as the owners and authorities are determined to punish someone, and if he was only a miner belonging to the union it is sufficient for them; for I know of some men who had been taken from their bed and imprisoned, who were never near the riot.'

Tommy Hebburn addresses miners in 1832

In 1832 the miners made a further demand, and came out on strike. The owners, jealous of the growing strength of the union, had decided at the next yearly binding, no man, being a member of the Miners' Union, should be bound, and consequently should not be allowed to work at their collieries. The men who had joined the Association had by this time become convinced of the advantage of unity, and showed no disposition to leave the union at the behest of their employers. At a meeting held at Bolden Fell on March 3rd, Mr Hebburn urged upon his hearers the necessity of supporting the Union for the maintenance of each other, and asserted that no less than £10,000 had been paid in the last twelve months from its funds.

On April 14th at Black Fell, Mr Hebburn again addressed the men in encouraging terms: 'Let them [the owners] make a few sacrifices, and twelve months will teach them a great deal. Things will come round in such a way that there will be need of more miners than were ever employed in England before, as pits are now being sunk in the north and south of us in our own counties as well as in Yorkshire and Lincolnshire, all of which will want men to work them. It has been said that the miners ought to get knowledge. I will teach you how to do that. Let libraries be established amongst collieries, which can be done for a shilling [5p.] a year, I think that is obtaining knowledge at a cheap rate. In conclusion, I urge you to part quietly, and let the world see our determination to support good order.'

All the collieries being now at a standstill, the owners had in many instances engaged new hands to take the places of those on strike. But with the striking miners still retaining possession of their dwellings, which were now required for the strangers, there seemed but one of two alternatives left for the adoption of the owners, either to submit to their late servants, or to put those newly-engaged in possession of the houses. They determined on the latter course, and commenced the work of forcible eviction, which was first begun at Hetton.

Special constables were appointed, a strong force of London police were placed on readiness, assisted by a detachment of the Queen's Bays. While families and furniture were handed to the door in the presence of the authorities no resistance was offered, but as the evening drew near there were many ominous signs that the peace would be broken by night.

Bound man found dead

Many of the union men assembled in a large group, several of them well armed, and occasional shots were fired by them. A terrible vengeance was taken upon one of the few miners at Hetton Colliery who had consented to be rebound, named Errington, who was found the next morning dead. At the resulting inquest, a verdict of wilful murder was returned against George Strong and John Turnbull, as principals, and against John Moore and Luke Hutton, as accessories before the fact. These persons were committed to Durham Gaol under an escort of cavalry.

More special constables were sworn in, and arms supplied them; part of their instructions being that whenever they found a few miners standing together they were to take them and lock them up either in colliery stables, or in the empty houses. As a result of this, a large number of arrests were made, and those taken were treated with great injustice and indignity. Some of them were bound hand and foot against the mangers in the stalls all night, with neither food nor water, and if they attempted to make the least resistance, a cutlass or pistol was held to their faces.

After the ejection at Hetton, the ejecting party proceeded to Friar's Goose Collieries, about two miles east of Newcastle. On reaching the colliery they were met by a large number of miners who were assembled there. Mr Forsyth, who was leading the constables, delivered to his men two rounds of cartridges containing swan shot, with strict orders not to fire till commanded. While the police were ejecting the family of a miner named Thomas Carr, a large number of miners attacked the premises appointed as a guard-house, overpowered the sentry, and carried off the guns. The noise and shouting drew Mr Forsyth to the place, he drew his cutlass and endeavoured to make his way to the assistance of the police. He was twice knocked down in his attempt. The police were most unhappily stationed in a narrow lane. The miners stood and threw brickbats, stones, and other missiles. The constables, thus pressed, and considering their lives in danger, fired amongst the crowd. Some of the miners fired at them as they retreated, six of the constables were wounded, and Mr Forsyth was wounded in the head and leg with stones.

About twelve o'clock, a messenger galloped through Newcastle on his way to the Barracks, without his hat, with a huge cut in his face, and with one of his ribs broken from the injuries he had received. The soldiers set out without delay for Friar's Goose, attended by the Mayor of Newcastle, and the Rev. Mr Collinson, Rector of Gateshead; but no further disturbances had taken place, and by the time of their arrival the men had in great measure dispersed.

As a result of the evictions, men, women, and children were seen begging about the district; the men, hounded and hunted by the police and military, their wives insulted by the wives of the other men who ought to have had more generosity, and their bairns laughed at and mocked by other children.

The murder of Nicholas Fairless

On June 11th, 1832, about five o'clock in the afternoon, as Mr Nicholas Fairless, of South Shields, a magistrate for the county of Durham, was riding to Jarrow Colliery, he was accosted by two miners, who seized and dragged him from his horse, and felled him to the ground. He was left lying in an almost lifeless state, and from the dreadful nature of the wounds in the skull he expired on June 21st.

One of the murderers was apprehended, but the other escaped. A reward of £300 was offered by the vestry of St Hilda and the Government for his apprehension, but he was never found, though it is believed that he stopped in the district till after the execution of his comrade, and finally visited his body where it was gibbeted on Jarrow Slakes, after which he departed for America.

At a meeting at Chirton, North Shields, on July 8th, a Mr Cuthbert Skipsey, a miner belonging to Percy Main, who bore the character of being a very quiet, inoffensive man, at this time was trying to make peace between the parties, when George Weddle, a policeman, drew his pistol and deliberately shot him dead on the spot. He left a widow and six children. Weddle was sentenced to six months imprisonment with hard labour.

Jobling tried for murder

On August 1st, William Jobling was tried at the Durham Assizes and found guilty of the murder of Nicholas Fairless. He was sentenced to be hanged and his body afterwards hung in chains near the scene of the murder. The sentence was carried out on August 3rd, with Jobling exhibiting on his way to the scaffold the utmost resignation and fortitude. Just as the fatal bolt was about to be withdrawn, a person near the scaffold cried out 'Farewell, Jobling!' The voice was supposed to be that of Armstrong, for whom there was a large reward offered. After hanging an hour the body was cut down and conveyed to the gaol where it remained till the gibbet was ready. The body was then covered over with pitch.

On the morning of August 6th, at seven o'clock, the body was taken in a small four-wheeled waggon drawn by two horses, from Durham, escorted by a troop of Hussars and two companies of infantry. They proceeded by way of Chester-le-Street, Picktree, Sludge Row, Portobello, over the Black Fell, to White Mare Pool, and thence by the South Shields turnpike road to Jarrow Slakes, where they arrived at half past ten o'clock. The spectators were not numerous, there being perhaps about 1,000 persons present.

The body was lifted from the waggon, and cased in flat bars of iron, the feet were placed in stirrups, from which a bar of iron went up each side to the head, and ended in a ring, by which the body was suspended; a bar from the collar went down to the breast, and another down the back; there were also bars on the inside of the legs, which communicated with the above, and cross bars at the ankles, the knees, the thighs, the breast and shoulders; the hands were hung by the side and covered in pitch; and the face was pitched and covered with a white grave cloth.

The gibbet, which was fixed in stone sunk in the slake, was formed of a square piece of fir timber, 21 feet long, and a top projecting about three feet, with strong bars of iron up each side to prevent it being sawn down. At high water, the tide covered the base of the gibbet to about five feet, leaving the rest visible. The body having been hoisted up and secured, a police guard was placed near the spot. Jobling was the first person gibbeted under a new Act of Parliament, which ordered the bodies of murderers to be hung in chains. Jobling's body, when gibbeted, had on the clothes in which he appeared on his trial—blue jacket and trousers, the hcel quarters of his boots were down, his head thrown back so that his face appeared to be looking upward.

During a very dark night between August 31st and September 1st, the body was stolen from the gibbet and secretly disposed of by some unknown person; nor was there any effort made to discover the parties, as the authorities seemed only too glad that such a hideous sight was removed from the district.

Tommy Hebburn begs for employment

The strike was now fairly at an end, and the large number of new hands which the owners had brought from other counties, gave them an opportunity of choosing who they liked amongst their old servants. Indeed, so overstocked was the labour market, that large numbers could not get work for a time. Thus many of the miners and their families were on the point of starvation, besides having no houses to live in, their furniture still remaining in farmers' byres and hay lofts, in public house long rooms, and by the roadsides.

This state of things happily did not continue very long, for the coal trade striking out very brisk at the time, the greater portion of them got employed, with the understanding that they should have nothing more to do with the union. But on no account could the leading advocates of the union get work. Mr Hebburn and others who had fought so hard and faithfully for the welfare of the whole body of men, were now prevented from getting work at any colliery in the two counties. Hebburn commenced to sell tea about the colliery districts, but in many instances the men dare not countenance him, whilst others who had the chance neglected him till he was almost driven to starvation.

The great man who had led the miners during their struggles of 1831 and 1832, now very shabbily clad, no one to converse with, broken down in spirits, proscribed and hunted, had to go and beg at the Felling for employment. The viewer, knowing he was a man of his word, put this proposition to him: 'I will give you work if you promise to have nothing more to do with the unions.' Hebburn paused for a moment before consenting; but he did consent, and on those conditions he was employed at the Felling.

But the seed of the unions had been sown, yet Hebburn did not live to see the results of his labours. In his calm reliance of the future he said:

'If we have not been successful, at least we, as a body of miners, have been able to bring our grievances before the public; and the time will come when the golden chain which binds the tyrants together will be snapped, when men will be properly organised, when coal owners will only be like ordinary men, and will have to sigh for the days gone by. It only needs time to bring this about.'

These were almost the last remarks Tommy Hebburn ever made in public.

3

VIEWS OF NORTH-EAST COALMINES IN
EARLY 1800s

Thomas Hair, an artist, lived in Camden Town and exhibited his
paintings at the Royal Academy three times between 1841 and 1849.
In 1844 he published a series of Views of the Collieries of
Northumberland and Durham *with the following narrative by M.*
Ross, editor of Historical and Descriptive Sketches of
Newcastle-upon-Tyne:

Air Shaft, Wallsend

Wallsend Colliery

We commence our series with views of the collieries at Wallsend, a spot famous in antiquity, and still more famous in modern times. Wallsend derives its name from being the undoubted site of the termination of the vallum, or wall, erected by the Roman emperor Hadrian, AD 120, and fortified and strengthened by Severus nearly a century afterwards.

The colliery occupies a field a little to the east of Carville Hall, commonly called by the inhabitants the Well Laws, or more properly, the Wall Laws, signifying the Wall Hill.

The winning of the colliery at Wallsend nearly sixty years ago [1784] was attended with great expense and difficulty. So discouraging did the prospect appear, that the ancestor of the present proprietor, William Russell, Esq., after embarking in it, took measures for abandoning an enterprise which was destined afterward to constitute one of the chief sources of his princely fortunes.

The Church Pit, Wallsend

The High Main Seam was found throughout the property nearly six feet thick, of the most unexceptionable quality, and under the most favourable circumstances as to mining. Owing to the far-famed prosperity of the colliery, the designation of 'Wallsend Coal' has continued for many years a passport to the quickest sale and the highest prices. To distinguish the coal sent from the colliery, it was for some times called 'Russell's Wallsend'. It is now, however, termed in the coal certificates, 'Bensham Wallsend' and 'Bensham Main'.

The view of the Church Pit, so called from its vicinity to the parish church, comprises nearly all the paraphernalia of an extensive colliery. On the railway line in front, the efficiency of that mode of transmission is exemplified by the fact of a ponderous waggon full of coals being moved on a gentle incline by the hand of a single individual. A railway from another colliery crosses the above by means of a wooden bridge. Behind, and in the centre, is the shaft frame, supporting the pulleys which overhang the pit. Over these wheels the ropes are passed by which the men, corves, etc., are lowered or raised to or from the bottom of the mine.

Contiguous is a lofty brick chimney or funnel, attached to the upcast shaft, and having a smoke disperser at the top, through which the impure air from the workings of the pit is ejected. The railed platform near the top is used for cleaning or making repairs in the chimney. On the right is the engine-house, containing the machinery for working the ropes; and close adjoining are the boilers etc, wherein is generated that immense power which raises all the produce of the pit to the surface.

In Casson's Plan of the Working Collieries of the Tyne and Wear, the depth of Wallsend Colliery is stated at 630 feet. Previous to an explosion in the Bensham Seam in 1821, only one shaft had been sunk, but that disaster having shewn the necessity of increased ventilation, the pit was laid in until other shafts were sunk, of which there are now five used in ventilation.

That disasters from firedamp have been of too common an occurrence at Wallsend Colliery, may be gathered from the following extracts from the *Local Records* of the late Mr John Sykes:

'**October, 1782** – An explosion of gas took place at Wallsend Colliery, by which one man lost his life. The coal being set on fire, the colliery was drowned up to extinguish it.

'**November, 1784** – An explosion took place at Wallsend Colliery, by which three men lost their lives. Another explosion took place in December, when two men lost their lives. These explosions were supposed to have taken place at the spark of a steel mill, by the light of which people were working at the shaft. The bodies were not discovered for several months.

'**June, 1785** – Two men died from an explosion at Wallsend Colliery. John Selkirk who was "playing the mill" at the time, survived the accident.

'**December, 1875** – Two more men lost their lives.

'**April, 1786** – An explosion at Wallsend claimed six lives.

'**October, 1790** – An explosion took place at Wallsend Colliery by which seven men lost their lives.

'**September, 1803** – An explosion took place, and thirteen men lost their lives.

'**August 5th, 1818** – An explosion of inflammable air took place in Wallsend Colliery by which four men lost their lives. This is the only explosion that is known to have taken place at the Davy lamp. A boy fell with the lamp, burst a hole in the wire gauze cylinder, and the explosion instantly took place.

'**October 23rd, 1821** – A dreadful explosion took place in Wallsend Colliery by which fifty-two men lost their lives. The explosion shook the ground like an earthquake, and made the furniture dance in the surrounding houses. The bodies of the deceased were most dreadfully scorched, and many of them strangely distorted. Forty-six of the bodies were buried at Wallsend, fourteen of whom, being relations, were buried in one grave; some of the remainder were buried at the Ballast-hills, and some at Wallsend old church, amidst sorrowing spectators.'

The following is from An Account of the dreadful Explosion in Wallsend Colliery *by John Sykes:*

June 18th, 1835 – The most fatal explosion of hydrogen gas took place at Wallsend Colliery that had ever occurred in Northumberland, and by which 101 men and boys lost their lives and four others were seriously injured. Eleven horses which were in the pit at the time were also killed. The banksman at the Church Pit shaft was first apprised of the explosion by a loud report, accompanied by a rush of after-damp to the mouth of the pit, which carried his hat from his head over the pulleys. The alarm in the village and neighbourhood was extreme.

Mr Buddle with assistants went down the C Pit; but the workings were found in so ruinous a state, that many tons of rubbish had to be brought to bank before the bodies could be got at. Some of the bodies were black, shrivelled, and burnt. On June 20th, three men and a boy were brought up alive. They were all burnt,· and the intellects of two of them appeared to be deranged. One of them, whose leg it was found necessary to amputate, died on July 3rd.

On Sunday, June 21st, crowds of people repaired to Wallsend to witness the funerals of those whose bodies had been recovered. The little communities around the northern collieries generally intermarry amongst each other, and thus become connected by the ties of relationship. Hence, scarcely a house could be found in the place in which the calamity was not felt, or an individual who had not lost some friend. In the afternoon about sixty bodies were conveyed on carts to the parish church for interment. A black pall was, in each instance, thrown over the coffin. In some cases, three were taken from one house. The coffins were furnished by the owners of the mine, who also contributed £1 in addition for the interment of each body.

The waggon-way from the C Pit to the banks of the Tyne is above half a mile in length. From the Church Pit which is near the river, the waggons are transmitted to the staith by means of an inclined plane. The staith itself, represented in our view, is like many others which fringe the steep shores of the Tyne between Newcastle and Shields, a lofty and strong timber framing projecting into deep water. A man is lowered down with the waggon, whose business it is to unhasp its moveable bottom, and thereby let the coals drop into the hold of the vessel. This apparatus is called a 'drop'. It was the invention of the late ingenious William Chapman Esq. of Newcastle who took a patent for it about the year 1800.

A 'spout' is generally attached to these staiths by which keels and other small vessels receive their ladings. Brand says: 'When a waggon lets fall its contents down one of these spouts, the noise at a distance very much resembles a clap of thunder.'

The keelmen of the Tyne have often complained of the navigation being interrupted by the staiths below the bridge; though the real cause of complaint, perhaps, was the dread of their own occupation being superseded by the majority of vessels loading at the staiths. A case was tried in August 1824 at York before Mr Justice Bayley where the jury returned the following singular verdict: 'We find that part of the navigable channel of the Tyne, opposite to Wallsend, has been straitened, narrowed, lessened, and obstructed by the gears described in this indictment; but we find, nevertheless, that the trade of the town of Newcastle, and the harbour of the Tyne, has at that time greatly improved.'

Our view (Wallsend Drop) comprises a laden Scottish ship at the staith, and a French vessel waiting her turn.

Drops at Wallsend

Willington Colliery

Willington Colliery

M. Ross continues:

This colliery is situated about a quarter of a mile east from the village of Wallsend. It was begun about 1806, and has been wrought by three shafts, including a water shaft to the Bensham seam. The shaft and engine represented in our view occupy the summit of an eminence overhanging a deep dean, through which a rivulet makes its way to the Tyne near Willington Quay. The shaft is 108 fathoms deep to the thill of the main seam, which is here six feet thick.

In sinking a staple from the High Main or Wallsend seam to the Bensham in 1831, an explosion of gas occurred, about nine o'clock in the morning of September 20th in that year, by which three men and eight horses were killed on the spot, and another fourteen men were severely burnt, four of whom died afterwards as a consequence.

Besides the catastrophe above noticed, only two more are recorded to have occurred here: December 3rd, 1829, when an unfortunate accident happened by which four men lost their lives by an explosion accompanied by a rush of water from some old workings. The other incident occurred on the morning of March 30th, 1840, when three men and five boys were severely burnt, and one of the former died the following day.

Percy Main Colliery

Percy Main Colliery

Proceeding eastward from Willington, we arrive at Percy Main, or Howden Pans Colliery, which is situated about a mile and a half from North Shields. Mackenzie, in his History of Northumberland, *noted:*

Howden Pans is seated in a vale under a hill, from which circumstance it derives its name; How signifying a hill, and Den a valley; the word Pans has been added from the numerous salt-pans which were once in it.

Howden was fomerly eminent for its extensive glass-works, which principally belonged to the Henzells. In Wallsend old church-yard there is a grave-stone of a Henzell, a broad glass-maker, of the date of 1684. The poor of this township were long supported by this respectable family. In latter times, Howden has derived its support from the ship-building business, which was carried on here for many years.

During the American war several fine frigates were built here, one of which, the *Argo*, was pierced for 44 guns; and since that time, some excellent war-vessels and large Indiamen have been constructed in these docks. The Wesleyan Methodists have a small chapel here, erected in 1805; and those of the New Connexion have a preaching room. A chapel dedicated to the Independents was also erected here a few years ago.

The sinking of the old shaft was completed in 1799. A formidable quicksand, which lay at a depth of 30 fathoms from the surface, with a feeder of water of 1,500 gallons per minute, greatly impeded the sinking and increased the expense. The sand was passed and the water dammed back by a cast-iron tub—the first that was used in the coal-trade for sinking through quicksand.

The depth to the High Main coal is 120 fathoms, and 160 to the Bensham seam, which is the deepest that has yet been worked. The workings extend under the bed of the Tyne. In some parts the seams rise at a considerable angle, and the workings on the rise side of the pit soon ascend much above the bottom of the shaft. This circumstance was productive of a singular phenomenon in 1807.

The colliery having been set on fire, it became necessary to drown up the workings to extinguish it, and the shaft was filled with water to the depth of 30 fathoms. When the engine began to draw the water out again, it worked for several weeks without apparently making any impression, the water sometimes rising and sometimes falling. At length an immense eruption of inflammable air issued suddenly from the mouth of the pit, which continued for 10 minutes to vomit a prodigious quantity of gas, when it as suddenly ceased, and all was tranquil again.

Burdon Main Colliery

Collingwood or Burdon Main Colliery

This colliery is the easternmost on the north bank of the Tyne, and is situated in the township of Chirton. It was here that Ralph Gardiner wrote his curious work entitled *England's Grievance Discovered, in Relation to the Coal Trade*, printed in 1655. Its expositions, not only with respect to the Coal Trade, but also on many other subjects such as the disgraceful trials and executions of persons then accused of witchcraft, and the grotesque punishments of the Newcastle Cloak for drunkards, and the Branks for scolds, are extremely interesting. Gardiner, however, paid the penalty of discontented persons who presumed to arraign the conduct of those above them, and his career was terminated by the hangman at York

The colliery was commenced in 1811 by Messrs Bell, Robson, and Co.; and the extent of its influence, connected with that of the neighbouring colliery of Messrs Lamb and Co., may be estimated by comparing the population in 1801, which was 1152, with that in 1831 when it stood at 4973.

Coals had been worked there during the 18th century, and, on opening one of the shafts in the year 1814, the skeleton of a man was discovered at a depth of 30 fathoms. The Old Pit, situated on the banks of the Tyne, has not been used for drawing coal for some time; that operation being performed at the A Pit, at some distance to the west, and also at the West Chirton pit. At a depth of 13 fathoms lies 'the 70 fathom post,' but which is here only 40 yards thick. The workings extend beneath the bed of the Tyne to about low-water mark. The coals are brought to bank by an engine of 30-horse power, and are conveyed to the spouts at North Shields by a railway, the greater part of which is an inclined plane.

An explosion occurred here in 1815, and is thus described by G. Johnson Esq., in his evidence before the Parliamentary Committee on Accidents in Coal Mines: 'The accident happened in consequence of an overman, with deputies and others, having gone down the pit to endeavour to secure timber and iron, and other materials, that were likely to be lost in consequence of a sudden creep having come on that part of the mine; they were then working with candles, the inflammable gas exploded, and those poor men lost their lives.'

St Laurence Colliery

The colliery is situated adjacent to the river Tyne, and in the eastern suburbs of Newcastle. Here was anciently a chapel dedicated to St Laurence, 'founded by the ancestors of the late erle of Northumberland toward fynding of a prieste to pray for all christian sowls, and also to herbour such persons as wayfayring men in time of need as it is reported'.

The pit is held of the Mayor and Corporation of Newcastle, and is carried on by Messrs Todd, Dunn, and Ridley. The period at which the Wallsend or High Main seam was wrought is supposed to have been more than a century ago. This is the only colliery in the district which has wrought the Six Quarter seam. At a distance of 800 yards from the shaft, a succession of downcast dykes cause the coals to be raised up a perpendicular staple, 14 yards deep, by horse gin, fitted up, for the first time in this part of the country.

This was one of the first collieries which introduced the system of working with square tubs, the shafts being fitted up with cages, and the tubs, guided by wooden spears, and placed one above the other, worked simultaneously out of the three seams. The colliery is commanded by two winding engines, capable of drawing 350 tons of coal per day; and the coals are delivered on board the vessels by an inclined plane 400 yards long. They are called on the London market, 'Todd and Watson's Wallsend', 'St Laurence', and 'Picton Main'.

St Laurence Colliery

Gosforth Colliery

Gosforth Colliery

This colliery is situated about three miles from Newcastle, and on the west bank of a romantic dean, through which the Ouse Burn winds its way to the Tyne. The sinking was commenced in 1825, and the coal was won on Saturday, January 15th, 1829. Great expense was incurred in this undertaking, from circumstances which have given a peculiar character to the pit.

The High Main seam was come to at 25 fathoms from the surface, but, near it, the seam was thrown down in an inclined direction, by a dyke, to the depth of 1200 feet. This Main Dyke was first discovered at Stella Grand Lease Colliery, and has been successfully traced through Denton, West Kenton, Gosforth, Killingworth, Backworth, and thence into the German Ocean [i.e. the North Sea]. It is owing to this dyke that the High Main Seam is found at collieries of Gosforth, Coxlodge, Fawdon, Wideopen, etc.

From John Sykes's *Local Records*, we find the remarkable winning of coal here was celebrated in a singular manner. On February 6th, 1829, a grand subterranean ball was given to the workers and others.

'The ballroom, which was situated at a depth of 1,100 feet below the surface of the earth, was in the shape of an L, the width of which was 15 feet, base 22 feet, and perpendicular 48 feet. Seats were placed on the side of the room, the floor was flagged, and the whole place was brilliantly illuminated with lamps and candles.

'The company began to assemble and descend about half past nine in the morning, and continued to do so until one in the afternoon. Immediately on their arrival at the bottom of the shaft, they proceeded to the face, that is the extremity of the drift, where each person hewed a piece of coal as a remembrance of the descent, and returned to enjoy the pleasures of the ballroom. As soon as a sufficient number of guests had descended, dancing commenced, and was continued without intermission till three o'clock in the afternoon, when all ascended once more to the upper regions in safety, much pleased and gratified with the amusements in which they had partaken. The Coxlodge band was in attendance; and cold punch, malt liquor, and biscuits of all kinds were in abundance. There were present between 200 and 300 persons, nearly one half of which were female!'

To expedite the drawing of corves, there are two shafts, and the waggonway to the Tyne is about 3 miles in extent. The colliery is the property of the Rev. R H Brandling, and the coals are called on the London Market 'Gosforth Wallsend'.

Jubilee Pit Coxlodge Colliery

Coxlodge Colliery

The present Coxlodge Colliery—a continuation of the old Kenton Colliery—is situated about three-quarters of a mile west from that at Gosforth, and in the north moiety [i.e. half] of Coxlodge township. The royalty of the whole township belongs to Ralph Riddell Esq., of Felton, and the colliery is wrought by the Reverend R. H. Brandling and partners.

A colliery was once attempted in the Fountain Close, a short distance from the Three-mile Bridge, on the north turnpike, and from the workings of which the water was procured with which, before the establishment of the Subscription Water Company, Newcastle was almost entirely supplied. Water had previously been brought to the town from Great Usworth Moor; but that being found inadequate, a lease for 227 years was granted by the corporation, in 1770, to Mr Ralph Lodge and other proprietors at an annual rent of 13s. 4d., 'to dig and make a reservoir at the south end of the Town Moor, and to lay pipes for bringing water to it from the Coxlodge grounds, and from the reservoir into the town; also for supplying water for a certain number of fire-plugs ordered by the Corporation'. The water is conveyed by pipes through Coxlodge estate, and across the Town Moor, to what is still called the New Water Pond.

The Jubilee Pit, so called in commemoration of the jubilee held on George III attaining the 50th year of his reign, is 68 fathoms deep; and the Regent Pit, named in honour of the Prince of Wales, afterwards George IV, is 92 fathoms. The coals are called in the markets, 'Riddell's Wallsend', 'Coxlodge', and 'West Kenton'. In 1836, 39,707 tons of coal from this colliery was shipped in 118 vessels, at a shipping price of 9s. 9d. per ton.

Wideopen Colliery

The hamlet of Wideopen is about five miles north from Newcastle, in the parish of Long Benton. The colliery is situated on the east side of the Great North Road, and is worked by Messrs Perkins and Thackrah. Sinking was commenced here in April, 1825; and the first coals drawn in May, 1827. There are two shafts for drawing coal, and another for a pumping engine. The depth to the High Main seam, which here averages 3ft 10ins in thickness, is 80 fathoms. The screens are covered in so as to protect the men and boys working at them from the weather; and they are lighted at night by gas, for which purpose a neat gasometer has been constructed near the pit. The total length of railway from the colliery to the Tyne, near Percy Main estate, is about 10 miles. The coals are titled on the market, 'Perkins, Wallsend'.

Fawdon Colliery

The township and village of Fawdon is situated about three-and-a-half miles from Newcastle, and in the parish of Gosforth. High Fawdon, Fawdon Square, and Low Fawdon, are pit villages which owe their existence to the colliery. The A Pit was commenced in March, 1810; and the High Main coal was reached in May, 1811. The B Pit was sunk in the years 1813 and 1814, and is about the same depth (48 fathoms) as the A Pit. During the sinking a fossil tree was discovered. No coals have been drawn at this pit for many years, but it is used as a furnace pit for the purpose of ventilation. The waggons are drawn from the screens by an inclined plane to Kenton-bank-top, or Blakelaw, by means of a fixed engine. The coals are called in the London Markets, 'Newmarch's Wallsend', being wrought by the firm of Newmarch, Sons, and Co.

Benwell Colliery

This colliery is situated nearly three miles from Newcastle, and is one of the most ancient on the Tyne. It contains the whole series of coal seams in a workable state, except the Three-quarter coal. All the seams from the High Main to the Bensham, crop out in the north bank of the river, between the Roman station of Condercum on the top of the hill, and the staith. Benwell was the scene of the celebrated poem called The Collier's Wedding, by Edward Chicken, a standard work in Northumbrian poetry, and graphically descriptive of the manners of pitmen in the last [i.e. 18th] century.

Benwell Staith

The seams above the level of the river were mostly worked out in former times; and the uppermost, or Main Coal, was accidently set on fire 160 years ago [1684], and continued to burn for 30 years. According to Foster's Section of the Strata: 'The fire at last extended itself northward into the grounds of Fenham, nearly a mile from where it first appeared. Red ashes and burnt clay, the relics of this pseudo-volcano, are still to be seen on the western declivity of Benwell Hill; and it is credibly reported, that the soil, in some parts of the Fenham estate, has been rendered unproductive by the action of the fire.'

On January 19th, 1830, a paper by John Buddle, Esq., was read at a meeting of the Natural History Society, Newcastle, describing a whin dyke which passes through the Beaumont seam here. This dyke passes under the Ninety-fathom dyke, and re-appears at the Ouseburn, and again at Simonside, near Jarrow, being found in the intervening collieries of Byker, Lawson's Main, and Walker.

The Beaumont seam was so called from having been first worked at Montague Main Colliery, in the adjoining estate of Denton, by the celebrated Mr Beaumont, thus mentioned in Grey's Chorographia:

'Mr Beaumont, a gentleman of great ingenuity and rare parts.'

The only explosion on record occurred on October 27th, 1826, when two young boys were killed, and several others injured. The coals are conveyed by inclined planes from the pit to the staith, where they are put on keels to be carried to ships lying below Newcastle bridge and at Shields. The colliery is worked by Messrs Surtees, Dunn, and Co; and the coals are called 'Adair's Main' in the London markets.

Walbottle Colliery

This colliery is situated in the parish of Newburn, about four miles west by north from Newcastle. It is of considerable antiquity, the Duke Pit having been a working shaft upwards of 100 years. Our view exhibits the bottom of the Coronation Pit shaft. The colliery has been remarkably fortunate in its exemption from explosions. There are three working pits, at which the coals are drawn by an aggregate of 83 horse power. The waggon-way from the Coronation Pit to the staith at Lemington is about two miles long; and waggons are conveyed thither by horses and inclined planes. The coals are forwarded to the ships by keels. Messrs Lamb and Co. are the proprietors of the colliery, and the coals are known as 'Holywell Main', 'Newburn Main', 'Holywell Reins', and 'Holywell Reins Splint'.

Wylam Colliery

The pleasant village of Wylam is situated close to the north bank of the Tyne, in the parish of Ovingham, and about nine miles west-by-north of Newcastle. The colliery, the property of Christopher Blackett, Esq., proprietor of the estate, is in the village; and to a considerable distance beyond it.

The antiquity of this colliery is attested by about twenty old pits belonging to it; and some of those in present use are known to have been so for above 90 years.

The workings of coal in Tynedale was carried on at a very early period. After the grand crisis of the capture of Calais by King Edward III, his queen, Philippa, resided chiefly in England. The following is taken from Lives of the Queens of England, by Agnes Strickland:

'Our country felt the advantage of the beneficient presence of their queen. Philippa had in her youth established the woollen manufacturers; she now turned her sagacious intellect towards working the coal mines in Tynedale, a branch of national industry whose inestimable benefits need not be dilated upon.

'These mines had been worked with great benefit in the reign of Henry III; but the convolutions of the Scottish wars had stopped their progress. Philippa had estates in Tynedale; and she had long resided in its vicinity during Edward's Scottish campaigns. It was an infallible result, that wherever this great queen directed her attention, wealth and national prosperity speedily followed.

'She obtained a grant from her royal lord, giving permission to her bailiff, Alan de Strothere, to work the mines of Alderneston, which had been worked in the days of King Henry III and Edward I. From this reopening of the Tynedale mines by Philippa, proceeded our coal trade, which, during the reign of her grandson, Henry VI, enriched the great merchant Whittington and the city of London.'

During the great flood of November 17th, 1771, which destroyed Newcastle bridge, and devastated the whole vicinity of the Tyne, the water reached one of the shafts of this colliery, and inundated all the workings, containing 300 acres. It was estimated there were 1,728,000 hogshead of water in the several seams of coal.

A downcast dyke of 40 fathoms which crosses the Tyne between Close House and Wylam Colliery, brings the seams which are wanting on the east side of it, down into the colliery. The Horsley Wood seam is supposed to be the last, or lowest, in the series. In its roof are various marine shells, sometimes occurring in great quantity.

The railway to the staith at Lemington is five miles in length, along which waggons are drawn by locomotive engines. In Mackenzie's History of England is the following description of the locomotive engines at Wylam: 'Each engine draws ten waggons, that carry eight chauldrons of coal, or 21 tons. Sometimes a dozen or more waggons are dragged by one engine. A stranger is struck with surprise and astonishment on seeing a locomotive engine moving majestically along the road, at the rate of five miles an hour, drawing along from 10 to 14 loaded waggons; and his surprise is increased on witnessing the extraordinary facility with which the engine is managed. This invention is a noble triumph of science.'

Locomotive at Wylam Colliery

Jarrow Colliery

On the south side of the Tyne, Jarrow Colliery occupies an important geological situation, being nearly in the centre of the great trough or basin formed by the coal measures, and where they are consequently found at their greatest depth.

Though the vestiges be few and meagre which mark the ancient sanctity of Jarrow—and though the former stillness and solitude of the place be exchanged for the bustle of Commerce, the clangour of modern mechanical and scientific inventions, and the hum of a dense population—yet the apathy of that man is not to be envied who can unmoved look around upon the spot where one of our earliest churches was built and beautified by Benedict Biscopius and his pious confrères, and from whence the Venerable Bede threw the halo of his learning, his industry, and his piety upon the otherwise dark ages of Anglo-Saxon history.

A notice occurs of a colliery at Jarrow and of the rents etc. of Durham Cathedral, dated 1618. This was an irregular seam of coal, lying near the surface, in the neighbourhood of Monkton, and which was partially wrought in those days. At the time Gardner wrote his England's Grievance, about 1655, the Black Staith was the only one marked in the parish. The present pit, the Alfred, was won by Simon Temple Esq.; and the colliery was opened on September 26th, 1803. It was sunk to the Bensham Seam, which is found at a depth of 175 fathoms from the surface. In this colliery is remarkably illustrated the growth and progress of the Heworth Band. It begins at the river Tyne a few inches thick, but gradually increases in its passage south until it entirely divides the seam. Beneath the churchyard at Jarrow, the coal was wrought under it, and it is there 30 inches thick; but in the space of a few hundred yards south, it was proved to exceed 20 feet in thickness, and the two parts of the seam are never again united in the southern district.

The following list of explosions here has been collected from Syke's Records:

September 25, 1817—six men lost their lives.
April 28, 1820—two persons killed.
January 17, 1826—on this occasion, forty-two men and boys were

killed, and forty-six horses and two asses were also killed.

March 15, 1828—eight men lost their lives.

August 3, 1830—This explosion occurred about twenty minutes before six o'clock in the morning, in the Bensham Seam, when forty-two men and boys were deprived of life. Twenty-one of the men were married, leaving widows and sixty-six children. . . . It appears that the catastrophe was caused by 'a bag of foulness' (as a latent accumulation of the inflammable gas is termed by the pitmen).

Jarrow Colliery

Hebburn Colliery

Hebburn Colliery is situated about a mile west of that at Jarrow. Coals appear to have been worked here at an early period; and these mines probably formed part of the supposed passage alluded to in the following extract from Thurlow's *State Papers*: 'In 1656, a mad design was entertained by — Clavering and Adam Sheppardson, to contrive a way from the cole-pitts about two miles from the castle [of Newcastle], underground to the castle of Tynemouth, for to relieve the enemy with provisions of food if required, and for that purpose there was a great store of provisions laid in, and to be laid in Hebburn-house, and eighty firelocks and a great number of stilettoes laid in Fellen-house.'

The present colliery was commenced in 1792. The winning was considered one of the most arduous and difficult that had up to that period been attempted, the quantity of water drained amounting to upwards of 3,000 gallons per minute, until stopped back by the then infant art of 'wood tubbing'. . . .

The quantity of inflammable gas evolved during many years of inexperienced practice, caused innumerable and heavy explosions; and the workmen, hardened by custom, frequently saw without alarm streams of blue flame emanating from the furnace. At that time the business of the colliery was principally carried on by the steel-mills, upwards of 100 of which were in daily use, and the ventilating current, according to custom, was carried entire through all the ramifications of the mine.

This was the first colliery visited by Sir Humphrey Davy during a sojourn at Hebburn Hall, the seat of C. Ellison, Esq.; and it was from bottles of gas taken from one of the blowers of the B Pit dyke, that the celebrated chemist made his experiments and analysis. The first [Davy] lamps, therefore, were sent down here to be tried by Mr Matthias Dunn, then resident viewer.

At the C Pit, represented in our engraving, the drawing engine is of 30 horse power. There are two other working shafts. The 'Black Staith' is one of the oldest on the Tyne. The colliery is wrought by Messrs Easton and Co.; and the coal is called on the market 'Hebburn Main'.

Hebburn Colliery

St Hilda Colliery, South Shields

The enterprising Simon Temple Esq first won a colliery here on the
ground of the Dean and Chapter of Durham, which was hence
called Chapter Main Colliery. The first coals were conveyed to the
spout, amidst great rejoicing, on April 23, 1810. The great expense
of the undertaking, however, compelled that gentleman to stop
payment; when the concern fell into the hands of Messrs Brown, of
London, proprietors of Jarrow Colliery, who sold the lease to Messrs
Devey. The present colliery belongs to Robert, William, and John
Brandling, Esqrs. The pit was bottomed at the Bensham Seam on
July, 1825; the shaft being about 143 fathoms deep. The average
thickness of the seam is 6 feet; and the workings extend to the south
of the shaft, which is situated a short distance from St Hilda's
Church, South Shields.

The colliery was always considered as peculiarly safe; but on the morning of Friday, June 28, 1839, about nine o'clock, the banksman observed the smoke of the furnace, mixed with small coals, ascending the downcast portion of the shaft, announcing the fatal certainty of an explosion. From the situation of the colliery, in the heart, as it were, of a populous town, the alarm spread with fearful rapidity; and the multitudes rushed to the spot to ascertain the extent of the catastrophe.

The mute despair, or frantic grief, of the assembled parents, wives, children, and friends, were intensely agonising; and as the bodies of the sufferers were one by one brought to bank, and conveyed in carts to their recent homes, the scene became almost too much for contemplation. . . .

In the course of the day, the whole of the bodies, 51 in number, were exhumed. An inquest was opened on Saturday, and adjourned to the following Monday, when it was ascertained that by far the greater number of those in the mine had perished by after-damp, only a small proportion being killed by the explosion. . . .

The verdict stated: 'It evidently appears that the explosion . . . has been caused by the incaution of one of the workmen in going with a lighted candle into what is called the tenth board of the mine, which had become foul.' Nineteen widows and 44 orphan children were left, for whom a subscription was entered into, which in a few days amounted to about £400.

St. Hilda Colliery

Pumping Engine at Friar's Goose

This engine, the most powerful on the Tyne, is situated about 1½ miles east from the town of Gateshead. It was erected 20 years ago [1824] for the purpose of drawing off the water in the High Main Seam of Tyne Main Colliery; and it was by means of it that the colliery at St Lawrence, on the north side of the Tyne, has been recovered.

The depth of the shaft is 55 fathoms, and there are three sets of pumps, each of 16½ inches diameter. Another engine of 70 horse power was erected here in 1842; and an engine for draining the Low Main Seam, at the depth of 100 fathoms, has also been erected at Gateshead.

A beautiful and extensive prospect may be had from the upper rooms of those erections, the interest of which is not a little heightened by the fact that a considerable portion of the foreground, on both sides of the Tyne, is excavated by the workings of the colliery to which these engines belong.

Team Colliery

Coal appears to have been wrought in the Team and Ravensworth districts for several centuries. A grant of way-leave from a colliery at Ravensworth occurs from Bishop Ruthall in 1530. The first waggon-ways, and the second steam engine used in the north, belonged to the Liddells; and Colonel Liddell and Hon. Charles Montague were the founders of a partnership vulgarly called the Grand Allies.

The Street Pit (represented in our engraving, and so called from its contiguity to the site of the Roman road) is situated about four miles south from the borough of Gateshead. The seams at present working are the Five-quarter and the Low Main. About a quarter of a mile north of the Street Pit is the Betty Pit, where the coals are drawn by an engine of Boulton and Watts construction, of 26 horses' power. The coals are shipped on the Tyne, at Poulter's Close, about five miles from the colliery; and there is also a waggon-way leading from this pit, to the staiths at Dunston, about two miles west from Gateshead.

Ellison Main Colliery

Ellison Main, or Sheriff Hill Colliery, is situated on the summit of Gateshead Fell. Sheriff Hill is so called from being the place at which the sheriff of Northumberland was formerly accustomed to receive the judges of assize on their way from Durham to Newcastle. The colliery is at present leased by Messrs Lamb and Hutchinson under Cuthbert Ellison Esq. of Hebburn Hall. The Isabella Pit was sunk between 50 and 60 years ago [i.e. *c.* 1790] and is 125 fathoms deep to the Hutton Seam. This seam is not used in the collieries north of the Tyne, but is a very valuable seam on the Wear.

On the morning of June 27, 1815, an explosion took place, whilst Mr William Foggett, the viewer, and his two brothers, were down, all of whom were killed by the blast, and eight of the workmen were also suffocated by the after-damp.

On July 19, 1819, after the hewers had left work, an explosion occurred which proved fatal to two men and thirty-three boys who happened to be in that part of the mine. Upwards of twenty men and boys were in other parts of the mine, but fortunately escaped, a few only being slightly injured by the concussion and after-damp.

The waggon-way from the Isabella Pit to the Tyne is three miles in length.

Brandling Junction Railway

A meeting of the nobility, clergy, and freeholders of the county of Northumberland, was held in the county courts, Newcastle, on August 21, 1824, at which the respective merits of a railway and a ship canal, to be formed between Newcastle and Carlisle, were discussed, and a committee was appointed. On the 26th of March following, another meeting was held, when the report of the committee in favour of a railway was unanimously agreed to. The royal assent was given to an Act for that purpose on May 22, 1829.

Various portions of the line having been formed and partially used, the whole was at length formally opened, from the Redheugh, near Gateshead, to Carlisle, on June 18, 1838; and a branch has since been formed on the north side of the Tyne, by which the trains arrive at Newcastle. Meanwhile, the Brandling Junction Railway was formed, connecting Gateshead with Monkwearmouth, and having a branch to South Shields. A connecting line, from the Newcastle and Carlisle Railway Company's station at Redheugh, to the terminus of the Brandling Junction Railway, on the east side of Gateshead, completes the line between the German Ocean [i.e. North Sea] and the Irish Sea.

A stationary engine of 60 horse power, represented in our engraving, draws the waggons laden with coals and other merchandise from the west up an inclined plane from Redheugh; and from this engine they are drawn by locomotives along bridges which extend across the principal streets of Gateshead to the Brandling Junction station, near which there is a coal-staith on the Tyne, opposite to Newcastle Quay.

Newcastle upon Tyne
Brandling Junction Railway

Garesfield Colliery

This colliery, the property of the Marquess of Bute and Miss Simpson of Bradley, is situated in the township of Winlaton, parish of Ryton, about seven miles south-west from Newcastle. It was commenced in the year 1800. The depth of the shaft is 25 fathoms and there is also a day level at the eastern part of the workings.

The royalty is partly in Winlaton lordship, and partly in Chopwell royalty; and the seams worked are the Stone Coal, the Five-quarter, and the Brockwell, the last being the lowest in the Newcastle coalfield. The waggons are transmitted, by means of horses and inclined planes, to Derwenthaugh staith; and the coals are thence carried by keels to the ships.

Walridge Colliery

This colliery is situated about 1½ miles from Chester-le-Street, and was opened on August 1st, 1831. On this occasion, a great number of inhabitants of Chester-le-Street and the neighbourhood assembled to witness the proceedings. About noon, the first waggon-load of coals were drawn off, amid the cheers of the populace, accompanied by a band of music. A party of gentlemen afterwards dined at the Lambton Arms, Chester-le-Street, in celebration of the event; and the workmen were also regaled with roast beef and plum pudding, ale, etc.

The colliery is held under lease of Colonel Joliffe and Lady Byron by George Sowerby Esq and Partners. There are two coal-pits and one engine-pit.

The number of collieries along the Great North Road seem long to have attracted the attention of travellers. 'From Durham,' says one, 'the road to Newcastle gives a view of the inexhaustible store of coals and coal-pits which employ near 30,000 persons in digging for coals; and from hence not London only, but all the south part of England, is continually supplied.'

Pelton Colliery

The colliery is situated about two miles west-south-west from Chester-le-Street. It was commenced by Messrs Kingcote and Co., but is now carried on by James Reed Esq. and Partners, who have, since they came into possession, effected many valuable improvements in the concern. The ground was broken for the air-shaft on August 12, 1835. The depth of this shaft is 64 fathoms . . . and the seam wrought is the Hutton. The coals are transmitted by the Pontop and Shields (the Stanhope and Tyne) Railway, a distance of about 13 miles, to the staiths at South Shields.

Hartley Colliery

Before we proceed to describe a few collieries on the Wear, it may not be uninteresting to notice that at Hartley, situated about six miles from North Shields. It is worked by John Jopling Esq. and Partners. The present shaft, 53 fathoms deep to the Low Main Seam, was sunk in 1830; a previous shaft, 80 fathoms deep, having been abandoned. The seam here is 4 feet 6 inches in thickness. The waggons are drawn to the staiths at Seaton Sluice, which is about a quarter of a mile distant, by horses. This singular harbour is situated at the mouth of Seaton burn, which, running down from the west, formerly discharged itself into the sea by a sudden turn due north.

Sir Ralph Delaval endeavoured to improve the haven by the erection of a pier; and, by the construction of a strong sluice and flood-gates, to scour the channel at low water, it having being found liable to be choked up by sand. The late Lord Delaval, at great expense, cut a passage through the solid rock in a direct line from the rivulet to the sea, and thus provided another entrance to the harbour, by which ships may enter and depart. This new passage, which is crossed by a drawbridge, is 52 feet deep, 30 feet broad, and 900 feet long. Indeed, this haven which is capable of accommodating from 12 to 15 vessels of 300 tons burthen, is a natural and artificial curiosity. 'Worth gaun a mile to see!'

Drops at Sunderland

The first staiths for the shipment of coals on the Wear were erected on the site displayed in our View in 1812. The scenery on this part of the Wear is peculiar and striking, and has often excited the attention of tourists. The lofty and precipitous crags of limestone rock which impend on each side of the river, indented by quarries, and interspersed with limekilns, bottle-houses, and loading gears; the number of ships, keels, and other craft, passing and repassing in the deep and comparatively narrow bed of the river; and that splendid monument of public spirit, science, and taste, the Iron Bridge, built under the auspices of the late Rowland Burden Esq., of Castle Eden, in the years 1793-6: all combine to form one of the most animating and impressive pictures to be found in this part of the country.

The railways were brought to the western brink of the deep ravine, called Galley's Gill, where an extensive depot was erected; and a strong bridge of timber, at a considerable inclination, was laid across the Gill, forming an inclined plane, down which the waggon-way was passed, and through a tunnel in a projecting rock (see View) to the spouts.

The erection of these works caused a considerable sensation amongst the keelmen and casters of the Wear, then, for the first time, forced into competition with shipping staiths; and several similar establishments having been talked about, on the afternoon of March 20th, 1815, a great number of persons, chiefly belonging to the above professions, assembled in a riotous manner, and proceeded to pull down the wooden bridge; which they effected by means of ropes. They also set fire to the depot and machinery for lowering the waggons down the inclined plane; and one house in the neighbourhood was pulled down, and several others unroofed. Many persons were injured by falling timbers, and one man was killed. At a late hour in the night, a party of Dragoons arrived from Newcastle, and dispersed the mob. The injury was estimated at £6,000.

Since that period, the depot has been restored, and the bridge superseded by an earthen mound; the road beneath being kept open by an arch of brick. On August 16th, 1819, John King was executed at the new drop, in front of the courts of Durham, for the wilful murder of James Hamilton, on the night of Sunday, the 16th of the preceding May, in a cabin attached to this building.

There are now eight drops extending from the lower or eastern side of the Gill, and three on the western side, to which the coals are brought by another branch of the railway. The coals at present shipped here are those from the Earl of Durham's collieries, and those of Henry Stobart, Esq, at Lumley. The export of the Marquess of Londonderry's coals from hence is now discontinued; but those from Framwellgate Moor Colliery are expected to be brough hither. The drops here are capable of shipping 150 keels per day. They are differently constructed from those on the Tyne, the waggon being suspended from the extremity of a strong framing of beams, which turns on a central axle, and lowers its load to the deck of the vessel.

Drops at Sunderland

Pemberton Main Colliery

This interesting colliery is situated on the north bank of the Wear, about half a mile from the Iron Bridge. It was commenced in May, 1826. The following account of this remarkable mining adventure is given in the *History and Description of Fossil Fuel*, p. 187: 'The shaft at present sinking at Monkwearmouth Colliery, near Sunderland, has attained a considerably greater depth than any mine in Great Britain (or, estimating its depth from the level of the sea, than any mine in the world). The upper part of the pit is sunk through the lower magnesium limestone strata which overlap the south-eastern district of the great Newcastle Coal-field. . . . In October, 1834, they reached a seam of considerable value and thickness, at the depth of 1578 feet below the surface; and, presuming that this newly-discovered seam was identified with the Bensham Seam of the Tyne (or Maudlin Seam of the Wear), they are rapidly deepening their shaft in anticipation of reaching the Hutton, or most valuable seam, at no distant period. The outlay of capital in this spirited undertaking has been immense—it is said not less than £100,000.'

The waggons are transferred from the pit mouth to the Wear on an inclined plane. In 1836, 51 ships with 13,707 tons of coal from this colliery arrived in the Thames; the average shipping price being 11s. 6d. per ton.

South Hetton Colliery

It was supposed, till of late years, that the magnesium limestone, extending over the greater part of the eastern district of the county of Durham, cut off the coal measures; or that, if coal existed beneath it, such coal must be deteriorated both in quality and thickness. The winning of this colliery, however, by Colonel Braddyll, and more recently that at Monkwearmouth, by Messrs Pemberton, have completely refuted this opinion, and have given an impulse to mining speculation in this hitherto unexplored field.

Hetton Colliery is situated in the vale of Houghton, about 50 miles east-north-east from the city of Durham. Before its commencement there was not a house within a mile of the spot which now teems with a numerous population. Considerable attention was excited during the sinking of the pit, the shaft of which is 180 fathoms deep.

The waggon-way from this colliery to the staiths on the Wear was opened on November 18th, 1822. It extends over a space of 8 miles, and in its course crosses Warden Law, one of the highest hills in the county of Durham. Five of Mr George Stephenson's travelling engines, two 60 horse power fixed reciprocating engines, and five self-acting inclined planes, were the means of transit. On the formation of Seaham Harbour, however, a railway was constructed thither from this colliery, a distance of about 6 miles. In 1836, 674 ships, with 201,737 tons of Hetton coals, arrived at the Thames.

The artificial harbour at Seaham is situated 6 miles south from Sunderland, and was commenced in September, 1828. A town has also been constructed on the lofty cliffs above the harbour; the first vessel loaded here, the Lord Seaham, proceeded to sea on July 25th, 1831, and a market was established in November, 1843.

The Letch Pit

This colliery, which receives its name from a letch, or brook, in its vicinity, is situated about a mile west from Hetton, and is the property of the Marquess of Londonderry. It was sunk in the summer of 1824; and the shaft is 80 fathoms to the Hutton Seam, which is here 4 feet 4 inches thick. The water passes from the workings by means of a drift between this pit and Pittington Colliery. The coals are shipped at Seaham Harbour by means of the railway from Pittington and Hetton. The quantity in heap, amounting sometimes to 1,500 scores, gives the colliery that volcanic appearance which we have endeavoured to represent in our View.

Broomside Colliery

Broomside Coliery, situated near to the Durham and Sunderland Railway, about two miles for the Letch Pit, is also the property of the Marquess of Londonderry.

The importance of a railway beween Durham and Sunderland having been suggested, successive meetings were held at Sunderland, and the sum of £81,600 (four-fifths of the estimated expense, £102,000) was subscribed in shares of £50 each; an Act was passed 'For incorporating certain Persons for the Carriage of Goods and Commodities, by means of a Railway, from the city of Durham to Sunderland near the Sea, with a Branch to join the Hartlepool Railway, in the Township of Haswell, all in the County of Durham. The Durham and Sunderland Railway Company has the power to make and use a railway, with staiths, wharfs, and shipping places, in the following townships: Gilligate (otherwise St Giles), Sherburn, Pittington, Moorsley, Moorhouse, West and East Rainton, Hetton-le-Hole, Little and Great Eppleton, Murton, Haswell, Dalton-le-Dale, Seaham, Seaton, Houghton-le-Spring, Wardenlaw, Burdon, Silksworth, Tunstall, Ryhope, Bishop Wearmouth, and Sunderland near the Sea.'

Whitwell Colliery

This colliery is situated near the Durham and Sunderland Railway, 2½ miles south-east from the city of Durham, and commands a splendid view of the beautiful cathedral, the castle, and the surrounding scenery of that ancient city. It comprises the whole of the extra-parochial place or township of Whitwell House, the property of the Master and Brethren of Sherburn Hospital. The sinking of the A Pit was commenced on May 2nd, 1836.

The coals are called in the market 'Whitwell Wallsend' and are produced from the Low Main and Hutton Seams; the High Main having been worked to a slight extent since the opening of the colliery in 1837. The coals are transmitted on the Durham and Sunderland Railway, a distance of 14 miles, to the latter place. The first were shipped on November 6th, 1837.

The Newcastle and Darlington Junction Railway (now in course of formation, and which will complete the railway communication between London and Newcastle-upon-Tyne), passes through the royalty, and within a quarter of a mile of the A Pit. This pit is almost entirely free from hydrogen gas or fire damp; and the accidents from other causes have been very few. Only one life was lost in sinking the A Pit, and three others since the commencement of the mine.

Beamish Colliery

Though situated in the midst of collieries which ship their coals on the Tyne, being about 8 miles south-south-west of Newcastle, yet the Beamish coals are sent, by means of fixed engines, inclined planes, and horses, to Fatfield on the Wear, a distance of about 6 miles. The colliery was commenced in 1763, by Morton Davidson Esq, from whose family the 'Grand Allies' held the lease for many years, and is now the property of Sir Robert Eden, Bart.

A water-wheel (represented in our View) is turned by water drawn by a level from the upper seam, and has been used for draining the lower seams; but it has latterly been found insufficient for that purpose. Of later years, the Beamish district has only been partially worked, other pits having been commenced at Stanley, further to the west.

St Helen's Auckland Colliery

We now proceed to notice some of the collieries which export their coals from the Tees, and which occupy a long-neglected district of the Durham coal-field. Vavasour's mine on Cockfield Fell, mentioned in 1375, is the first inland colliery on record.

We have been favoured with the following interesting account of the Auckland Coal District by Joseph Lawson Esq: 'This district may be said to commence at Coundon, a little east of Bishop Auckland, and extends westward to Butterknowle Colliery, a distance of 10 miles; it will contain not less than 70 square miles of surface, under which, in most collieries, there are two, and sometimes even three or four, workable seams, varying in thickness from 3 feet 6 inches to 6 feet, and equal in quality to any coal wrought in Great Britain. Within the last 20 years, considerably under one hundred coal-workmen were all that were engaged in the district getting coals; and the whole of the produce of this important coal-field was carried away either in carts or the backs of mules and asses. Large numbers of them, taking the by-roads in order to secure a little of the scanty herbage, and avoid payment of gates, were, in those days, to be met, carrying two or three bags each. They frequently found their way to a distance of 50 miles from the pits, where, from the excellent quality of the coal, a ready market was secured.'

The colliery of St Auckland is one of those which would never have been called into existence but for the formation of the Darlington and Stockton Railway. It is now the property of Sir George Musgrave, Bart., and a portion of the royalty belongs to Sir T. J. Clavering, Bart., and the Rev. Matthew Chester. The sinking was commenced by Joseph Pease Esq (late MP for South Durham) and Partners. The distance of this colliery from the shipping place on the Tees is 26 miles, and to facilitate the transmission, 533 coal-waggons are used. The coals were formerly shipped for London and coastwise, but latterly a considerable quantity have been sent foreign. A large depot trade is also carried on, by which the coals are sent as far south as York; and the coke manufactured here is used by most of the railways for 60 miles south.

St Helen's Auckland Colliery

Old Etherley Colliery

The Phoenix Pit, Old Etherley, of which we give a View, is situated about 3 miles west from Bishop Auckland, 24 from Stockton, and 28 from Middlesbro', to both of which latter places coals are sent from this colliery by the Stockton and Darlington Railway. It was undertaken by Henry Stobart Esq and Partners. The Five-quarter Seam is very little wrought, in consequence of its being of an inferior quality; but the Main Coal Seam is wrought extensively, and is an excellent coal. The coal is shipped coastwise; and considerable quantities are disposed of by landsale in Yorkshire.

Drops at Middlesbro'

The town of Middlesbro', on the south side of the estuary of the Tees, forms the terminating point of the Stockton and Darlington Railway.

The first rail of this Company was laid on May 23rd, 1822 by T. Meynell, Esq. A writer in *Frazer's Magazine* for May 1844 says: 'To the success of the "Stockton and Darlington Railway" may be traced the rise of all others. To the originator of this line is due the honour of being the founder of the railway system. . . . We hope the time may never come when the millions at home and abroad, who enjoy the advantages of railways, shall have forgotten that they owe them to Mr Edward Pease of Darlington. . . . It remains a striking instance of foresight that, without any experience, and with "all the world before him where to choose", he selected what, to the ordinary observer, is an unpromising district, and made the first and most successful railway.'

The branch was opened from Darlington to Croft on October 27th, 1829. On May 1st, 1830, the Haggar Leazes Branch was opened by a procession. The length of the main line is 30 miles, cost about £125,000, and crosses the Tees at Stockton by a bridge; it is thence carried along the south side of the river at Middlesbro'.

In the year 1767, a navigable canal was projected to pass from Stockton, by Darlington, to Whinston, with collateral branches from Cotham Stob to Yarm, from Darlington to Croft Bridge, and from Thornton to Piersbridge. The expense of the project was calculated at £63,722; and from want of funds it was relinquished, without an application to the legislature.

Middlesbro' is as yet scarcely noticed upon the maps, though, like Goole upon the Ouse, it is rapidly rising in importance. The drops represented in our View, since it was taken, have been superseded by docks. The staith was about 450 yards long, extending along the water's edge; but the most remarkable feature of the drops was, that the coal-waggons were raised by a steam-engine from the railway behind to the upper floor of the staith, and thence lowered again to the decks of the vessels in the river.

Drops at Middlesbro'

Whitworth Park Colliery

This colliery is situated about 6 miles south-west from the city of Durham, and the royalty belongs to R. E .D. Shaftoe, Esq., of Whitworth. The sinking was commenced June 10th, 1841, by the 'Durham County Coal Company' and the depth to the Hutton Seam is 86 fathoms. In 1842 the colliery was laid in and dismantled by the company, after an outlay of nearly £40,000; but in a very brief space it was re-let to, and refitted up by, a private company, who are entering upon their speculation with sanguine expectations of success.

Clarence Railway

In 1824, a bill was introduced into parliament for the formation of a railway to extend from Stockton to the districts in the central and northern parts of the county; but owing to some informality [i.e. drafting error] it was thrown out. In 1828, however, it was again introduced and carried. On February 18th, 1829, Lord Lowther brought in a bill 'to enable the Clarence Railway Company to vary and alter the line of their railway, to abandon some of the branches thereof, and to make other branches therefrom'.

By this act, the proprietors were authorized to form a line of railway, including branches, from 47 to 49 miles in length; and its estimated cost was £243,000. It has, however, been recently stated to have cost half a million pounds, The main line from Port Clarence, on the Tees, to Sim Pasture, in the parish of Heighington, is about 16 miles in length; and there is a branch of about 3 miles from it to Stockton. Another branch, 9 miles long, leads to Coxhoe; and two others respectively lead from it to Chilton and Byers Green.

The Clarence Drops on the Tees

4

CONDITIONS UNDERGROUND FOR BOYS

A Royal Commission on Children's Employment reported its findings in 1842, shocking the nation with some horrific tales:

Fifty years ago [1792] the labour of lads in coal-pits was excessive, and its duration long then, as now, when lads of as young as six or eight were sent down below to work. His occupation was to open and shut a door to preserve the proper circulation of air, whilst the coals were passing from the workings to the shaft. He was called a trapper, and had 5*d*. a day for his wage. His labour is only light, but he must generally remain until the work is all done, and the pit is closed for the day. After going through this early stage of a pitman's life, he then becomes a driver or putter. The former attends a horse that draws the coals in corves or baskets to a crane or the shaft; two of the latter take the coals from the workings themselves without the assistance of a horse. Here the misery of the putter begins, and generally continues until he is 17 years of age, when he is considered fit to be a hewer. Previous to going down the pit, his education, when he had any, consisted of a little reading got from the village school-mistress. After he went to work, little time for education could be spared, unless, for want of demand, the pits were not at full work.

The 1842 Commission heard this evidence about Nichol Henderson of Monkwearmouth Colliery:

Age sixteen. Is bound as a putter, but unable to put yet. A year ago the horse ran away; knocked him off; trailed with the waggons. Off work for 10 months. Is lame now, and will always be lame. His leg was set wrong at first. One leg is shorter than the other. The pit makes him sick. Was very healthy before. Has been here for nearly six years. The heat makes him sick. The sulphur rising up the shaft as he goes down makes his head work. Feels worse when he first goes down at three o'clock in the morning; when he comes up at six in the evening he feels sick. It is nearly seven o'clock when he gets home.

Very seldom when he gets home can he eat very much, this is from the heat and long hours down the pit. Gets to bed at different times, generally lying down by the fireside first. Mother calls him about 3 a.m., when he feels very sleepy and often so sick that he cannot eat when he gets up. Sometimes he can eat his bait down the pit, sometimes not. Sometimes so sick as to bring up his victuals again from his stomach.

About half a year since, a lad, John Huggins, was very sick down the pit, and wanted to come up, but the keeper would not let him ride (come up) and he died of fever one week later.

Knows some boys who have been sick in this way, and of three boys who were killed when the rope broke as the corf was going down, and they fell to the bottom of the shaft; the rope falling on top of them.

One of the colliery officials, Henry Morton, of Biddick, near Lambton, gave the management side of the story:

Works at one of the Countess of Durham's collieries. Thinks that the usual employment of the children in coal-mines is perfectly consistent with their health. Making very good wages, they are enabled to have good and sufficient maintenance. Working at the night shift does not make much difference, the air and ventilation being the same at one period as another.

Within an experience of 14 years in the Countess of Durham's mines has not observed any instances of prejudicial effects from the hours, or mode of place or working . . . has never heard of boys straining or rupturing themselves in these pits. Does not think any alteration in the hours of labour necessary for children. Would not object to a law restricting children from going down the pits before 10 years old, but would rather leave it to the discretion of the Viewer to accept or refuse them; any such law would press heavily on parents who had large families. Any medical or educational certificates would be totally unnecessary. Parents are anxious to send children to school, but they have no good schools; and boys might obtain instruction after going to work. Does not think that the work in the pit incapacitates them to receive instruction after the day's labour, especially with regard to putters, who usually only work 8 hours.

There is no prospect of any mode of carrying on collieries so as to dispense with the labours of very young children; any restricting law that should produce a scarcity of children would prevent many pits from being carried on beneficially; old men to supplant trappers, and what are called 'swing doors', are inapplicable. Pitmen become perhaps thin, but are extremely active and muscular, and are in general quite as healthy as other labourers; of course they are subject to accidents. Does not think pit-people are necessarily lower in stature than others, and their work does not produce that effect. They consider themselves vastly superior, in the scale of society, to agricultural labourers. Drunkenness is a prevalent vice, and dog-fighting is a favourite amusement.

Alexander Ball, a putter, gave this account to the Commission:

Aged 18 and 4 months; makes about three shillings [15p.] a day. Gets up at 4 a.m., goes down the pit at quarter past four, begins work at five. Has breakfast before he goes; takes bait in a bag with him and a bottle of coffee. Has that about 11 a.m., cannot stop before that if the hewer has hewed many coals. Eats the rest when he wants it or takes it in his hand as he is working.

Loose (end of shift) at 6 p.m. Has worked at Hebburn and Wallsend. The first thing he does every morning is to prepare the tub by taking off the drags; then goes in-bye, perhaps a mile, to where the hewers are at work. There, with the help of the hewers, fills the tub; then puts it along the tramway, perhaps 70 yards, then returns for another.

Went down Walker pit when he was 9 years old. Was a healthy boy, is well now, generally, but is sometimes bad in his inside. Sometimes cannot walk well for this pain. Sometimes it comes on at home, other times at the pit. Monkwearmouth is a very hot pit; hotter than Wallsend, Hebburn or Walker. Heat sometimes gives him cold. Puts on jacket when he comes up pit. All work quite naked (except the drivers, trappers and flatmen) with the exception of a front covering of flannel and shoes. The putting is hard, but the hardest thing is the heat; and the hours are very long. Sometimes he has a doctor; has been lamed twice rather bad. Once off for five weeks; the second time eight weeks. Is lame now in some degree, from slipping his foot on a plate. Can read an easy book. Writes very little; writes his name. Does not go to night-school, but sometimes goes to Sunday-school.

5

MINERS ... 'HOUSELESS AND HOMELESS'

as told by Richard Fynes

To resist the tyrannical aggressions upon their rights, the miners formed themselves into an organisation called the Miners' Association of Great Britain and Ireland in 1841. The Northumberland and Durham miners raised £500 towards what they called a law fund. This was one of the most gigantic unions that ever was known at the time, and had for its leader some of the ablest men, Martin Jude being at its head. He had around him some of best men in the colliery districts, such as Mark Dent, Thomas Pratt, James Ballantine, George Thompson, George Charlton, Matthew Elliott, Edward Richardson, William Mitchell, Christopher Haswell, Thomas Hay, John Tulip, T. Clough, Robert Archer, Alexander Stoves, William Hammond, and many others.

In the year 1843, the owners of Wingate Colliery, in the county of Durham, decided on having wire ropes for hauling cages to bank. To this the men, who were foolishly prejudiced, objected, which was the cause of a long strike. In the same year the men at Thornley Colliery, one of the largest in Durham, came out on strike. Warrants were issued against 68 persons for absenting themselves without leave, on November 24th.

Mr J. E. Marshall appeared on the part of the owners, and Mr Roberts, the miners' advocate, for the prisoners. Mr Marshall in opening the case said the men were bound under the ordinary pit bond.

Mr Roberts applied to the bench to stop the case, urging that as a weighing machine was not stamped according to the provisions of the Act, the bond was illegal.

Mr Heckles, resident viewer of Thornley Colliery, after been sworn, had this to say: 'On November 13th I received a letter from the workmen, written and signed by James Bagley, as secretary to the workmen. The answer I made was: I wondered why they didn't get someone who could write a letter plainer. I sent word to say that if the letter meant anything, they would have to send a deputation. On the evening of the following day, fifteen men called upon me, and half of them spoke. The overman, according to instructions, deducted two shillings and sixpence [12½p.] fine for the day lost. On the evening of the 23rd, a large body of workmen came up and asked why the fine had been deducted. I told them they were asking the road they knew (a voice in court: 'Just like you!').

As Mr Roberts objected to this evidence because the men were not present, the Chairman said they would take the evidence for what it was worth. (A voice: 'That's not much if we get justice!').

Cross-examined by Mr Roberts, the viewer said: 'I do not know whether the weighing machine now being used was stamped as required by an Act of Parliament. I have been five years at the colliery, and it has never been stamped to my knowledge. I don't doubt that one man may have been fined twenty-two shillings [£1.10] for two days.' [*Colliers were fined if it was found that excess stone was mixed with their coal.*]

Mr Roberts called a number of miners who gave this evidence:

John Cockson—I don't think a man can get a living if the bond is carried out in its strictness. If a quart of splint is to be fined for, I am sure a man cannot get a living. I will go to gaol before I will work under any such bond.

Matthew Dawson—I recollect twenty-two shillings being laid out for one man; there were other tubs came up with as much in as his; more might have been laid out.

John James Bird—I doubt very much that an average man can make a living under this bond. One of the causes for the men not going to work was that the scales were not put up. I will rather go to prison than work under this bond.

William Wearmouth—The bond has not been enforced before for a quart of stones. I will rather stop in gaol for ever than work under this bond.

John Stephenson—No man can earn a living under this bond. The black brass and splint comes down amongst the coal. In some places the men work by the light of a Davy lamp, it is impossible to separate the black brass from the coal.

William Ord, William Kay, John Bates, William Toplis, Augustus King, and many others gave similar evidence.

After a lengthy summing-up, the Chairman said that the law had been broken, and that the defendants must stand convicted; and the sentence of the Court was that they should be imprisoned for six weeks.

Immediately after the trial Mr Roberts obtained a writ of habeas corpus, and the men who were in prison were removed to the Court of Queen's Bench where, upon an informality [i.e. an error in the way the charges had been worded], they were acquitted.

The many grievances referred to in the long police-court case were fast becoming unbearable by the men. It was not only that their wages were reduced, and that they were cheated and defrauded at every turn by unprincipled and dishonest agents, but they were subjected to such an amount of contemptible and petty tyranny, such mean despicable domineering, which was all the more galling and irritating from its very meanness. . . .

The miners determined to have their grievances thoroughly laid before the public, for they thought there was no other way of getting any redress unless the public took up their case. They had the great majority of the Press to fight against, and the strong power of capital. The coal-owners, when speaking of the [1844] strike, would say: 'We will never yield to the men, we will force them to comply, no matter at what cost.'

Wholesale turning to the door continued in almost every colliery village; pregnant women, bedridden men, and even innocent children in the cradle, were ruthlessly and remorselessly turned out. Age and sex were disregarded, no woman was too weak, no child too young, no grandma or grandsire too old; but all must go forth.

One poor woman, expecting to become a mother every hour, was turned to the door at one colliery, and another was dragged by the neck 100 yards along the railway; and proofs might be multiplied to show that every vile scheme was tried, and every mean trick resorted to, in order to throw the men off their guard, and exasperate them, so that in a moment of excitement they might be induced to break the peace. . . .

Such then was the position of affairs at this time. The men, houseless and homeless, hungry and careworn, many with wives and children pining for food which they could not get for them, were still convinced of the justice of the cause they had adopted, and still determined to fight in that cause. Often, when the men were away at public or district meetings, the policemen, with their ruffian auxiliaries, would swoop down upon a village and turn all the defenceless inhabitants to the door, so that when the husbands or fathers returned they would find their dear ones huddling together amongst broken furniture, beneath some hedge. But ill-treatment seemed to have no effect in breaking the spirit of the men, but rather to brace them up with sterner resolution.

6

DOWN A NORTHUMBERLAND PIT

W. White, 1859

The mouth of a pit in work is always a busy scene owing to the rapidity with which the coal is hauled up and hurried away to the shoots or waggons; and here the laden trains and the already large heaps were growing every minute longer and larger with the supplies brought from underground.

Up came the cage with its burden; then old Robert, bidding the brakesman pause, placed me on one side of the cage, himself on the other, told me to take hold of the bar that crossed between as a basket-handle, and down we shot into the darkness and a depth of 48 fathoms. I felt a sensation as if about to faint. The sudden deprivation of light was painful, and the more so in going from the full blaze of a July sun; and when the cage touched the bottom I could see nothing but what looked like two torches flaring in the distance, and the sense of bewilderment was increased by noisy cavernous rumblings, the hurried heavy tread of horses and shouts of boys.

I stepped from the cage and was led across a tramway to a wooden bench and bidden to sit down. Then the noises multiplied by the shoving of waggons into the cage, and by the crash and shock with which the heavy machine decended, almost, as it seemed, before it could have risen to the top.

When we had sat about ten minutes, I began to see, but very

dimly, that we were seated at one side of a great tunnel-like excavation stretching to unknown distances to the right and left, opening immediately in front of us upon the foot of the shaft, and containing a tramway along which the waggons were drawn, and pushed to the cage. Above my head, fixed to the black wall of shale or stone, whichever it might be, hung two flaming oil-lamps, the torches which I had fancied far off; and by their light the man Jem, who had led me from the cage, was working bravely at his task of sending up the coal. I could see a constant stream of smoke creeping to the shaft, and there passing up as though a chimney; for mines must breathe, and if pure air is drawn in at one shaft, foul air is discharged at another by the heated current of a furnace; and it was through the smoky stream of the upcast shaft that we descended.

Old Robert gave me a lighted candle, stuck in what looked like a wooden battledore, took another himself, and led the way along the black cavern on the right. I had to stand still when the waggons rumbled past, and shrink close to the wall, and make myself as small as possible, so dreadful did they seem to me in my ignorance of the route and my doubtful vision. Robert, holding his candle over the train as it passsed, discovered many a breach of rules: that is, men lying on the waggons to save themselves the trouble of walking.

At times we came to a wooden partition built all across the passage, which carries a door, hung so as to keep constantly shut. Behind each of these doors sits a boy to pull the string when men or waggons approach, and he lets the door fall to again as soon as they have passed. Neglect of duty might occasion an interruption of ventilation, and endanger the mine.

In some places the roof rises high into the darkness where masses have fallen; and stout timbers are set up to give support, or a strong stone wall is built up, making you aware of strenuous measures for safety. In some places roof and walls are firm and compact, and there is no more than room for a man between the wall and the tramway; in others there are great gaps on each side half-filled with fallen rubbish. And there are places, as old Robert stopped to show me, where air-channels tightly constructed of wood pass across the way overhead.

By and by, we turned from the mainway into a branch level, narrow and low, where you cannot stand upright, and where ponies and not horses draw the waggons. Following this we came to 'the broken', that is the place where hewing was going on, where in all directions you saw what appeared to be large black chambers and branching passages. Loose heaps of coal lay about, from which men and boys were loading the waggons, and the ponies drew off one short tram after another, along the crooked and uneven tramway to the main way.

The hewer sits on his haunches and dislodges large lumps of coal by the aid of his pick, or he bores a hole and loosens a mass by gunpowder. At intervals he leaves a huge square pillar to support the roof, and when these have served their purpose long enough, he digs them away also, and the roof sinks down with the pressure from above, and the disembowelled place becomes a goaf or abandoned working.

7

NEW HARTLEY DISASTER, 1862

The following is a Newcastle Daily Journal *account by T. Wemyss Reid (later knighted), who kept an hour-by-hour diary of events in one of the most horrific disasters in mining history:*

At eleven o'clock in the forenoon of Thursday, January 16th, 1862, the most terrible calamity that ever visited any coal-mine in the country occurred at the Hartley New Pit, a large colliery belonging to Messrs Carr of Newcastle upon Tyne, and situated near Seaton Delaval, in the county of Northumberland.

The immediate cause of the accident was the breaking into two pieces of an enormous beam of cast-iron, used in a large engine employed for pumping water out of the pit. One-half of this beam, which weighed more than forty-three tons, projected from the engine-house right over the mouth of the shaft. It was this half, which, from some unexplained cause, suddenly snapped off from the centre, and fell headlong into the shaft.

The fall of an enormous mass of metal, twenty-one tons in weight, down such a place necessarily produced results of the most fearful description. Unhappily, its fall also tore away from the sides of the shaft the stone with which it was lined, and this falling mass of rubbish came into contact with the cage, containing eight of the miners belonging to the fore-shift who were ascending to the surface. In an instant it crushed the cage into a battered and indistinguishable piece of metal. Four men in it were thrown down the shaft and buried amid a mass of falling debris.

A jack-rope was lowered down to the cage with a loop attached. One man, named Sharp, got in, but, in coming away, he got fast, was pulled out of the loop, and, falling on the wreck below, was killed. Two men, Ralph Robinson and Thomas Watson, were got out of the cage and brought to bank safe, but in a very exhausted state.

Rescuers on going down the pit found that, while the approach to the highest seam was clear, the shaft from that point was completely filled up with rubbish. Had the obstruction been lodged below the Yard Seam, and only above the Low Main Seam, no difficulty would have been encountered in rescuing the prisoners, as there was a road, by means of a ladder, called a staple, leading between these two seams, so that there was a communication independently of that afforded by the shaft.

Broken beam

The accident had happened at the most unfortunate time possible, for, in addition to the back-shift, the fore-shift workmen were almost all in the pit.

Crowds of picked men from all the surrounding collieries came to offer their services, and those were at once accepted, Mr Emmerson, the able assistant of Mr Coulson, the master sinker of Durham, superintending the arrangements. The men at once set to work upon their Herculean labours, and so energetically did they work that, by this time (Friday evening) they have got a very large portion of the debris cleared away, and hopes are entertained that in at most four hours they will be able to reach the 204 prisoners in the pit.

Great confidence is felt in Mr Amour, the back-overman, who is down the pit, and who, it is felt, will preserve order as long as possible.

Saturday, January 18th — noon

Another night has passed without any considerable change in the condition of the 204 unhappy men, who at this moment lie buried in the pit. All night long the work has been carried on without intermission, and a fair progress through the obstruction blocking the shaft has been made.

During the night the prisoners were heard jowling, as it is technically termed, communicating the fact of their still being in existence to those above them by making as much noise as possible. The jowling, however, ceased entirely at eight o'clock this morning, and for the last four hours nothing whatever has been heard.

The bodies of the two Sharp brothers, and of Ralph Robson, three of the men who fell from the cage, have been recovered; they have not yet been brought to bank, but are deposited for convenience in the upper seam, to which there is now free access.

When day broke this morning a mournful and impressive scene was presented at the mouth of the pit. Two huge fires burning near the shaft cast a sickly flame of light upon the tall engine-house, and the cage, which was broken on Thursday, now lying a battered heap of metal upon the heap. Occasionally the hoarse cries of the men at the engines, as they gave their signals from below, rang through the keen frosty air, and the gin, the jack or the crab, as the case might be, responded to the order.

Though work is going on below actively and unceasingly, there are but little signs of it at the mouth of the pit, near which are congregated only the viewer and the underviewer, a police inspector, two or three reporters, and a few gentlemen connected commercially with the colliery.

The labour of clearing the shaft is conducted by a relay of two men, picked as crack hands out of all the collieries in the neighbourhood, being lowered one by one, perilously and slowly, down the black pit, by means of a heavy chain. Suspended by ropes in order not to touch the rubbish, which might fall at any moment, they go down as far as possible, and then as quickly and as gently as they can, clear away the obstruction, placing it in a corf (basket) which is at once received by their comrades stationed at intervals above them, and being passed quickly upwards is shot into the top seam, which is still clear.

Bit by bit, the brave men bent on rescuing their comrades at whatever risk to themselves, advance, though every step is attended with the most terrible danger to their own lives. But an accident like this brings out the noble qualities of the Northumbrian pitman. For a time he rises above himself, and with the calm grandeur of heroism takes his place at the work upon which so much depends, just as a matter of course, and seemingly without the slightest idea that he is performing an action for which, long ere this, men have become famous.

Volunteers from all parts of the district have hastened to the catastrophe. All this morning, little bands were seen approaching the place from north, south, and west, and as they arrived they simply and modestly announced that they had 'come to help'. As we were standing in the rude cabin on the top of the pit-heap, which affords the only shelter to be obtained, nine men came in from a colliery of considerable distance. 'You sent for three,' they say, 'but we thought you might want more.'

The uncertainty still shrouding the fate of the unhappy men is as great as ever. At any moment the fatal obstruction may give way with a run, and leave the passage clear for the egress of the prisoners; on the other hand, there may be beams or other immovable objects matted together, which cannot be removed in time to save life.

Last night, from six to ten o'clock, about 10 feet were sunk. During the night very little progress was made, but early this morning, Mr Coulson, of Durham, the celebrated master sinker, went down the shaft himself, and under his direction the work has gone on rapidly, some 15 feet having been cleared away.

Around the pit buildings a crowd of men are gathered, talking to each other in undertones, speculating upon the fate of their comrades. Whenever the gin needs to be turned they volunteer for the service, for the horses are thoroughly worn out with the labour through which they have gone. At other times the men stand idly and silently, apparently quite unconscious of the bitter blast which is sweeping in from the sea with chilling force. Occasionally, one or two women, with tearful faces, come to the village to know if anything has transpired regarding the fate of their loved ones, and then, with fixed stony countenances, slowly return to their desolate homes.

The appearance of the village itself indicates the presence of some overpowering calamity. Few villages are more noisy or cheerful than those connected with collieries, but here a deep and solemn silence prevails. No children are at play, every door is shut, and the one or two little shops at which the inhabitants supply themselves are partially closed. Through the windows can be seen the clean bed, which is always remarkable in the cottage of the north-country pitman, while upon the table in front of the window, in almost every case, the breakfast things prepared for the prisoners on Thursday morning are still standing waiting for them. Now and then the face of a woman, marked by the same cold agony that distinguishes them all, is seen above the blind. Two days and two nights these poor women have waited; and now their grief, loud and passionate at first, has settled into the stillness of despair.

Occasionally, one of the men who have been working in the shaft goes to his home in the village. He passes on the way one house where the drawn blinds indicate that death has already visited it. It is the home of one of those killed in the cage. The door opens and a young man appears, and looks at the averted countenance of the other. There is no need of words to tell that, as yet, there are no tidings. It is indeed a calamity, the terrible nature of which cannot yet be realised, that has visited the village. In every house some seat is vacant, and all know the agony of hoping against hope.

One o'clock
The train which has just arrived has brought a large number of visitors to the spot. Amongst them is Matthias Dunn Esq., Government Inspector of Mines. Little progress has been made during the last hour in getting down the shaft, but the men generally are more hopeful, and those who direct them are confident of being able to move the obstruction ere long.

Five o'clock
A party of men have just come to bank from below, and we learn from them that, during their shift of two hours, a progress of three feet has been made. This is much above the average, and is highly encouraging. When, however, we ventured to ask one of the men who had come up, and who had a deep personal interest in the question, for he has a near relative in the mine, what the chances were of the 204 men and boys being brought up alive, his eyes filled with tears, and, shaking his head, he turned silently away.

Six o'clock
The outward appearance of the scene has changed much within an hour. All the visitors have gone, and darkness set in. Once again it is resigned to those whose few duties to the lost men or the public compel them to remain on the spot. It is bitterly cold, and a few flakes of snow are falling; but our patient little group of watchers is still gathered round one of the huge fires waiting. In a rude cabin, close at hand, are collected the men who are engaged on the different shifts of work, each quietly awaiting his particular turn. Once in two hours a party of strange-looking objects, enveloped in

huge 'black skins' made of leather, and heavy helmets made of a
similar material, are hauled up to the surface, and these, making
their way to the cabin, change their wet clothes, while their places
below are taken by others.

Midnight

Hope at last, thank God! The men have, for the last five hours, been
labouring without intermission at the clearing of the shaft. They
have met with many obstacles on their way, and the falling of a part
of the shaft wall has stopped them sadly. About two hours ago,
however, in answer to their own repeated calls, the dreary silence
which for thirteen hours had been preserved by the imprisoned men,
was broken, for a feeble but distinct jowling was heard from below.
Since that time the responsive cries from the unfortunates have been
repeated; and. thus inspirited, everyone is working with redouble
vigour. By Mr Carr and Mr Humble it is considered impossible that
any communication can be made between the searchers and the
sought before five or six tomorrow morning; so that another dreary
night must pass away before anything decisive can be known.

In the meantime everything has been prepared under the
superintendence of Dr Davison for the reception of the prisoners
immediately on their release. Ambulances, stretchers, hot tea,
brandy, blankets etc are all at hand in abundance; and in every
cottage in the village similar preparations have been made.

The neighbourhood of the pit is now very quiet. Fires are lighted
all round the base of the heap; and beside each are clustered
worn-out men, many of whom have never been in bed since the
occurrence of the accident, vainly endeavouring to shield themselves
from the pitiless east wind which is blowing in from the sea with a
bitterness that is almost unbearable.

Sunday morning—five o'clock

Another night, the third which has passed away since the accident, is
slowly wearing away, and we are still waiting. Little has transpired
during the night, and the men are getting on very slowly. There is
one good sign, however: the jowling from the prisoners has been

repeated during every shift; so that is evident they are still keeping up their hopes. Great obstructions, however, lie in the way of their deliverers. A large quantity of the stone wall which lines the shaft has fallen, and added itself to the mass of rubbish which blocks it up.

All around the pit-heap the watch-fires are still burning; and the patient waiters, looking more solemn and despairing than ever, are clustered near them. They have have stood the severity of one of the bitterest nights we have had during the present winter; and as yet show no signs of giving in.

Now and then there emerges from the gloom the figure of a female, who, after another sleepless night, has come forth to learn the news. Her face, as she hears of how little has been done to save those whom she so tenderly loves, assumes an aspect which can never be forgotten by those who have once seen it.

Noon

A bright beautiful Sabbath morning has come to us; but in the work that is going on around there is little evidence of the sacred nature of the day. The labour of removing debris in the shaft is going on as steadily and earnestly as ever; but alas! since the fall of stone last night, very little progress has been made. The bucket of a pump, which leads from the open seam to near that in which the men are supposed to be, has been the object of much fruitless labour. The shift which has just come up report still more unfavourably on the progress made.

The neighbourhood of the pit-heap wears a different aspect. An immense crowd is gathered all round the base of the mound on which the buildings stand, watching the working of the engines, and chatting and talking as if it were some curious spectacle they were witnessing. All along the line of the Blyth and Tyne Railway, which passes within a dozen yards of where we stand, an unceasing crowd of people is streaming towards the colliery. Men, women, and children, are in the group; and they have come from all parts of the country to gratify their morbid curiosity. The trains which have arrived have brought vast bodies from Newcastle, Blyth, and

Shields; and it is computed that not less than twenty thousand persons have visited the scene of the calamity every day.

The Hastings Arms, the only inn within a couple of miles, is literally swarming with visitors, passages and staircases being alike impassable; and, with a callousness that is positively shocking, all are drinking, joking, and enjoying themselves as if they were out upon some holiday. Quite distinct from the ordinary visitors are those who are waiting for the release of the friends they love. They are gathered together by themselves, and their feelings must be deeply wounded by the heartlessness displayed by the strangers around them.

One o'clock

Mr Coulson has just come up, and he reports pretty much as might be expected. He says: 'We have four feet to go straight through before we reach the bucket platform; when we get there we hope there may be very little more rubbish. It is 15 feet to where the men are from our present position; and we've heard them jowling four times this morning.'

Mr Coulson further thinks that it will take at least four or five hours to reach the platform; and, under the most favourable circumstances, another four hours to get to the men themselves.

A report has got about that the men will probably be reached in one hour. It is totally untrue, and it is amazing how little the people here know of what is really going on. A dozen ridiculous and impossible stories are related of things which are said to have occurred.

Word has just been given of those gentlemen who are present upon the ground; Mr Fryer, viewer, Teams Colliery; Mr Pearson, foreman of Hawks, Crawshay and Co.; and Mr Pringle of the same firm; Mr Dixon, engineer at Messrs Hawthorn's; Mr Johnson, engineer, Mr Sanderson, viewer, and Mr Marshall, engineer, all of Seaton Delaval Colliery; Mr Potter, owner and viewer of Cramlington Colliery; Mr Crone, West Moor Colliery; Mr Hurst, Backworth; Mr T. Y. Hall; Mr M Dunn; Mr Ramsey, Wallbottle; Mr G. B. Forster, Cowpen; Mr Cochrane, Elswick; Mr T. E. Forster

Seaton Delaval; Mr Maddison, Burradon; Mr Mundill; Mr Jobling, Bebside; Mr Middleton, Bedlington; Mr W. R. Horsley, engineer; Mr George Golightly, engineer; Mr W. Watson, Newcastle; Dr Davison, Dr Pyle, Earsdon; and Dr Gibson, Birtley.

Five o'clock
Another shift has come to an end, and there are still some unfavourable symptoms. A fresh giving way of the stone in the shaft-side has taken place; and the men are thus once more retarded. In about an hour from this time it is hoped that the workmen will get at the regular debris once more and advance steadily towards an end. It is, however, considered that at the present moment we are no nearer obtaining the release of the unfortunate men than we were at this hour yesterday morning.

Few can conceive the appalling nature of this simple statement. To us who have had to wait hour by hour spending the usually quiet Sunday in this unwonted manner, the day has been long and dreary enough, but what must the unutterable horrors have been to the 204 captives immured in their living tomb? The question of their ability to stand out much longer is seriously discussed by all, save the chief men on the spot, who, happily, entertain a firm conviction that they can resist hunger for a very much longer time than they have yet been incarcerated.

Then, as to the air, the immense body of water falling into standage, and gradually rising, as it increases in volume, drives before it the fresh air in the pit, which, passing over the heads of the confined men, rises through the rubbish in the shaft. This is the only danger at present; of course it can hardly be believed that every man amongst the 204 will be brought to bank alive, but we would fain hope that the number who have succumbed to the terrible privations they are enduring is very small.

The crowd of listless, curious, unfeeling gossipers, who have swarmed round the place during the whole day, is now beginning to disperse. They have been kept out of proximity to the pit by a body of the county police, under the active and intelligent supervision of Mr Superintendent Wookey.

Nine o'clock

The accounts from the pit continue about the same. No communications can, however, be had with the men before four o'clock tomorrow morning, at the earliest. Mr Carr and Mr Humble have been here during the whole day, and have thoroughly superintended the arrangements. They have been ably assisted by Mr Taylor, the check-viewer of the colliery.

Monday—Ten a.m.

Again we have seen morning dawn without any tidings of relief for the prisoners. Late last night the stone which has been such a terrible bar to the progress of the workmen was cleared away, and since then there has been little trouble with it. Immense difficulty is experienced with rubbish, as so much of it consists of the timber of the brattice, which has become wedged together.

A poor man has just arrived from the Potteries in Staffordshire. He has a number of friends in this place, and hearing of the accident, has travelled all night for the purpose of ascertaining whether any of them are in the pit or not. He has not been here for 16 years, and has just come back to his native place on this mournful occasion. Another poor creature, named Smith, whose son and grandson were down the mine looking at it at the time of the accident, has sat upon the heap ever since it happened. The bodies of the five men killed in the shaft on Thursday were brought to bank about one o'clock this morning.

Noon

There is at last a ray of comfort. Mr Coulson, while down the shaft a few hours ago, saw some smoke ascending, and it is therefore certain that the prisoners have a fire lighted. If this be so, it affords great grounds for hope that a large number of the men are alive. They had near them the body of one pony, and they would be able to subsist upon it for a considerable time; whilst the bodies of several of the horses were undoubtedly within their reach up to yesterday afternoon at any rate.

One o'clock
Mr Coulson has just sent word up from the shaft that he expects to be at the men within two shifts, or four hours. This is cheering intelligence, and we trust that it may prove correct.

Five o'clock
Again we have to report the falsification of fondly cherished hopes. There can be no doubt that the workers are very little further on than they were eight or nine hours ago. Mr Coulson is still down the pit, and every effort is being made to push the sinking onward. A large number of visitors from Newcastle were on the platform, but as they interfered with the movements of the signal-men, they were compelled to leave.

Seven o'clock
The weary watchers, who have waited so long and so patiently for the glad tidings they expect, are still disappointed. As night once more is closing in, and as the merely curious are leaving by the crowded trains, a deeper gloom is settling upon the faces of the watchers than has ever appeared there before. They have watched, and watched, and watched, day by day, night after night; and numbers have never known an hour's sleep since Thursday morning.

It may not be amiss to give a short descriptive sketch of this place which is now a centre of the deepest interest to all the inhabitants of the British Isles.

The pit is situated close to the line of the Blyth and Tyne Railway, and within a stone's throw of Hartley Station. All the buildings are surrounded by, and indeed, appear to be erected upon, a huge pit-heap, composed of stone and other useless substances wrought in the mine. The first object that attracts the attention of the visitor as he climbs up this heap are the gins which are used in lifting material gathered by the sinkers in the shaft. Round these are always standing a number of men ready to assist at any moment in turning them; for as the work is continually going on, it is impossible for the wearied horses to keep up with the continual demands on their strength.

The old Castle Eden colliery, dismantled 1892

The new Castle Eden colliery in course of development

Houshold coal depot Blackhall

Return terminal aerial ropeway, Blackhall

Blackhall colliery from north

Shotton colliery from south

Horden colliery from south west

Ellington colliery baths, the first in the North East

Filling coal into a conveyor on a long wall face

Delivery of mothergate rubber belt conveyor into tubs

Hand drilling a hole in coal for the explosive charge

Ashington Main workshops, blacksmiths bay in 1924

LNER staith and coal belts, Hartlepool Docks

Coaling jetty LNER Hartlepool Docks

View from Bowes Neuk of Bedlington Doctor pit in the 1950s

Rescue Brigadesmen, Bill Burfield, Frank Ramsay, George Fulthorpe and Jack Evans attend a gas explosion at Choppington pit in October 1948

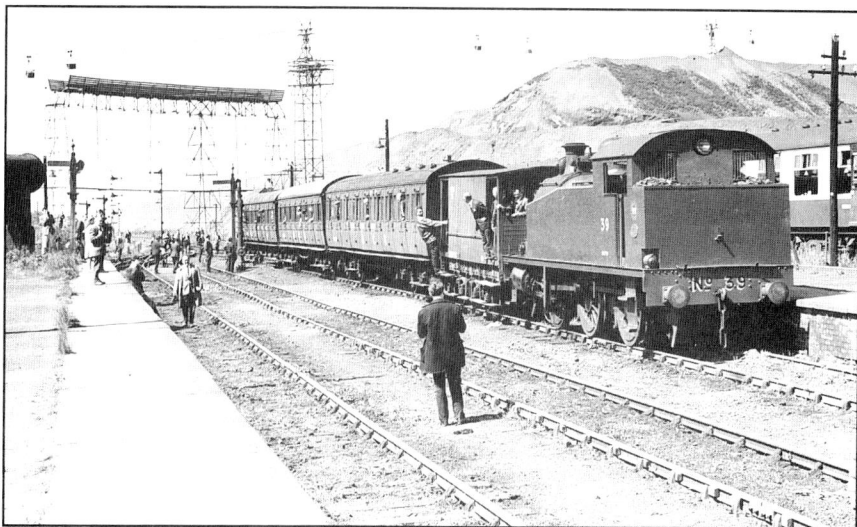

Hirst platform, Ashington in June 1967   *Photo by S. Carr*

A Lightening strike in the early 1970s provided these men from Bates colliery with a miners picnic

The Pitmen's Derby won by Frisure in 1954 ridden by Gordon Richards

The first conveyor at New Lynemouth colliery 1934. Manager Bill Gibson on right in skullcap

Another shift over 1940s

Outside netties were cleaned out at night in 1940s

The clarty streets of Longhorn colliery

Miners at North Seaton colliery in 1920. Back row: R. Cuthbert, S. Butters. S. Maclean, Front row: T. Pyle, J. Taylòr, T. Maclean and T. Wealans

Ashington coal company waggon late 1920s. Larry Bell centre

The 'A' team at Ashington colliery 1930s, three Robinson brothers, two Hindmarsh brothers and Haffy Hindhaugh 2nd right

Lads were trained at 14 years of age in the art of putting a pit pony into the limbers

Durham Miners' Gala 1920s

Bill and Ann Gibson lived in the Klondyke miners cottages in the 1940s

Miners at Easington colliery, just after the announcement of the closure

Northumberland Miners' Picnic held at Ashington 1998

Durham Miners' Gala 1994

General view of New Hartley Pit

Not far from these are the boilers of the now useless pumping engines; and at the other side of the heap are the joiners' and smiths' shops, and a small engine called 'the jack,' also used in hauling up materials. It is here the greatest number of hapless waiters congregate, clustered in anxious groups, their longing eyes following every man as he disappears down the shaft.

Passing this painful spot, we scramble up a heap of coals to the iron platform at the head of the shaft. Here is a curious sight presented. In the background is the yawning chasm, black and dangerous-looking, down which the mighty beam fell with irresistible force. Huge timbers, torn and twisted like pieces of paper, evidence, in small degree, the violence and frightful velocity with which the fatal mass of metal dropped through the air.

Standing here, beside the huge fires which cast a brilliant light upon the scene, and diffuse an uncomfortable warmth, are the superintendents at bank, Mr Humble, the resident viewer, Mr Forster Jnr., Mr Carr and Mr Taylor. Close by are two signal-men. Occasionally a totally unintelligible shout comes from the workers below, the lights of whose candles may be dimly seen far away down. The shout is instantly interpreted by the signal-men, who cry out in strange hoarse tones: 'Bend up the jack' of 'Lower the gin' and 'Heave up the crab', as the case may be.

Just behind the shaft is the lofty engine-house. Entering this, and climbing up the stairway past a perfect labyrinth of machinery, we come at last to the remaining portion of the broken beam. To our inexperienced eyes, several suspicious-looking flaws appear. It has, however, been examined by the best judges in the North of England, and has been pronounced as fine a piece of casting as could possibly be had. How then has it broken? That is a point which must be discussed at the Inquest.

Today a telegram has been received from a Mr Hill of Bristol, advising Mr Humble to bore a small hole down the shaft through the debris, and by means of it pour soup down to the men. Had it been feasible it would long ago have been attempted.

Nine o'clock
The news assumes a more cheering aspect. The work has been going on steadily for some hours, and has been advancing better than could be expected. As the men go on they rejoice to hear a falling-away of the rubbish beneath them. This shows that there is a hollow space. Another hour, or at the most two, must decide the dreadful question of the fate of the 204 prisoners. As may be believed, the most intense excitement prevails.

Ten o'clock
It is impossible to conceive the impatience with which we all are waiting for the intelligence which is so near at hand. The very heart sickens and the hand palsies as we write these lines, and anticipate a dreadful conclusion to our long and painful watch. We fear that there is now no benefit to be derived from withholding some information we have possessed from the first. The jowling, so often distinctly heard up to 8 a.m. on Saturday, ceased then. This was known to very few from the first, but all were desirous to put the best face upon everything.

Eleven o'clock
We have an exciting incident. The men waiting outside have just

come up in a body to ask why they were not told everything. Mr Coulson offered to let two of their number go down the shaft; and two, having accordingly been chosen, have just gone down.

Midnight

We have just witnessed a scene outside quite in keeping with all that has taken place in this sad affair. While the two men chosen, Charles Gallagher and John McLeod were away down the pit, the dense mass of watchers were in a perfect agony of impatience. Looking down on them from a small bridge running from one platform to another, such a scene is presented as defies description. The crowd, madly moving in a body, like caged hyaenas, are swaying to and fro by an irresistible impulse. Now and then someone cries out in hoarse tones of discontent, and asks where the men are who have gone down. Someone replies from the bridge that they have not come up yet; and again an agonised shudder runs through the people.

At last the deputation return. In a moment a deadly silence reigns and a sea of upturned faces is revealed by the flare of the watch-fire. One of the two men stepped forward, and said, in clear distinct tones: 'Men, we have been told there is stythe (gas) at the bottom. Now, we've been there, and there is none. There's water enought to drown a man, but no stythe.'

A low sound, that can be better compared to a growl than anything else, came from the crowd. And then Mr Baker Forster, speaking from the bridge, said: 'There is no fear for the men, if it is not for the stythe, and I can see no stythe; but let me tell you the truth—I fear there is some.'

A man from the crowd cried out: 'Is it true that they jowled yesterday morning?' Mr Forster again spoke and told them that they had; that Mr Wilkinson had told him so, and he would not have told him a lie.

Tuesday—Three o'clock (a.m.)

It seems as if some fatal bar was hanging over all the efforts made to relieve the prisoners. The work is still going on, but seemingly we are as far off the long-desired object as ever.

Mr Humble said to the waiters: 'The work has gone favourably, and the hole is considerably larger; there is fair hope of the next shift getting on still better.'

'What about the stythe?' asked one of the men.

'I asked no questions and heard no complaints.'

'Are they all alive?' a shrill, high-toned female voice exclaimed.

The enquiry was drowned in a chorus of exclamations of 'Oh, they don't know that.'

Poor fellows! the momentary rebellion of last night has entirely subsided, and they are once more passive and uncomplaining. It is a bitter night, the snow is lying on the ground and flying through the air, but no one will move away, and there is hardly a women in the hamlet who is not on the spot.

Four o'clock (a.m.)

While we were sitting penning the above lines, an incident of truly appalling nature happened. A man ran up to the platform and cried out: 'All the men are alive; they've got the shaft clear, they're all safe.'

The few sleepy watchers awoke in an instant, and a rush was made to the shaft mouth. Hardly a moment had elapsed, however, before the hopes of all were rudely dashed to the ground.

How the strange rumour had at first originated is not known, but just at the moment at which it was propagated, a signal of distress was received from below, and on one of the men being quickly borne up, it was found there had been a great fall, and that the shaft was almost, if not entirely, clear; but at the same time came the paralysing intelligence that a deadly gas had, immediately upon the fall taking place, rushed up the shaft, and by its insidious influence more or less injured all the men.

The intelligence was soon visibly confirmed, for, a few minutes after, one of the self-devoted sinkers was led to the little cabin, staggering between two comrades, who were endeavouring to support him. Another and another came up, whilst others were carried off, some of them totally insensible, to the blacksmith's shop. One man was carried past us on an ambulance. He seemed to be in a deadly sleep. His face was pale, his eyes shut, and his hands lying listlessly before him. Merely to look at him, it might easily have been supposed that he was a lifeless body. Doctors Davison, Ward, Nicholson, and Ambrose were at once in attendance upon the sufferers, and by their means were quickly restored to consciousness.

The names of those affected by gas are: Mr William Coulson (son of the master-sinker); Richard Wilson; Richard Dickson; John Little; and Matthew Dunn.

Seven o'clock (a.m.)
We have just seen Mr Atkinson, the Government Inspector for Mines for Durham, and Mr John Taylor. Both gentlemen seem confident that there is yet hope for the prisoners. The lightness of gas would naturally cause it to rise upwards, and it would, therefore, necessarily be met with when sinking. If this be so, all yet may be safe.

Noon
The people here have hardly yet recovered from the terrible shock received from the sudden cessation of all work at the very moment that their expectation stood most a-tiptoe.

As might be expected, the people took the news of this morning's disaster very badly.

This morning a cat was sent down the pit to a great depth. After staying there for some time it was brought up, and then found not to have suffered materially. It was 'stupid' and silly, hardly able to stand, and seemingly intoxicated. This shows that the gas is in full force, and we regret to say that it greatly weakens the chances in favour of Mr Atkinson's theory of a mere surface stratum of the carbonic-oxide gas.

One o'clock
The shaft which was considerably damaged is being repaired. There seem to be no hopes of saving the lives of the 204 lost ones. Very

few authorities here continue to hold out any hope of our coming upon the men alive. In the words of one of the chief men upon the place: 'The case is as bad as it can be.'

Wednesday—Ten o'clock (a.m.)

Our last night's watch has not been so dreary as the preceding one. Busy men have been at work all through the silent hours, pushing on the process of bratticing (a means of ventilation) with the greatest rapidity. The furnace at the mouth of the shaft is now throwing down into the pit 10,000 feet of fresh air per minute.

A party of viewers, mining engineers, etc., consisting of Messrs Telford, Sanderson, Baker, Forster, Marshall, Cole, and Lowther, are awaiting now in readiness the moment the furnace-drift or the Yard Seam has been reached in safety, for the purpose of searching for the lost men.

Half past eleven

Further news of great importance has arrived from below. Emmerson and two men named Davison and Burn went down lower than ever. Emmerson, after looking by the flickering light of his candle, for a short time, found two axes, a saw, and a back-skin, evidences that the poor wretches had been labouring at this spot in endeavouring to effect their own deliverance.

Just as he had secured the above articles, he felt that he was being overpowered by the deadly gas, and was forced to leave. Coming to the surface, he was so much exhausted as scarcely to be able to speak. On examination it was found that the axes belonged to two of the buried deputy overmen, John Sharp and Thomas Tranent. Great confidence has been felt ever since the accident, in the ability of the latter man. This is evidence that that confidence was not misplaced, but that he has been doing all he could to recover the men. They have evidently been driven by the bad air into some part of the workings. They may yet be there alive.

Noon

Mr John Taylor, Mr Emmerson, and Mr C. Hewitson are just going down in order to report as to the condition of the pit. If all goes well, another shift must do it. Upon the platform there are none except those whose presence is absolutely necessary, and the reporters. It is a cold damp morning, and a heavy rain is falling, but the heap is still surrounded by people from the village.

While writing, we are informed that Mr Humble has also gone down the shaft to inspect and report. The doctors go down in the following order, two at once: Dr Ambrose of the Endeavour; Dr Lambert of Seaton Delaval; Dr H. Ward of Blyth; and Dr Nichols of Bebside. They are at present putting on their dresses. Dr Davison and Dr Ward Sen. are on the platform. Drs Smith and Trotter of Blyth have just arrived by the special engine. The two Misses Richardson have come to the spot as volunteer nurses.

Two o'clock
A workman has just come up, and he reports that, before long, they will be at the furnace drift. The ventilation is becoming better, and when the Yard Seam is reached the door leading to it will at once be removed, and a draught thereby caused.

Four o'clock
Mr Humble, Mr Taylor, and Mr Coulson have just come to bank. Their report once more thickens the gloom overhanging us. They state that they were down the furnace drift a certain way, but found air so bad that they were compelled to retreat. They found some tools belonging to the unfortunate men. They could not, they state, go more than two or three yards, in consequence of the gas, which makes it impossible that anybody can live in such atmosphere.

A meeting of pitmen has just been held. A resolution, expressing confidence and gratitude for the efforts now being made to release the prisoners was passed; and a strong wish was expressed that two men might be permitted to go down and report. They have accordingly just gone.

News of a heart-rending nature has come at last. It confirms our worst fears, disappoints our faintest hopes. William Adams, one of the brave shift-men, has just come up. Accompanied by two companions, pushing their way along at great danger to themselves, for the air was very bad, they went along the drift till they came to the furnace itself, and there they found the bodies of two of the entombed men. They managed to get to the Yard Seam, here they opened a door and found more bodies strewn in in all directions. Walking over them they came to another door, which they also opened; and when they got there they found bodies, to use Adam's words, 'thicker and faster'. In all the ghastly company not one spark of precious life remained; all had laid down and died.

Adams said, 'It was a heart-breaking sight. No one need blame anybody for the delay; it's an awful dangerous road we went. After we got to the Yard Seam we found the air cooler and better. The bodies were lying closer and closer, none in each other's arms, but side by side. I think we saw about fifty, all considerably swollen.'

Some time will be required before any of the bodies of the lost ones can be brought out. On the platform all the long-cherished hopes having for ever vanished, there is revulsion of feeling which words will not describe.

Half past five o'clock
Mr Humble has just sent up for more men. The work of removing the bodies seems likely to be commenced. Warned by this, we have taken up a place in the 'horse-hole', where the men who are being lowered down the shaft leave bank. It is a strange place. A long, crooked cavern, lighted by two huge fires, and cumbered by heaps of beams, chain cable, machinery, etc. Stumbling along this we come to the shaft itself, a huge, yawning chasm, black as pitch, which opens at our very feet.

Scarcely had we written this brief description when Mr Humble and Mr Hall, a viewer from Trimdon, came to bank. Both were much affected by the air. When Mr Humble had had some tea he exclaimed, 'Oh, dear! Oh, dear! So many of my fellow creatures dead. Oh, my cannie fellows.' In answer to Dr Pyle, who was attending to him, he said they were all dead.

They had been right into the great gallery of the Yard Seam, and had found all the men and boys. All without exception were dead;

and were lying near the shaft, where they had waited so long for the help which never came in life. They were lying side by side, but the boys of each family appeared to be clustered around their relatives. The corn-bins were empty; but in the pockets of the men some corn was found; it is evident, therefore, that they were not starved. In addition to this, the pony, upon which such reliance had been placed, was found dead, but untouched.

The men have all been dead a considerable time, probably since Sunday morning.

A quarter past six

Mr Maddison, of Burradon, and one of Mr Coulson's sinkers, have just gone down. It is intended to bring the bodies to bank as soon as possible; and for this purpose, a number of new leather slings has been sent down. Word has come up that more air-boxes will be required before the fearful work is commenced.

Half past six

Mr John Taylor, the brave and able check-viewer, has been speaking to the people from the platform. In mild, gentle, sympathising tones, he told them the dreadful news. The intelligence fell like no thunderbolt on the people. The shock was given on Thursday morning when the dreadful news flew like lightning through the desolate village.

In the village, the grief was still to a certain extent exciting. Numerous visitors are sitting in each cottage. Now, we find the house from which seven have gone forth never to return. Troops of friends are here, administering in abundance all the consolation which earthly means can afford.

Seven o'clock

The stythe in the shaft is very bad, and the men are being drawn up every minute ill from its effects. It is said that there is a possibility of the bodies being coffined before they are brought up.

Half past seven

It appears that the two men who volunteered to go down are

reported that there was a very bad smell indeed from the bodies. They had no appearance of being starved, but all appeared to have lain down and slept themselves to death.

A curious rumour was current among the spectators this afternoon: we only mention it because it may reach Newcastle. It was asserted that the first person to reach the bodies was a London diver, supposed to be upon the spot. Nothing could be more false than this. Adams was the first man to ascertain the actual occurrence of the most appallingly sudden calamity which the British Isles have known for many years. Adams, however, goes under the nickname of London Will, and so the mistake appears to have arisen.

The following telegraphic message has been received on behalf of Her Majesty Queen Victoria: 'The Queen is most anxious to hear that there are hopes of saving the poor people of the colliery, for whom her heart bleeds.'

Villagers read the Queen's Message

Thursday—ten o'clock (a.m.)
A mass meeting has been held. Mr Turnbull, a pitman at Cowpen, occupied the chair. All was very orderly. It appears that, during the night, the men have been very unreasonable, and, by insisting upon having men sent down again and again, they have actually stopped the work for fully twelve hours. Dreadful scenes are occurring. Fathers coming to the shaft, almost frantic, to seek their children, wives wailing for their husbands, and sons for their parents. It is a most painful scene, now that despair has finally settled down upon it.

Noon
In the hurried and imperfect parcel which we despatched an hour or two ago, we made mention of the conduct of the bereaved around the pit-heap. We regret to say that it has been, in some cases, scandalously bad, and that great danger and delay has, in consequence, been entailed upon Mr Coulson and his workmen. There can be no doubt that some of the men are most wickedly unreasonable. They wish the sinkers to go to the bodies at once, without a moment's delay, and commence immediately the work of bringing them up to the surface. Surely the annals of Hartley New Pit are black enough.

Late last night, one man—we can speak no harsh words about him, for he has four sons amongst the lost—came upon the platform and acted in such a manner as shewed that grief had completely unhinged his intellect. Had he not been restrained, he would undoubtedly have thrown himself headlong down the shaft.

Mr Coulson has agreed that a barrier be erected to keep all parties needlessly approaching the pit at the moment the corpses are drawn out. The bodies will not, however, be fastened in their coffins until they are identified; and it is proposed that Mr Humble and some other person, equally able to settle any point, should go down the shaft and identify all the bodies they can, writing their names upon slips of paper, that the dead will eventually be identified, as most of their features are dreadfully disfigured. This is particularly the case with the boys, who are all greatly swollen about the head and face. However, the men did not express themselves as perfectly satisfied. They wish each body to be brought to the barrier as it is got up, and the name to be called out, in order that any friends of the deceased who may be there may have the opportunity of seeing the remains. Whether this request will be granted or not is yet undecided.

One o'clock

The men in the shaft are still very busy. Every minute the water in the shaft is rising higher, and before long it is certain that it must be up to the Yard Seam. If this should be the case, the bodies cannot possibly be recovered for several months, as the water will have to be pumped out first. There is now some difficulty in obtaining men to go down the shaft. The work is dangerous, and no lives are to be saved. It is earnestly hoped that labour will not be allowed to stand still upon such grounds.

Half past one

Another mass meeting has taken place. The chair was again taken by Mr Robert Turnbull. He told the men that a meeting was to be held in Newcastle tomorrow, for the purpose of commencing a fund to support those rendered destitute by this calamity. He asked if some people who were acquainted with the district would go among the cottages and get a correct list of the widows and children under sixteen.

The Lord Bishop of Durham and the Mayor of Newcastle have just arrived. Lord and Lady Hastings have sent a messenger to express their deep sympathy.

An identification committee of twelve men has been appointed.

Four o'clock

The scene presented by the neighbourhood of the colliery is now a very strange and striking one. On the platform there are fewer people than ever. The officials of the colliery, worn out by their strained labours, are now endeavouring to obtain the rest which they must so require.

All round the buildings, upon every accessible portion of the heap, immense crowds are gathered. Some of them belong to the village; and we recognise faces we have known before amongst the patient waiters; others are new visitors from the surrounding district. They stand in one dense mass talking softly to each other, and seldom moving from the same spot. Amongst them, plying their activities and vocations with avidity and apparent success, are the hot-pie men, and others, who are gleaning on the grim harvest field of Death. Many painful scenes are taking place. Women are weeping, and strong men shedding tears. We see one poor woman who has just come by train, and who is advancing with a sad story. Her husband was one of the men who had gone down the pit for the first time upon that fateful Thursday morning. She is not aware yet whether he is amongst the killed; but, in a perfect paroxysm of grief, she seeks the information from those who can give it, while she strains a wailing infant to her bosom. Alas! her worst fears are realised, for she learns that she is now a widow, and that her husband's body is lying lifeless at the bottom of the shaft.

Eight o'clock

We have just learned the results of the melancholy labours of the committee appointed at the mass meeting today, for the purpose of ascertaining the number of widows and orphans left dependant, owing to the death of their protectors in this sad accident. It must be understood that only children under 16 years of age are noticed in this statement:

103 *widows*
257 *children*
 27 *sisters*, supported by brothers
  2 *orphans*
 16 *parents*, supported by sons
  1 *aunt*, supported by nephew
  1 *grandmother*, supported by grandson
 ───
 407

Four hundred and seven poor creatures are thus deprived, at one fell swoop, of their only means of support, and are left to rely upon the coldness of charity. Well may the British public rise to the feeling of responsibility thrown upon it. A whole district has been cast into mourning—a village suddenly deprived of all its manly strength.

Another telegraphic message has been received from the Queen: 'The Queen has been deeply affected by the dreadful news from Hartley. Her Majesty feels the most sincere sympathy for the widows and orphans. What is anyone doing for them? I will write by tonight's post.'

Midnight
The coffins have already begun to arrive. The night is very wild; and for the first time since the accident, scarcely anybody at all is upon the pit-heap.

Friday—noon
There has been little to chronicle in our progress during the last twelve hours. The shaft is now entirely secured, and the men have got down to the point from which they intend to send up the bodies.

The men have been very quiet through the night, the few malcontents amongst them having been completely silenced. Mr Mason, the incumbent of Earsdon, has been speaking to the men upon the pit-heap in reference to the matter of burial. He told them he feared the churchyard would not be able to hold all the bodies, and by an order of the Government no bones at present lying in the place could be disturbed. It is probable, if they wish for additional ground, His Grace the Duke of Northumberland will grant it.

Half past two
We regret to announce another disturbance amongst the men. One or two disaffected parties have commenced an agitation which has just resulted in another outbreak. Mr Turnbull had just gone down to give the report. Several of the crowd were dissatisfied, and one of them, William McKie, who has a father and brother down the pit, demanded to be allowed to go down. Mr Coulson at once refused

this. The man threatened to jump down; he was, however, secured and taken away.

Five o'clock

We are still performing our dreary and unenviable task of chronicling the history of this sad catastrophe. The number of visitors today has not been great, but we may mention, as evidence of the interest taken by the country in this catastrophe, that reporters from *The Times*, the *Morning Chronicle*, the *Mining Journal*, and a Huddersfield paper have been here today, while two artists from the *Illustrated London News* have been sketching various scenes about the place yesterday and today. The usual staff of Newcastle reporters is, of course, still upon the ground.

A melancholy sight is at present being presented at the base of the platform. Cart after cart, laden with black coffins, are disgorging their gloomy contents at the mouth of the horse-hole.

Saturday—six o'clock (a.m.)

The men had to contend all through the night with their usual difficulties; this morning at last, however, we begin to see daylight. The end of the whole dreary business, so far as regards the pit itself, is approaching.

The work will go on very slowly, as not more than two bodies can be brought up at a time, so that more than twenty hours will be occupied in it. All coffins which contain identified bodies will have the name written upon the lid; the rest will be left open for inspection. A large staff of medical gentlemen are in attendance to see that the bodies are properly coffined.

Two o'clock

The frightful work of bringing up the bodies has now commenced. Instead of sending the coffins down the shaft, as was first proposed, the corpses are to be brought up just as they have lain in the pit, and coffined on bank. The scene is a very frightful one, and will occupy a long time. The men who 'ride' with the dead men are being supplied with whiskey, to enable them to fulfil their ghastly duty.

Midnight

The longest road has an ending, the most dreary day a nightfall; and so, at last, we approach the closing scenes of the tragic history of the Hartley New Pit catastrophe. From the early morning to the present hour, the day has been occupied in one sad task: that of raising the bodies of the hundreds of men and boys who, last Saturday, came by their death in the Yard Seam of this ill-fated colliery.

At the base of the platform, the sad sight we noticed yesterday was again presented. One long deep country cart after another was drawn up at the stable-door and unladen of the coffins which it bore; and at last a climax was reached by the arrival of a special train, conveying nothing but coffins made at a distance. These coffins were not highly polished, nor were they yet like those of the lesser catastrophe at Burradon, mere white wooden boxes, nailed together in such a manner as hardly to be able to stand the slightest strain. All of them, though made of the commonest deal, were strong and substantial; and all were neatly and decently stained with the deepest black. Some of them had been specially made for such bodies as could not be identified down the pit. The top of the lid turned back upon hinges, thus rendering the face entirely visible, whilst no other portion of the body was exposed to view.

About half past ten, when all other things were prepared, we began to watch for the disappearance of the first coffin down the pit. We were destined to see a far more fearful spectacle.

As the end of the rope drew near the surface, one of the men was seen riding upon the little sling on which the sinkers have so fearlessly ascended and descended. Just below him, carefully attached to an iron chain, was a strange and hideous object, which at first we could not recognise; in a moment, however, we saw that it was the stiffened form of one of the victims of the carbonic-oxide that was dangling in mid-air before us. In a moment he was landed on the platform. It was dreadful to look upon his skinny attenuated form, which seemed so small beside the gigantic men around, his almost fleshless hands curiously marked in white and blue, and his fixed immobile features, the closed eyes of which denoted that he had slept while treading the valley of the shadow of Death. He was thrown down upon an open shroud, spread upon the ground, and while he was being rapidly rolled up in it, some one called out his name, which was methodically entered in a book by one man while another chalked it upon the lid of a coffin into which he was forthwith lifted. Thus laden, the coffin was placed upon a small rolley, and pushed along the wooden bridge separating one portion of the pit-heap from another. At the further end, the name inscribed upon the coffin was called out; someone stepped forward from the dense crowd of waiters, and claiming the body as that of a relative, it was placed in a cart, and conveyed to the home it left in health and strength ten days ago.

So quickly was all this done, that the bystanders had scarcely time to recover from the effects which it had produced upon them, when another cry from the shaft mouth of 'Stop the gin' announced that another ghastly freight had arrived. Once more, standing by the shaft, we again saw the ropes gliding stealthily upwards; this time bearing with them a double burden. Lashed together, face to face, we saw the bodies of two of the dead. Both wore upon the countenance an air of perfect repose; and while sitting upright in the sling, it was hard to see the difference between them and the iron-nerved 'rider' who sat so composedly between them.

After this, a constant succession of frightful burdens were borne up from below. To detail them all minutely would be more than revolting; let our readers only be glad that it was not their lot to be compelled to stand upon the platform today to witness all these ghastly sights. Men and boys of all sizes and ages were brought up to the bank. Some had died with a smile upon their faces; others frowning in terror or anger.

Hour by hour they were brought forth, it seemed as if some unholy, premature resurrection was going on, for which the Lord of Life and Death would certainly call upon us to account.

Over and above all, strange cries arose: 'A longer coffin wanted here,' and 'This body is far too small for such a big coffin.' 'Bring some more chloride of lime', and a hundred similar exclamations added to the confusion of the scene.

We must not omit to mention that during this dreadful process, very great assistance has been derived by all from the sharpness of a little boy, not more than fourteen years of age, who was employed to collect and keep the tallies of the pitmen, and who seems to have known almost every man and boy upon the place. As each body was brought up, he called out the name with unerring certainty, and there was scarcely a dozen whom he could not recollect.

The body has been found in the Yard Seam of William Armour, the back-overman, and his son. When he was searched, a common thin memorandum book was found in his pocket. On opening it, the eager searchers found entered upon the last page, in a straggling handwriting, the following:

'Friday Afternoon at Half-past Two — Edward Armstrong, Thomas Gladstone, John Hardy, Thomas Bell and others took extremely ill. We also had a prayer meeting at a quarter to two, when Tibbs, Henry Sharp, J Campbell, Henry Gibson, and William Palmer . . . Tibbs exhorted us again, and Sharp also . . .'

This memorandum, brief and imperfect as it is, possesses an immense interest. It shews, as on many occasions of a similar nature, that the horrors of death beyond imagination have been lightened by the only consolation man could have in such an hour: they had with them One greater than they, who alone could solace and console.

Sunday—ten o'clock (a.m.)

All the exhausting excitement of the struggle to get at the prisoners is over. We have got at them, though too late, and we have seen the dreadful week brought to a close by a scene so fearful that pen and pencil alike refuse to do full justice to it. Now, we have seen the mournful task of the sinkers completed during the night; the bodies of the whole of the men have been brought up.

The exact number of bodies recovered since yesterday is 199; these, added to the five men killed in the cage, and already brought up, give a grand total of 204 lives lost in this terrible accident.

Monday—five o'clock

A shot-box belonging to James Bewick, a pitman residing at Hartley, has been found. The following inscription was found to be scratched: 'Me Dear Sarah — I leave you . . . .'

After the accident, the Hartley royalty was abandoned by Messrs Carr, but was subsequently leased by the owners of Seaton Delaval Collieries. Work recommenced in 1877 with a fresh winning of the Yard Seam by means of the Hastings and Melton shafts. The shafts were afterwards deepened to the Low Main Seam. The old Hartley workings were entered in 1900. The scene that presented itself to the miners was strange and weird. In many parts of the workings, tubs and gear were found standing ready as if for the resumption of work which had been hurriedly abandoned more than 38 years previously.

8

COLLIERY VILLAGES
Ashington and Pegswood

Source: *Newcastle Weekly Chronicle*, Saturday, September 6, 1873

The two villages which we have this week selected for description are not entirely new villages. They are, so to speak, old friends with new names, and also with new faces. The old names were significant of old ideas, old associations, and, unfortunately, of old colliery houses. Limited resources in the old time meant inadequate machinery, imperfect development of rich mineral stores, and, consequently, a want of that large-handed liberality and speculativeness which we now see exhibited in the development of our great modern collieries. Notable indeed has been the change within the last few years in the district north of the Wansbeck. Where, formerly, only a few small landsale pits existed, we now see large collieries, with gigantic pit gearing and towering chimneys that belch forth clouds of thick black smoke; and where, formerly, a few wretched hovels marked the site of a colliery village, we now see comfortable brick cottages springing up like huge blue-topped mushrooms. We pass through the district in early spring, and see nothing but fields in which grass grows rankly; we pass again when summer days are shortening into autumnal length, and to the blades of grass are chimney stalks, surmounting a rich crop of brick or concrete cottages. Such has been the fate of Fell 'em Doon and the Banks, the old has given way to the new system, and money has not only given them a new name but has also infused new life and energy into them so that they now keep pace with most of the pits in the county.

To begin with Ashington, then, we find the village pleasantly situated in the midst of an open stretch of country about four miles and a half to the Eastward of Morpeth. Together with Sheepwash it forms a township. In 1801 the population was only 76. At the present time it is very little, if any, short of 1,400. In its early days as a colliery village it was known as Fell 'em Doon, under which appellation it commenced operations well-nigh a quarter of a century ago. Since then, however, the original shaft has ceased to be used as a coal-raising shaft. Its old gearing still stands as it stood of yore, but its timbers seem old and a trifle groggy, as though the old water which rises from below had flown to their head and made them untrustworthy. The seat of active operations was removed about six years ago half a mile to the eastward, and there new shafts have been sunk, and a new village has sprung up, but has not yet done growing.

In deference to its age and infirmity, we will first take a glance at the old place, which need not detain us long, its dimensions not being great, and the style of its houses so much like many of those we have seen lately. The house accommodation at the old place is comprised in two old fashioned back-to-back rows, standing at right angles to each other, and furnished with some half-dozen ash-pits and privies at the backside of the place for the use of the entire community. Each house is arranged to contain two families, one in a downstairs room and an un-ceilinged attic at the front side, and another holding possession of two similar apartments behind. There is no through ventilation; the windows are of the small, old-fashioned type, and during the hot summer weather they are like so many ovens erected for the baking or kippering of the numerous families who have been packed into them like so many herrings. There is however a movement towards the new place, and as each of the old houses becomes vacant, the men intend to impress on the owners the necessity of breaking through the wall of partition, and making the old houses double their present size. The end house of one of these old rows was the only school which the village possessed, but on the day of our visit it was closed and had been so for some time. The six months of grace allowed by Mr Forster, however, in the interest of the Established Church, when he passed his Act, have been of service to the Church party in this district, and a splendid set of Church schools have been built in Ashington, and will shortly be open to the children of the village, who will doubtless be educated with an eye to their becoming future adherents of the Church which has its local interests looked after by his sporting reverence of Bothal.

His Grace of Portland is the owner of the soil, the royalty is held under the usual restrictions as to school and stores, and, however, the dissenters of the village may strive to get an unsectarian school in the place, they may depend upon it there will be no site for them to build on. Passing on to the colliery we note by the way numerous tall posts with boards nailed across the top, bearing in large characters the words 'No road this way'. There are several pleasant foot-roads through the fields from Ashington, which have existed from time immemorial, but in accordance with the line of policy which the Duke by his agents is trying to carry out in regard to the footpaths on his estate, attempts are being made to stop them all. As yet however those attempts have been disregarded, and it is to be hoped that the Ashingtonians will stick to their right of way; for however important it may be that hares shall breed unmolested, to provide sport for the leisure hours of the aristocratic person, it is of much greater importance that the small rights of way which the plebeian public still possess over diverse estates should be protected.

At Ashington New Colliery, operations are being carried on at an amazing rate. At present only the high seam of coal is being worked. Nearly 250 hewers are employed in it, and they manage to send to bank some 600 tons of coal per diem [daily], which is run down the waggon-way to the North-Eastern main line, and whirled away to the docks or to such other places as the requirements of the market may demand. An extension of operations, however, has been in contemplation for some time, and to further this end a new shaft has been sunk to the low seam, though on the day of our visit it was far from finished. We looked down the abyss, and at a depth of some 250 or 300 feet saw a host of adventurous bricklayers suspended on a platform doing their work by the light of candles, which from the top appeared like brilliant fireflies lighting up the operations of an army of lilliputian builders. When this shaft is finished and mining commenced, of course more men will be required, and this will mean more new houses, and on a spot which a few short years ago knew nothing but green fields and the work of the farmer, there will soon be a large village with a population of from two to three thousand souls. Verily old Fell 'em Doon in his days of decay could but little imagine the greatness in store for his offspring. So must it always be, we suppose—the old giving way for the new, and when the change is so much for the better, as in the present instance, we 'welcome the coming, speed the parting guest'.

Ashington is a somewhat compactly-built village, each row standing in a regular succession, like a regiment of soldiers, formed in open order ready for marching past in slow time, when the bands begin to play. In open order we said, but we had nearly forgot that one row is a quarter-distance only, as though the Captain had judged his distance wrongly, and drawn up his rank too near the one in front. However, this mistake has not been repeated, there is plenty of space between each row for all the sanitary arrangements required, and space also for the pure air of heaven to flow through the houses. The row facing the road, with gardens in front, may be taken as showing a fair sample of the sort of cottage which is required for our pitmen nowadays.

The majority of the houses in this row contain, on the ground floor, a good-sized kitchen, with cement floor, and a pantry, large enough to hold provisions sufficient for even a large family with large appetites. Down at the back side runs an open drain, which at first sight seems objectionable, but we were informed that all these drains (and every row has one behind it) are kept under strict supervision, and no filth is allowed to accumulate in them. Behind this again are the privies and ashpits, so that all the decencies of life and safeguards of health may be said to be provided for. The upper storey is reached by a staircase springing from a small passage, upon which the front door opens. Ascending the staircase, the steps of which seem, from their narrowness, to have been made for Chinese feet, we find the upper storey divided into two comfortable rooms, one of which may be available for a sitting room, if not required as a bedroom. Five houses in this row contain each five rooms, and it has not yet been our lot to see five more comfortable colliery houses anywhere. As we enter by the front door, we have on one side a kitchen, large and comfortable; on the other side is a sitting room, large enough for a small prayer meeting; and at the top of the staircase, which has a small independent window of its own, are three nice bedrooms. There is in addition to this, the pantry and other conveniences behind, and a piece of garden ground in front. Such houses as these could not have been had in Newcastle for less than eighteen pounds a year.

One of the rows is composed of cottages a size larger than those first described, for men with families, the only notable difference being that a roomy kitchen is built on at the back side. There are several rows of new brick cottages in course of erection, and there will be more to build as soon as these are finished. There is also in progress a row of houses built of concrete. The concrete walls are the work of the North of England Concrete Company. The wood is contracted for by Haggie Brothers. From what we were able to learn, no more houses of this class are to be built after the present lot is finished. They are too expensive, which is a great pity, for they are indeed a very superior class of colliery dwelling. The manner in which they are built is rather curious, and suggestive of the total abolition of bricklayers and masons. In the first place, an iron framework is erected, and iron plates inserted the width between them, being the thickness of the wall to be built. A mixture of cement and gravel, or such rubble as may be most easily obtainable on the spot, is then poured into the space between the plates, and as soon as the concrete wall thus formed has had time to set, the plates are raised another stage, and so the building process goes on until the desired height is attained, the joists and other timbers being embedded as required. The walls thus formed of course present a very rough appearance, and to obviate this they afterwards receive on the outside a coat of cement, the inside being plastered in the usual manner.

Each of these concrete houses has four large rooms, two on the ground floor and two above, reached by a staircase leading from a small passage inside the back door. The front room on the ground floor is to be fitted in one of the corners formed by the chimney projection, with a stationary chiffonier, surmounted by what I took to be intended for a sort of wardrobe or, perchance, a stationary bookcase. Running the whole length of the row, at the back side, is a high concrete wall, against which ash-pits, privies, and coal-houses (also concrete) are erected. The outside appearance of these houses is decidedly elegant. The design of the chimney stacks is positively ornate, and when these model dwellings are completed we venture to say they will surpass anything to be met with at any other colliery in the county.

From this description it will be gathered that Ashington is a model young village. We have no hesitation in saying that it is. But then there are spots even on the bright sun itself, and there are drawbacks even to Ashington. Principal among these is the intermittent nature of the water supply, which is dependent upon the working of the colliery engines. So long as the pit works and the engine runs, all is well; but when it stops, the water supply stops also, and at week-ends a sufficient stock must be taken in to serve until the pit starts again. Then there is but one shop near the place, and it is away at the old place. The old story of monopoly is told here, as at numerous other places, where the land belongs to men who ought to have lived in feudal times, when they had their serfs to oppress, and not in days like these when every such restriction is an insult to the free inhabitants of what we fondly deem a free country.

The men of Ashington are nearly all Co-operators, yet they cannot get a store on the estate. But this is not a fatal blow to men who believe in an institution the first principle of which is self-denial, and therefore we were not surprised that a large number of the miners here are members of the Choppington Store three miles away, and that another large number are members of the Sleekburn branch of the omnipresent Cramlington Store, whose carts penetrate even into the sacred preserves of His Grace of Portland. Chapels as yet do not flourish at Ashington, and the members of the various denominations in the place meet for worship in the old schoolroom, or such other places as may be convenient. Equally conspicuous by their absence are public-houses, and no one seems to grieve that the spirit of enterprise has left the village unprovided in this respect.

There is, however, a reading-room in the village with a list of 102 members, which is a large proportion. Last year their income amounted to nearly £70, a sum which provided them with a balance in hand of some £15. This is a cheerful state of affairs, and members entertain a confident hope that the owners may be persuaded to build them an institution and lecture-room worthy of the colliery. Such is Ashington by daylight, and when night comes we are happy to state that night is handsomely provided for, receiving as he descends a warm greeting from each gas-lighted cottage. Your fancy paraffin lamps are out of date at Ashington Colliery, and thoughtful owners who wish to make their men as comfortable as circumstances will allow have taken care that one of the cries of the village shall not be 'Light, light, more light'. Having seen this much of Ashington, we step out briskly for Pegswood, two miles away, with its big chimney blowing a rare cloud of smoke on the hill top yonder.

A pleasant countryside is this, and Pegswood stands in a very pleasant corner of it, perched on the top of the rising ground which surmounts the beautiful wooded valley of the Wansbeck, a short distance to the north-west of Bothal. The surface of the earth round and about Pegswood has been much probed and bored at diverse times by men anxious to rifle the interior of its contents of black diamonds. In all probability, the hillside has been much worked in remote times, though upon a small scale, for the benefit of the people of Morpeth. Indeed, the memory of the very oldest inhabitant goeth not back to a time when coal was not got there or thereabouts.

The first attempt at systematic mining, however, seems to have been made when the Bank's Colliery was sunk, some fifty-five or sixty years ago [i.e. *c.* 1815], and since then the royalty seems to have passed through many hands, until within the last few years it passed into the hands of Mr S. H. Frazer of Newcastle, who has wrought such a change that the old 'Bankers' would not be able to recognise the 'Banks' of their youth. Pegswood Colliery now gives employment to 160 hewers, who accomplish something like 380 tons per diem, which are shunted from under the screens on to the North-Eastern Railway, which passes close to the pit. And here we would remark that the erection of a station for the use of the village would be an inestimable boon to the inhabitants thereof. Morpeth is the nearest station at present, but it is three miles away, and as there is no shop or store in the place, a weary distance has to be trudged every weekend by those who desire to go a-marketing. The miners now do a great deal of travelling at the end of each week, and with a rapidly increasing population, the erection of a station would prove a gain to the railway company.

The old workings which passed out of use when the new pit commenced operations six years ago, stand about half a mile further northward, and were unworkable by reason of their being flooded. At one time the men employed in the new workings became alarmed lest a too near approach to the old workings should let the water in upon them, and drown them, like so many rats, without chance of escape. To obviate this, however, a drift has been worked from the interior of the workings towards the bed of the Wansbeck, about a mile away. The difference in level between the surface of the river and the old workings is four feet.

Drifting has for some time been carried on simultaneously at both ends, and a fortnight ago the excavators managed to make ends meet at a distance of 400 yards from the river side—a result highly creditable to the engineering skill of Mr Gibson, the colliery manager. Through this drift then will the surplus water make its way to the river, and all fear of an inundation is at an end. At present only one shaft is in operation at Pegswood, but another has been sunk to the lower seam which is at a depth of 39 fathoms from the surface. In a few months this seam will be under way, and houses are springing up in the village with wonderful celerity. In all there are seven rows of houses near the colliery, but many of the miners employed in the pit live in villages at a distance—some of them even walking to their work from Morpeth, three miles away.

As a village, Pegswood is decidedly irregular; it lacks the neatness and Quaker-like precision of Ashington, and the various rows of cottages are more closely built, straggling about at all sorts of angles from each other. Two rows contain houses of two rooms, one on the ground level, with a cement floor, and a bedroom above of the same dimensions, which is reached by a narrow ladder built in like a staircase, and having its starting-point in a back passage, which also contains the projecting pantry. Ashpits and privies are built on the space between the back sides of the rows; it would seem that many of the inhabitants are too lazy in habits to throw their refuse into the proper receptacles. The other five rows consist of houses much the same as these for size; but they are made more convenient for families, by having the upper storey divided into two distinct apartments. One old row is without privies or ashpits, and the longest of the new rows is also without those very necessary conveniences, though the bricks for their erection are lying ready at the back side. These are the only two styles of houses, to be found at Pegswood, and on their construction cheapness has been carefully studied.

They are, however, a great improvement upon the old system, though inferior to the best specimens of the new order of colliery architecture. In addition to the colliery houses, however, the miners have single houses leased here and there from the Duke of Portland or his agents, and a group of four, situated in a field at the top of the Quarry Bank, may be safely taken as the worst specimens of human habitations to be found within the whole length and breadth of Northumberland. Four wretched bothies are there, with low walls of brick and stone, open in places to every breeze that blows, whether it be the balmy air of summer or the biting breeze of winter. Miserable floors of brick, stone and wet clay; covered with old thatched roofs, which admit the rain through a hundred gaps, and dimly lighted by little more than one square foot of glass. Were it not for the smoke from the tell-tale chimneys, the stranger would gaze upon them as relics of the olden time, left standing as places of shelter for benighted cattle, or pass them by wondering why they were left to cumber the ground.

In one of these houses we found a miserable-looking Scotch woman, whose shortened locks told of recent fever. In apologetic tones, as though she were afraid of being turned even from the semi- shelter of those miserable walls, she admitted that they were 'awfu' places', but still they were better than 'oot bye a' thegither'. This woman's husband works at Pegswood. The next apartment, which originally formed a second apartment to this woman's house, was vacant, but someone from Morpeth was to come over and take possession of it ere night. Part of its walls had fallen or been blown down, and a good gap had been simply fitted with loose stones.

Next door to this was a similar kennel, which a broken-down-looking woman in vain attempted to make decent by a plentiful sprinkling of the damp uneven floor with sand, a process which only served to show the open character of the walls and roof, by defining the course of the rivulets which had flowed from the walls to the door in front of the fireplace. The poor old body seemed to be afflicted with hypochondria, and in a quavering voice, and with quivering eyelids, she informed me that she had lived eighteen years in the place, 'her and her husband, and now they did not like to leave it, though God knows last winter she had to stand with a broom in her hand and sweep out the water as it rushed in'. Poor old soul, her task must have been well nigh as hopeless as that of Mrs Partington, who strove to beat back the Atlantic tide with her mop. Yet these kennels stand upon ducal ground, and doubtless ducal hands receive rent for them, directly or indirectly, but no matter what the rank of the owner of the hovels, or the owners of the land, such miserable dwellings are a disgrace to our civilization, and reflect eternal shame upon the men who not only suffer them to deface the landscape, but leave them upon for human beings to dwell therein.

The same influences which tie the hands of the Ashington Co-operators bind the men of Pegswood, and the same desire to keep the education of the young in the hands of the Establishment which we saw at Ashington prevents the erection of a school here.

The Duke's agent says the owners of the colliery can build a school if they like, but it must be under the management of the nominees of His Grace; and so there is no school in the village, neither is there any chapel, and children must trudge to Bothal or Longhirst to learn their catechism, and be taught due reverence towards their betters, while the devoutly disposed must either go to Bothal, or Longhirst, or Morpeth, or be indebted to the visits of itinerant preachers. The only break in this dark social cloud is a Mechanics' Institute in course of erection at the village. This much the miners have been allowed to do, a small mercy for which the men of Pegswood can never be sufficiently thankful to His Grace.

9

DEPRIVATION IN EAST DURHAM PIT
VILLAGES IN THE 1880s

Dr James Arthur, Medical Officer of Health, 1883 Report to Easington Colliery Sanitary Committee:

At East Murton it [smallpox] broke out in the family of an innkeeper, attacking six persons . . . I immediately ordered this home to be closed, maintained a rigid isolation and had it thoroughly disinfected. It gave origin to four other cases in Murton. At Castle Eden Colliery a woman visiting Spennymoor took the infection home with her, and a young man in the same house got it from her. At Trimdon Foundry the epidemic extended to 22 cases. Before the outbreak your Committee had provided a special hospital at Easington.

During the year additional accommodation was provided. It is to be regretted that among the poorer classes there is great antipathy to enter the hospital. I would suggest that where this is refused a police constable be engaged to blockade any infected house. By sanitary means an epidemic disease may be kept out of this district but when it enters it must run its course. This is due to the people, who consider it a religious and social duty on the part of females to visit each other in times of sickness and especially when the obsequies of death must be performed, thereby disseminating disease germs in a way that only the most elaborate sanitary machine can possibly prevent.

In 1884 Dr Arthur made this report about Thornley:

Since April the colliery has been laid in. Considerable difficulty has been experienced in the cleansing of ashpits, this duty formerly being undertaken by the owners, who are now in a state of bankruptcy and the occupants of the houses objecting to do the work on the plea that they have never done it before. Should the occupants persist in their refusal, I should recommend that the house be declared uninhabitable and closed. . . .

June 1886

Fourteen more deaths, and all from enteric fever. The water supply I found on analysis to be bad or suspiciously near a drain. Several deaths occurred at Seaton and Castle Eden Colliery. At Seaton every house had a separate ashpit and privy. At Castle Eden the greater majority of typhoid cases were in the newest houses having separate ashpit and privy in enclosed yard; very strong evidence that this is not the most efficient form of sanitation for colliery villages. . . .

February, 1890, Murton

One hundred workmen's houses, the older ones, have been provided with privies, one for every two houses. The results of these structures on health I shall watch most carefully. It is important to retain as much space as possible with these alterations. . . . It is undeniable that this disease is absent where open channelling with a sufficient fall to ensure speedy removal, a plentiful supply of water and fairly efficient scavenging exist, and that its occurrence is invariably associated with the closed drain imperfectly constructed

Education of miners' children in east Durham

Report to House of Lords, 1842

In connection with the boys' school at Wingate Grange Colliery, a striking example of the peculiar jealousy and independent pride of pitmen may be adduced. The owners, anxious that the education of the boys should be as much an act of benevolence as possible, professed to exact only a penny a week from the men as an acknowledgement, and subsequently became very lax and indifferent in its exaction. The schoolmaster was also a man of superior education and gentlemanly address; a design appears in all this.

An under-clerk possessing a physical defect was discharged from the colliery. He established a school in the Methodist chapel, and in six weeks obtained 70 pupils at the usual rates of charges sliding between 2*d.* and 6*d.* per week—the owner's school having diminished in this time nearly in the ratio of the increase in the other. This person possesses the usual qualifications of a pit village school and is doubtless desirous of effecting good. Neither his ability nor his system can for one moment be compared to those of his competitor.

Four years previously these reports had been made to the House of Lords:

An infant school in a colliery village is such an entire novelty that the advantages for the women by the establishment of one at Wingate Grange is not understood by them. The first impression of the idea of removing their young children from under their own eye is doubtless a revolting one to their strong maternal feelings. The system of infant instruction should therefore be presented to them in a clear and enticing manner.

One master, Thomas Anderson, of the school at South Hetton, opens a night school which was considered to be in a flourishing condition. There were at my visit 21 persons from twelve to twenty-one years. The average attendance was about 30 and the oldest was thirty years. They are pitmen and their children, and there are occasionally three or four girls. The master professes to teach reading, writing and mensuration plain and spherical, trigonometry, land and subterranean surveying, charging 8*d.*, 9*d.*, and more than a shilling for these higher subjects. He is self-taught and, being lame, opens this school for a living. He thinks about one-third of his pupils are intelligent, but complained that few parents encourage the school.

10

PILGRIMAGE FROM NENTHEAD
(to Ashington)
Chester Armstrong, 1936

Chester Armstrong was a checkweighman at the Carl Pit in Ashington Colliery in 1936 when he began to write his autobiography in his allotment shed. He sent his manuscript to various publishers and it was eventually published by Methuen, entitled Pilgrimage from Nenthead. *Here are some brief extracts:*

I was born at Nenthead in Cumbria on July 2nd, 1868, in the middle cottage of the three that stand almost parallel with the Primitive Methodist Chapel. My father, William Armstrong, was born and spent his young manhood in a place called Ashgill. My father was one of the surviving members of a family of nine, but the greatest part of this family died in youth, of consumption, principally.

My mother's maiden name was Elizabeth Jackson, born at Farney Shield on a farmholding in West Allan, Northumberland. Her whole life of sixty-six years was one continuous act of heroism. She brought into the world a family of six: five sons and one daughter in their order of birth, the third son dying in infancy. I am the fifth son in this order.

When as a family we came to Ashington, the wrench on my mother's part was as great as it was with my father. She was a typical daleswoman. Yet it was she who impressed on her husband the urgency of taking the decision to leave the district, a decision taken on his account alone.

Once established in Ashington, the domestic burden my mother bore became heavier. It was increased by the fact that my father, my two brothers and myself, were employed at the colliery, involving all that it means of worry and work in the home. It meant a never-ending struggle to keep the dirt at bay.

Mother died in 1900 on the same day as John Ruskin. On the day of her funeral it was discovered that the grave was not dug, the sexton being absent on a drunken spree. He was found eventually, but we had to wait a considerable time in the chapel. Reaching the graveside under a biting wind, we were compelled to witness the humiliating spectacle of the semi-intoxicated grave-digger striving in a state of awakening repentance to complete the job. Just as the upper fringe of a January sun like a great red ball dropped below the horizon, the coffin was lowered into the grave.

I was six years old when I came to Ashington (1874). I saw the sea for the first time. We visited the colliery at the time the Carl Pit shaft was being sunk. The sinkers were but a few yards from the surface. I remember stepping gingerly to the edge of this hole, quite awe-stricken. Little did I imagine that my acquaintance with this hideous thing would be so real and prolonged in later life.

At Ashington, through the kindness of my mother's sister, Mrs Joseph Martin, whose husband tenanted a small farm-holding at New Moor, we were provided with a single room until we could procure other accommodation. Very soon afterwards we came to occupy one of the two cottages which stand close to the road end leading into New Moor. These cottages were part of a farm held by Mr Bruce, and one of the conditions of occupancy was that the tenant would place his services at the disposal of the farmer for at least one day in the year.

We had no sooner settled here than the need for finding employment at the colliery presented itself. My father, my two brothers and I were interviewed by Mr Robert L. Booth within the doorway of his office.

It was my mother's intention that I should continue my schooling in preparation for some employment more suited to me than manual labour. But there I stood, confronting the manager. My brothers, who had some experience of work in the Nenthead lead-mines, were fixed up with underground employment.

'And what about this other little fellow?' asked the manager, graciously. 'Surely we can find work for him about the heapstead?' My father hesitated just a little and then thankfully complied. All so simple, so terribly simple.

I presented myself accordingly on the following Monday morning at the heapstead. The experience of this dark December morning has left scars on my consciousness that yet remain. There was I, a mere mite for my years, and acutely sensitive. I managed somehow to find my way on the Screens (a means of sifting stones from coal), and from there to the pit-head proper in search of the Keeker. I was too full of bewildered amazement to sense the full meaning of it all—this came later. The thunderous din and clatter, the thick haze of dust through which I could just discern the men shovelling coals into wagons, and though the gas-jets flickered and flared, all combined to dull the senses to a due apprehension of it all.

In Ashington in 1880 there were many roads to Hell but only one to heaven. The means of avoiding the former and ensuring the latter were provided by the presence of two Nonconformist bodies: the Primitive Methodists, known as Ranters, and the Wesleyan Methodists. Almost adjoining the latter chapel was the Mechanics' Institute and reading-room, the east wing of which was used as a concert room. Apart from the Bothal National Elementary School, this Institute and concert-room afforded the only accommodation and facilities for edification and entertainment.

The concert-room, small as it was, was the centre and training ground for all the aspiring local talent in the village—good, bad and indifferent. 'Penny Readings' were then the vogue, composed of songs, recitations, and readings, the charge of admittance being one penny. Clog-dancing was popular and occupied a place on every programme, the artiste being dressed in spotless white shirt, velvet knee-breeches, with lurid coloured stockings to display to advantage the ample calf of the leg.

Occasionally, this concert-hall would be hired by some itinerant variety company, and at those times the room was taxed beyond capacity. A coloured troupe engaged the hall for a week. On the Monday evening the room was packed. We were treated to the usual plantation songs with banjo accompaniment. There was little or no enthusiasm among the audience, just a patient waiting for something more interesting to turn up. Just at that moment a bashful child came on and recited *Mary Had a Little Lamb*. The effect was electric, but when someone laughed in derision a storm broke out and pandemonium reigned. The company were fortunate to escape from the village without injury.

The only available space for outdoor recreation was a patch of land at the west end of the village, then known as the bowling-field. Quoits, a close rival to bowling, was also of keen interest to the miner, as could be seen by the clamorous contending groups of men when money was at stake. Fairs (or Shows, as they were called) with all their retinue of attractions, quack doctors, auctioneers and the rest, were held here. On occasion, travelling theatre groups would pitch their large tents, and remain as long as it was profitable to do so. Then there were such blood-curdling dramas as *Murder in the Red Barn*, to keep us awake at nights.

It was on this open space that association football had its birth in Ashington, a club being formed with the ambitious name of Ashington Rising Star. The first team were a motley crew, but tremendously keen. The goal-posts were long thin poles, painted like the old-time barber's pole; a piece of rope served as a crossbar. Though the game of cricket was played previously in small ways in a field behind the colliery, it was on this plot of land that the Ashington Cricket Club was born.

Since Ashington was the first colliery village I had seen, and coming from a village altogether different, I was struck by the contrast. Instead of scattered cottages there were long rows of houses running parallel to each other. They were a series of brick boxes mutually supported and constructed on a simple plan, without any regard for any external pleasing effect, and with a bare minimum of regard for what is required to meet the demands of home life. Running parallel to the houses were the open ash-middens and privies, the roadway between impassable in winter-time for mud. The whole appearance of Ashington gave an impression of dullness and monotony.

Housing conditions afford a glaring example of the little value the miner places himself on his own worth, and the much smaller value that society places on his services to the community. The housing of the miner everywhere constitutes a monument to the parsimonious reward that is meted out to the miner for what he gives in return.

The whole arrangement of Ashington has always reminded me of a huge compound. Each colliery row is numbered and there is nothing to give any house a separate identity save its number. Most of them are what is termed single houses, with one living room—which frequently serves as a bedroom—on the ground floor, and two bedrooms above. Owners are impelled—at their own expense—to erect a wooden lean-to, or back kitchen, to supplement this accommodation, and to enhance the prospect of decency.

During the period 1880 to 1893 the population of Ashington was more than doubled. This brought the urgency of adequate housing, which was effected on a large scale. But these new houses were built on almost precisely the same scale as the older houses, the only difference being that a backward step was taken when two large blocks were composed of two rooms only, the living-room on the ground floor and the bedroom above, presumably suitable for newly married people. There was a repetition of open middens and the same neglect of paving roadways.

And what of the housewife and mother? Her never-ending struggle against dirt and squalor in these colliery rows would tax the genius of Dickens to describe. The pity of it is that when houses of this kind are erected they must remain as long as they are capable of repair.

The coal trade at that time was rising to its boom periods of prosperity and enjoying a degree of monopoly in the foreign markets. Not only did Ashington Colliery interests share in this prosperity, but they were favoured with comparatively low costs of production. It had always appeared obvious to me that the opportunity was lost of making Ashington a model colliery, as an example to the whole mining community.

In the Hirst area was perpetuated the old and simple plan of constructing houses for miners: long rows or streets, some of them more than a mile in length, and so close together as to be severely congested. The larger part of this area is an outrage on society, a monstrosity. Many of these streets are named after some familiar trees and shrubs. Thus we have Sycamore Street, Laburnum Terrace, Hawthorn Road, and the rest. Surely it must have been a piece of sardonic humour on the part of those responsible for the christening, for anything less appropriate could hardly be conceived. As I now write in 1936, the external appearance of many of these streets is so dilapidated that they are well on the way to being added to the abundant supply of slum property in Christian England.

Owing for the need for haste in coping with a rapidly increasing population, Ashington was thrown up, so to speak, and thus presents a conglomerate character, without form, except that the long blocks of houses represent straight lines, almost utterly void of appeal to the aesthetic eye. In this period, what became known as High Market began to assume its present form. About this time [1887] the church of the Church of England (Holy Sepulchre) was built, together with the vicarage, adjacent to which is the cemetery. Among the first to be buried there was Joseph Riddle, who was fatally injured at the pit under the same circumstances as those from which I, by a miracle, escaped a similar fate.

Opposite this church now stood the new central premises of the Ashington Industrial Co-operative Society. It was an ambitious block of premises marking the most definite progress of the Co-operative Consumers' organisation in Ashington. The main building was composed of grocery, drapery and butchering departments, with a temperance hotel at the east corner and a public hall on the floor above.

This hall supplied a much-felt want at the time in the way of adequate accommodation for public meetings, lectures and concerts. It has since shed its identity by being converted into a drapery department, but could its walls now speak, they would echo the sentiments of some of the most reputed persons in England.

It was in this hall that the people of Ashington became directly acquainted with some of the new reformist organisations: the Land Nationalisation League, the Single Tax Movement, the Social Democratic Federation, and others. Ashington was then a forlorn hope for the Conservative Party, and these organisations were but the scattered advance-guard of the Labour Party which came into being in later years. Such was the political keenness among the miners that they were almost made to feel assured that a new social order was within immediate reach.

11

TRAGEDY AT WOODHORN COLLIERY, 1916

On Sunday, 13 August 1916, a gas explosion at Woodhorn Colliery, near Ashington, killed 13 men, eight of whom were deputies. The management tried to shift the blame on to four fireman who had not reported for work on the furnaces on the Saturday night. Lack of pressure to the ventilating pipes resulted in a build up of gas in the Main Seam. The following dramatised evidence is taken from the inquest held in September 1916, at the Harmonic Hall, Ashington:

Coroner Charles Percy addressed the inquest members:
I want to say at once, I propose, as I always do, to adopt my usual practice of giving a very wide latitude for the calling of witnesses, so that any person, having a direct or indirect interest in this calamity —this terrible accident—may call and produce before this Court what he considers will be any evidence which may assist us in coming to a conclusion.

I understand there are, on this occasion, a good many representatives of different interests relating to the colliery owners, and representatives of the men.

After the Coroner had called on William Cookson, colliery surveyor, of Windsor Terrace, Newbiggin, and Joseph John Hall, Sub-Agent of the group of collieries, the next witness, who gave evidence of cause of death, was Dr Robert Joseph Mills:

I took some rough notes at the time describing each individual case as they came to me. They were unidentified; I only knew them by numbers.

No. 1: Walter Hughes, who was brought out alive. He was suffering from fractures of both hands and left leg. Burns were very extensive all over the body, hands, feet, breast. We chloroformed him although he was practically unconscious.

No. 2 was Daniel Harrison: compound dislocation of left ankle. He also was taken out alive; wounds to the head and superficial fracture of frontal bones, severe scalp wounds, burns extensive, and of a similar nature to Case 1. I think the cause of death was shock from burns in these two cases.

No. 3 was Joseph Hodgson, suffering from dislocation of neck but no burning. He still had all his clothes on.

No. 4: Ralph Howard, dislocation of neck, fracture of skull, at right temple and base. Practically no burning.

No. 5: George Blair, fracture to the base of the skull, practically no burning.

No. 6: Thomas Armstrong, fracture of skull, deep indentation of frontal bone, extensive burns; fracture of skull was cause of death. He must have fallen forward by a blow from the roof, unconscious immediately.

No. 7 was Thomas's brother, David Armstrong, who died from shock, dislocation of neck; practically no burns.

No. 8: Joseph Harrogate, fracture at base of skull, fracture of both arms, fracture of left leg, burns on arms and face, severe.

No. 9: George Hudson, shock caused death at once, burns extensive, probably post mortem, fracture of left leg.

No. 10: Edward Walton, death due to the same cause, extensive burns in the lower extremities as if he had fallen and been burnt *post mortem* [after death].

No. 11: Robert Hindmarsh, shock and burns as in No. 10.

No. 12: George Marshall, shock as in No. 10.

No. 13: John George Patterson, driver of the pony, back of skull was badly fractured, most of his back burnt, and of course the pony was dead.

Question: Most of them, I take it, must have died instantaneously?
Answer: Oh, yes. Instantaneously. Although some fresh blood was found on the ground beside George Marshall, the man nearest the coal face
Q: Blood on the coal, you say. Tell me, Doctor, I am curious, why did you think fit to number the dead men?
A: I had not the names at first. When they were identified I put labels on.
Coroner: Thank you, Doctor.

The witness withdrew and Joseph John Hall was called and sworn.

Q: Your name is Joseph John Hall? Where do you live and what are you?
A: I am sub-agent for the colliery, and I live at Ashington.
Q: Previous to August 13th, had you been engaged in any special work at this colliery in the Main Seam?
A: The seam was opened out about five months ago, the object being that as the number of men had been greatly reduced by enlistment [in the 1914–18 war], this seam was started with the object of increasing the output.
Q: Tell me the character of the seam, is it gassy?
A: No. It is a seam very well known in the county. It is the first seam we ever commenced at Ashington, and it has been worked ever since.
Q: Has it been known to be free from gas?
A: It is worked by naked lights. It has been worked at Woodhorn to a smaller extent, also at Longhirst and Ellington, and it has been worked at Newbiggin.
Q: On the 13th, Mr Hall, was there anything unusual about the ventilation?
A: The ventilating fan was running on the surface, except that it had a reduced speed owing to the slackness of steam.
Q: Was the fan stopped during the Friday night or Saturday morning?
A: Yes, previous to the accident it was stopped from 6 a.m. to 11

a.m. for overhauling and repairs.

Q: Did it start as usual at eleven o'clock?

A: Yes, on the pay Saturday when the pit is idle is the usual time for doing necessary repairs to the ventilators and fans. Before the fan was stopped we started the furnace, which takes the place of the fan when standing.

Q: Can you give us any explanation of the shortage of steam?

A: The reason why the steam was short was the fact of shortage of firemen, and on the Saturday night, when the night shift came on there were only two men to work out of four required.

Q: You mean to say who turned up for work?

A: Yes, the other men were sent for.

Q: If you had got four men you would not have been short of steam?

A: No.

Q: Have you made enquiries about these two men not turning up?

A: Yes. But on Sunday morning we also had two men off out of six.

Q: On the Sunday morning, when the shift started at 6 a.m., how many men did you have then?

A: Only four men were doing the work of six.

Q: I want you, Mr Hall, to give me an opinion. I do not want a vague one. Do you consider that these men not turning up and securing the proper supply of steam had anything to do with the accident?

A: Yes.

Q: Can you give me the names of the two men who did not turn up on the Saturday night shift?

A: William Ritson was one and Rayford Dawson.

Q: And the two men who did not turn up on the Sunday?

A: George Lowrie and John Dent.

Coroner: I shall want you to have these men here. It is only fair to the Crown that they should hear what is being said. Summon them as soon as possible.

After some delay the men were brought to the court. William Ritson was called and sworn.

Q: Are you a boiler-minder?
A: No, sir.
Q: What are you?
A: A fireman. I am a screener and an auxiliary fireman; I fire occasionally.
Q: Was it in the ordinary course of your duty to go on shift as a fireman on the night of the 12th at five o'clock?
A: Yes, sir.
Q: Did you go?
A: No, sir, I did not feel exactly fit for the occasion, I just went and met a few friends and stayed away and sent no reason.
Q: How do you mean, not fit for the occasion?
A: We can get run down, exhausted, like.
Q: And you met a few friends?
A: I spent part of the day with them. Of course I should've been at work at night.
Q: Where did you spend the day with them?
A: Is that question necessary?
Q: When I ask you anything, it is necessary.
A: I was at the club.
Q: Spent the whole day in the club?
A: Not all the day, part of the day. It would be easy to say I was partly drunk and exhausted together. *Pointing to a reporter:* It's not nice evidence to put in the papers, and I would ask you to put it down there better, as it is going to be published, like.
Q: I have nothing to do with what is published. You are truthful, at any rate.
A: When you are exhausted it doesn't take much to . . . to turn your mind towards not gannin' to work at the pit. I'm a fairly good attender.
Q: I suppose you realise the importance of firemen being there in order to keep the ventilation going in the colliery?
A: We have never in any way looked at it like that.
Q: And now?
A: We'll aall take a different view after this.
Q: It never occurred to you that the fact of your staying away would

hurt anybody?
A: Aa realise that now.

Rayford Dawson was called and sworn.

Q: What are you, Rayford Dawson?
A: A fireman, sir.
Q: Where do you live?
A: No. 6, New Queen Street, Newbiggin by the Sea.
Q: And was it your duty to be at work on this Saturday at 5 a.m.?
A: Yes, sir.
Q: Were you there?
A: No, sir, I was ill with a bad face.
Q: What do you mean?
A: An abscess on the face.
Q: Was it broken?
A: No, sir, swollen.
Q: Did you give any notice that you were not going to be at work?
A: Yes, sir, I sent word up with one of the men to the boiler-minder.
Q: Who did you send word up with?
A: Hunter Barlow. We call him Burly.
Q: When did you tell him to take word up?
A: About four o'clock, I saw him when I was down the street getting some stuff for me face, and he said he was sure to tell him.
Q: He was leaving Newbiggin at four o'clock to start at five. So your message could only arrive when you should have started work?
A: Yes, sir, that was the only man I could get to send word up with.

John Dent was called and sworn.

Q: What is your name and where do you live?
A: John Dent, 40 Queen Street, Hirst.
Q: What are you?
A: I am a boilermaker by trade, sir, engaged in the Ashington Colliery as a fitter.

Q: Were you an auxiliary boilerman?
A: Yes, sir. I am a bit deaf.
Q: So I notice. Was it your duty to start a shift on the boilers at 6 a.m. on Sunday morning, the 13th of August?
A: Yes, sir, but I was unable.

Dent then produced a doctor's note which read: 'I hereby certify that from August 14th to the 16th John Dent consulted me for gastric colic, and I prescribed for him. He was unable to work up to Friday, 18th August. Signed: Frank Patton.'

Q: What happened on the day you should have been there?
A: I was confined to my bed on the Saturday.
Q: On the Friday you began work at 6 a.m. and finished at 5 p.m.?
A: Yes. And then I went straight home to bed.
Q: And you were not up again?
A: Not up to the Monday, when I went to see the doctor.
Q: Did you send word that you were not able to work?
A: I sent word with Mr Kidd on Sunday morning at 11 am.
Q: That was five hours after you should have started. Could you not have sent word at six o'clock in the morning?
A: No, I had nobody to go but the old lady, and I would not turn her out to take word. This is only the second time I have been off duty in six years. The books will tell the tale.
Q: It can be contradicted if it is not true.
A: That is so.

The witness withdrew and George Lowrie was called and sworn.

Q: Who are you and where do you live?
A: George Lowrie, of Newbiggin by the Sea.
Q: What are you?
A: A fireman at Woodhorn Colliery.
Q: Should you have been on duty at 6 am on Sunday morning.
A: I should.
Q: Why were you not there?

A: I slept the 'caller'. It was twenty past six when I woke. Of course we have no caller, you know: I slept in.

Q: Did you attempt to get to your work then?

A: No. I did not think it was any use bothering, after that time there would be another man in my place, I thought. They generally do that.

Q: Had you been drinking?

A: No, I am not accustomed to drinking.

Q: If you knew they were short of firemen, and when you woke at 6.20 a.m., don't you think it would have been useful if you had hurried to work?

A: That is true.

Coroner: Now I have given you men a chance to say why you were not at work. I thought it was my duty.

The witness withdrew and Granville Poole was called and sworn.

Q: Is your name Granville Poole and are you a junior Inspector of Mines?

A: Yes

Q: Have you assisted in the investigation of large explosions?

A: I have, on various occasions.

Q: On Sunday the 13th of August, 1916, did you go down Woodhorn Pit and make an examination of the site of the explosion?

A: I did, sir. And on subsequent occasions—six days in all.

Q: Did you examine any report made prior to the explosion?

A: I have seen no such report.

Note: Before entering any place of work, it was the duty of a deputy to examine the place for gas. If any was found, the men were sent out and a report filled in to that effect. No report was filed that day.

Q: You have heard the evidence about a six-inch-diameter compressed-air pipe ventilating the place where these men were to work. How effective would that be?

A: I think there was no ventilation at all in the headings where the men were. It was a high seam, over eight feet; if there was gas there it would rise to the roof, yet the compressed-air pipe lay on the floor, some twelve yards away from where the men were to plant girders.

Q: Would the absence of ventilation allow gas to accumulate?

A: Yes.

Q: We heard from acting manager J. J. Hall that he thought that the gas was released by a fall of stone; his theory was backed up by a mining expert, Colonel Blackett. Do you go along with this view?

A: *Referring to a plan of the pit:* It would assist if I went right through the indications. Going up this drift into the Main Seam, two men were found, Harrison and Hughes; they were badly burned. Thomas Armstrong was found here, a little higher up; he was burned, too. Harrogate, the pump man, was blown right up against a prop and he was badly crushed, a lot of bones broken, and he was badly burned, too. His pail was flattened like a piece of tin blown up against the wall, so there had obviously been a lot of force.

Q: We may take it that the fall of stone causing force would not do the injury to that man?

A: No, it could not account for it.

Q: And do you think, as has been put forward by Mr Hall and the coal company's witness, Colonel Blackett, that the rush of air from the fall of stone would cause that force?

A: Quite impossible.

Q: And where and how do you think the gas would be ignited in the first place?

A: Right at the face, here. A clay pipe was found here. I think that pipe was simply dropped; it is not smashed. I suggest that this man stood upon a tub, put his candle up to the roof, and said: 'Where has this girder to go?'

Q: And lit the gas?

A: Yes, inflamed it; and it developed its maximum intensity a little further outbye.

Q: And what significance do you place on the doctor's evidence when he said that there were signs of fresh blood on the coal at this point?

A: I can only surmise that this bleeding occurred in some entirely different circumstances and had nothing whatsoever to do with the explosion. A cut or scratch—just one of the many hazards of working down the pit.

After three days of inquiry, the jury retired at five o'clock on 21 September 1916, and returned fifty minutes later with the following verdict:

That the 13 men whose names have been repeatedly read—the said deceased men were accidently killed on the 13th day of August, 1916, while working in Woodhorn Colliery, by an explosion of gas in the Main Seam, and that such gas had accumulated through want of sufficient ventilation, and exploded through contact with a naked light and before any fall of stone took place. The Jury are of the opinion that the management should see in the future that written Reports should be made for every shift, special or otherwise. The Jury are also of the opinion that there has been a certain amount of laxity on the part of the management for not seeing to sufficient ventilation being maintained.

12

MONTAGUE PIT DISASTER, 1925

Thirty-eight men and boys were killed in the disaster at this colliery in the west-end of Newcastle. Here are the eyewitness accounts of two of the deputies who were down the pit when it happened. First, Joseph Robson:

At 10.25 a.m. Matt Errington shouted that he had 'holed'. I procee-ded to the spot and found a slight bleeding from the coal. I at once decided to send for the overman, and to do that I had to go back about 50 yards to seek my son, Jim, to carry the message. I had just given these instructions and was about to drill a hole in the coal to prove its thickness when I heard a loud report. I then realised what had happened: water had broken through.

I immediately rushed towards the spot, but had only gone about two steps when I met a wall of water about five feet high, and was plunged into darkness. I then had to face the fact that the position of the men in that flat was hopeless and, with this horrid thought in my mind, I realised my next move must be to get the boys and ponies out at top speed. On reaching the flat, my son, Jim, had just got that far and was waiting for me with the ponies and tubs, which helped him to make good his escape.

After seeing to the safety of my son and the remainder of the drawers—Brown, Wertera, and Black—and putter Tracey in the effected flat, I proceeded to get down the hitch. This was a death trap but, knowing I had four hewers down there—Joseph and John

Foster, George Young and Thomas Lacham—and putter Lochren, I could not leave them, so within two minutes, just in the nick of time, I got them to safety. Owing to being in complete darkness I found this very difficult, but, thank God, we managed.

I then proceeded towards the shaft. On the way I met Sam Evans the overman. about 500 yards from the spot where the water was first seen. This would be about 10.45 a.m. Overman Evans, not being able to proceed further owing to blackdamp, stated to me that the only hope was to go by the standage to get the men out of the Ropeway Flat. I offered to accompany him, but he suggested it would be better for him to take Jack Hall, the deputy of that district, and that I should carry on with what I was doing.

The story is now taken up by Jack Hall:

William Jackson, deputy, and myself and Wiliam Errington, timberman, were going inbye together when I felt the air change. I said to Johnson: 'There is something wrong, and I am going back to report it to Sammy Evans, the overman.' I went back and saw Evans and told him that the air was changing. Sammy and I came back to Irish Cross Cut, and we met the boys coming out from that direction. They said there was a burst. In the meantime Deputy Robson and some men came out.

Sammy Evans and I decided to go round by the return, to try and get the men out of the Irish Ropeway. I saw Jackson, the rolleyway-man, and asked whether he had seen my boy, Jack, who was driving that day. He said he was at the Ropeway pump. Sam and I then tried to get through some separation doors at the Ropeway headways. When we got there it was like a raging sea, and we could not get through. I said: 'If the boys are in there they are finished.'

I was nearly poisoned by gas, and the water was gushing through the bricks and the woodwork of the doors. We decided to go on to the return, and we went along till we came among some of the boys. Sammy and I went down to see Deputy Johnson, and he told me to get as many as I could and get out with them. I got 16 men and boys, including my son, and we all got out safely.

The boy, Jack, told me how he had seen Deputy Johnson for the last time running inbye to get the men out of the Board Flat. The water was then above his knees and was rising as he ran into the pit. He could have saved himself had he then gone out of the pit, but when he was last seen he was going further in, and the water was up to the deputy's kist, a box where tools and reports are kept.

The Newcastle Evening Chronicle *reported on 21 May:*

Scenes terrible enough to daunt the staunchest of hearts were revealed when the rescue brigadesmen, after toiling day and night for over seven weeks, at last broke into the flood-sealed tomb of 17 of the 38 victims of the Scotswood pit disaster. The story of how the dead rode to bank for the last time constitutes an epic in mining annals.

The bodies were found in the Irish Ropeway, and to reach them the workers, wearing their oxygen breathing apparatus, swam through polluted waters reaching up to a few inches from the roof.

One by one the remains of the ill-fated men and boys were placed in the oak-grained shells yesterday, and then the officials were faced by the problem of carrying the grim freight across the water barrier.

The difficulty was solved by bringing the coffins through the flood on a raft, and this was begun and safely accomplished by one of the strangest and grimmest underground journeys in the coalfield's history.

Union representative William Straker had this to say in his Monthly Circular:

It seems strange that during the 20 years since the 1905 Commission on Mines Dangers found in favour of such, nothing has been done to secure the plans of old workings abandoned previous to the 1872 Mines Act. If such plans had been asked for it is quite evident that the accident at Montague would have been prevented, as since the accident an old plan has been discovered of the workings from which the water came. This plan shows, to within a yard—so we have learned officially— where these old workings were.

With almost 60 children left fatherless, it was fitting that Straker headed his Montague Disaster Report *with this verse from one of Joe Skipsey's poems, entitled* The Caller*:*

'Get up!' the caller calls, 'Get up!'
And in the dead of night,
To win the bairns their bite and sup
I rose, a weary wight.
My flannel dudden donn'd thrice o'er
My birds are kissed, and then
I with a whistle shut the door
I may not ope again.

13

NORTHUMBERLAND MINERS' HISTORY 1919–39

By Jack Davison, a miner from Pegswood, near Morpeth, from his
book of the same title

I carry an indelible memory of the 1926 lock-out, my earliest
recollection at the age of four. Together with my friend, Andrew
Hall, also aged four, we left the soup kitchen still feeling hungry, so
we explored my mother's pantry. Save for some bread and an
opened tin of condensed milk on the top shelf, it was bare.

As we were both small we struggled and dragged what seemed
then an exceedingly heavy chair into the pantry. With Andrew's
assistance I reached the tin of condensed milk, and though we only
intended to take one or two spoonfuls, before we realised it we had
consumed the lot. When we realised our 'crime' we ran out of the
house leaving behind all the evidence of our raid on the pantry.

Later that evening when I admitted my act to my mother and
father. Instead of being chastised I was amazed to see my mother
crying and my father with tears in his eyes. How many such
heartbreaking scenes could have been told throughout the British
coalfield. Despite all their efforts to feed their children, despite all
the sacrifices towards the end of the lock-out, the hunger of the
children was becoming painfully evident. . . .

Some indication of how miners' children fared can be seen in the
Pegswood School Log Book of 1926. The Headmaster records:

'October 4th, Dr Stonehouse, the local Medical Officer of Health, visited the school to examine children suffering from lack of food.'

What of the adults who were making all possible sacrifices for their children? Many pigeon fanciers amongst the Northumberland miners killed their birds, save for one or two favourites, to help sustain the family larder. The few pigeons spared were left with open holes in the pigeon lofts to fly to the fields to forage for their own food. . . .

In this struggle mothers suffered the most, and not because they were moulded in the Andy Capp wife fashion; their sacrifices were self imposed. For many years after, the custom in numerous miners' homes was for the mothers to sit down to a meal after the family finished. The custom began in the 1926 strike, when the mothers put their children and husbands first for feeding. What was left, if anything, they ate. Not surprisingly, many of the women looked old despite being in their late twenties or early thirties. Their moral support for their men, and their militancy against the owners' proposed terms, was reflected daily in the mining villages.

They would organise their children and stand together along the colliery streets leading to the pit, and shout and hurl abuse at the blacklegs travelling to and from work. At both Ashington and North Walbottle, miners' wives were prosecuted for interfering with blacklegs. The militant attitude of the miners' wives, I feel, reflects more than anything else the justification of the miners' resistance. Already, before the attempted imposition of reduced wages, they were the main sufferers from the deprived miners' income. They had to balance the home budget, and in their household management they were already victims of deprivation. Many of them were working 16 hours or more a day in the home to try and make ends meet. Truly, they were the heroines of the 1926 tragedy.

Outside of picket or soup-kitchen duty or other trade union committees, father would be busy poaching, working coals from the outcrop or stealing them from colliery sidings. Allotments and gardens were always carefully cultivated. . . .

Whilst the youths and unmarried men were fully trade-union conscious, they did not carry the same responsibilities, yet many of them undertook to help in the feeding of the children in every possible way. Some worked at local farms during haymaking and harvesting, and were paid in meals and other food to bring home to the villagers. Where they worked for wages this was regarded as blacklegging, and protests against this action were received at county level from the Stobswood branch. The Agricultural Workers' Union protested against miners working on the farms in the Seaton Delaval area to the detriment of agricultural workers.

The call for more militant action came mainly from the young men, in their enforced idleness of the lock-ut. Understandably, under such circumstances . . .[there were] disturbances throughout the British coalfields and Northumberland was no exception. . . . The Northumberland Miners' Union Minute Book reads more like the *Police Gazette*:

May 7th — Thomas William Paxton, George Lockett, Bedlington miners, charged with preventing proper use of a vehicle. Five windows of bus smashed. Lockett sentenced to three months' imprisonment, others two months. D. Neason, miner, charged with interfering with bus driver and threatening to stop buses running from the Market Place, Morpeth. Neason claimed he was alone and was sentenced to one month's hard labour. At Killingworth Station level crossings a large crowd prevented the opening of the gates, and both the Newcastle and Edinburgh trains had to force their way through. . . . W. Harris, the signalman, was chased by the crowd, and it was alleged he was threatened that if he returned he would be thrown on the live wire. T. Helmsley, loco fireman, was discharged, as was W. Hall, Palmersville miner, who was one of the scout rovers who went to give assistance to quell the disturbance.

May 10th — John Gray, Joseph Mole, Samuel Wright and Arthur Dickinson, miners, charged with attack on food wagon at the Three Mile Bridge, Gosforth, and gaoled for three months. At Stakeford, J. Mounsey, R. Metcalfe, E. Kirkley, J. Allison, N. Richard, J. Robson and G. Rix were accused of impeding transit of a commercial van. The police found in Metcalfe's possession a catapult and some stones. The *Daily Mail* reported that the men were released on June 10th from Durham Gaol and presented with £1 each and given a public reception.

May 10th — Fourteen miners from New York and Murton Village were charged that out of a crowd of 900 people gathered near the Holystone they stoned a van and ambulance, breaking a window and injuring one of the driver's arms. Six Netherton miners were charged with obstructing the highway near Netherton by placing a telegraph pole across and preventing transit of a bus. Morpeth Court next day witnessed an amazing scene; whilst these men were being charged Superintendent Wight turned to the public benches and accused W. W. Bell, miners' representative and Chairman of Bedlington U[rban] D[istrict] C[ouncil], with also being concerned in the incident. Bell was immediately taken into custody and the whole case was adjourned for two days. At the following court session, Bell proved conclusively that he was one and three-quarter miles away at Netherton Institute at a meeting with three other men. He was discharged but the others were fined £5.

May 10th — the 10 a.m. train from Edinburgh was derailed three-quarters of a mile north of Dan Dyke level crossing between Annitsford and Cramlington. R. W. Martin, L[ondon and] N[orth] E[astern] R[ailway] engineer, stated that there were about 100 to 120 men at the scene of the derailment. . . . Press reports differ as to the number of passengers, between 500 to 600, and 300 to 400, but all were agreed that only one passenger was hurt. . . . It took the Judge one hour and twenty-five minutes to sum up. On July 2nd the accused received the following sentences:

A. Wilson aged 27, R. Harbottle aged 21, T Roberts aged 25, were sentenced to 8 years' penal servitude.

W. Stephenson aged 22, J. Ellison aged 29, were given 6 years' penal servitude.

O. Sanderson aged 25, W. Muckle aged 25, W. Baker aged 28, were sentenced to 4 years' penal servitude.

Outside of their protest of innocence the men took the sentences calmly but the women in the Court gasped at the severity of the sentences imposed. . . . The Executive reported on July 6th, 1926, that they were disappointed that the Home Secretary had refused their request to release these men; but in December of that year they were finally released from prison.

After the period of the General Strike it would seem that the regulations were not so stringently applied. There were, of course, many cases. Both the Stobswood and Seaton Delaval miners' branch secretaries, J. Parks and James Fisher, were imprisoned—Parks for alleged coal theft, and Fisher for alleged intimidation of a blackleg. James Fisher was refused employment after the lock-out and he was compelled to emigrate to Australia to find work. . . .

Not all disturbances were brought to the Court's attention . . . the Pegswood miners' branch minutes recorded on October 22nd that the local union officials reported that 50 men were on their way from Ashington to stop the outcropping of coal for commercial purposes at the Primrose Valley, near Morpeth. Upwards of 50 men left the Pegswood meeting to join the Ashington men . . . coal carts were tipped into the river Wansbeck, the outcroppers were manhandled and sent packing, and all the timber was withdrawn from the workings to seal the coal off for future working. Many similar instances could be reported throughout the county.

Northumberland union branches 1919–39

With very few exceptions, men working at pits employing fifty or more, formed their union branch. Even at small undertakings some men sought to join the nearest branch. For example, in 1919, men at Spittle Pit and Horsley Wood Pit were accepted as members of North Wylam Branch. Small pits like Longframlington, near Rothbury, remained outside the union for several years, and when the union branch was formed in 1924, the pit closed within six weeks.

The opening and closing of branches [as shown in the following table] was a fair reflection of the erratic position of the coal industry in Northumberland [between the wars].

1919

January 10	Barcombe Colliery	opened
January 27	North Tyne	opened
May 20	Byron Pit	opened

1919 (continued)

July 25	Newburgh	opened
August 15	Lead Gate	opened
September 24	West Denton	opened
October 13	Wallbottle Union Pit	opened

1920

January 23	Tramwell	opened
April 1	Gunnerton	opened

1921

October 5	Goodfellow	closed
November 16	Mickley Grange	closed
December 23	Walbottle Union Pit	closed

1922

January 21	Broomhill	opened
March 14	Union Pit	opened
March 18	Bebside	opened
August 12	South Shilbottle	opened

1924

January 11	Lambley	opened
April 15	Tramwell	opened
June 2	Longframlington	opened
July 30	Longframlington	closed
August 15	Blucher	closed
November 17	Amelia, Shankhouse	closed
November 17	Dudley	closed
November 17	Hartford	closed

1925

March 1	North Seaton	closed
May 23	Eccles	opened
July 20	New Delaval	opened
August 1	Rising Sun	opened

1925 (continued)

October 29	Shilbottle	opened
November 9	Throckley	opened
December 21	Hartford	opened
December 21	Dudley	opened

1926

January 19	Seaton Burn	opened

1927

July 14	Montague	opened
September 12	Heddon	closed
December 14	West Cramlington	closed

1928

April	Midgeholme	opened
September 17	West Cramlington	opened
October 16	Hauxley	opened
October 16	Newburgh	closed
November 28	Burradon & Coxlodge	closed

1929

May 14	Coronation Pit	opened

1931

December 31	Lynemouth	opened

1932

January 19	Bebside	opened
February 20	Edward Pit	closed
March 17	South Tyne	closed
June 21	Prudhoe	closed
June 21	Barrington	closed
June 21	Plenmellor	closed
June 21	Preston	closed

1933

August 21	North Wylam	closed
December 4	Barrington & Plenmellor	closed
December 4	Church Pit, Wallsend	closed
December 4	Preston & South Tyne	closed
December 4	Acomb	opened

1935

| February 11 | Low Midgeholme | opened |
| March 21 | Nelson Pit | opened |

1936

February 8	Scremerston	opened
March 28	Low Midgeholme	closed
June 19	Barmoor	opened
August 11	Wallsend G Pit	closed

1937

July 12 1937	West Sleekburn	closed
July 30	Melkridge	opened
November 24	Whitechapel	closed

1938

| February 8 | West Cramlington | closed |
| October 28 | Blucher | opened |

1939

| March 31 | Benwell | closed |
| October 3 | Dinnington & Seaton Burn | closed |

14

NORTHUMBERLAND MINERS'
MUTUAL CONFIDENT ASSOCIATION

Branch Secretaries as at 12 August 1929
SOURCE: Burt Hall records

COLLIERY	SECRETARY
ALGERNON, Backworth	J. Convey 2 Turner Street, West Allotment
ASHINGTON	J. Wallace 55 Eighth Row, Ashington
BARRINGTON	N. Reavley Gladstone House, Bedlington
BEBSIDE	T. Pattie 32 Front Street, Bebside
BEDLINGTON	J. Ricalton 29 Shiney Row, Bedlington
BENWELL	John Chapman, MP 121 Farndale Road, Benwell
BOMARSUND	T. W. Allison 16 West Terrace, Stakeford
BROOMHILL	John Jobson 141 Hadstone Row, South Broomhill

BURRADON	George Bell MP
	29 Middle Row, Dudley
CAMBOIS	G Bryson
	6 Watergate, Cambois
CHEVINGTON DRIFT	T Barrass
	26 Simonside Terr., Chev. Drift
CHOPPINGTON	W A Brown
	4 Sixth Row, Choppington
CHURCH PIT, Backworth	Fred Cuthbertson
	18 Duke Street, Shiremoor
CORONATION	J Baker
	20 Simpson Terrace, Blucher,
	Newburn on Tyne
COWPEN	John Mordue
	15 Cowpen Square, Cowpen
CRAMLINGTON, ANN	J. P. Dobson
	29 Terrace Row, Cramlington
CROFTON	N. G. Mordue
	20 East Row, Isabella Pit,
	Newsham
DINNINGTON	G. M. Scott
	19 Augusta Terrace, Dinnington
DINNINGTON, West Moor	J. P. Horner,
	1 Palmersville, Forest Hall
DUDLEY	T. Gray
	19 Middle Row, Dudley
ECCLES	J. M. Patterson
	15 Lamb Terrace, West Allotment
EDWARD PIT, Wallsend	Edward McAndrew
	48 Rawdon Road, Wallsend

ELLINGTON

Stephen Ryan
52 Ariel Street, Ashington

ELTRINGHAM

John Cameron
9 Eltringham Colliery, Prudhoe

HARTFORD

T. Elliott, JP
9 Everard Street, Hartford

HARTLEY

A. C. Smith
24 Hastings Gardens, New Hartley

HAUXLEY

George Hope
16 Leslie Row, Radcliffe

HAZELRIGG

J. Walker
7 Lambert Square, Coxlodge

HEDDON

A. W. Anderson
The Square, Heddon on the Wall

HOLYWELL

H. McKay
7 Lamb Terrace, West Allotment

LINTON

T. Patterson
2 Milburn Road, Ashington

LONGFRAMLINGTON

James N. Robson
'Devonia', Longframlington

MARIA, Throckley

J. Mitford
Somerset House, New Throckley

MAUDE PIT, Backworth

Augustus Smith
56 Killingworth Ave, Castle Park, Backworth

MICKLEY

H. Pattinson
Hall Yard Cottages, Stocksfield

MONTAGUE

J. McKay
123 West Road, Pendower, Benwell

NETHERTON HALL

W. P. Armstrong
7 Plessey Street, Netherton

NETHERTON HOWARD

H. Taylor
19 First Street, Netherton

NEWBIGGIN

C. B. Simpson
5 Thirlmere Terrace, Newbiggin

NEW DELAVAL

W. Wilkinson
28 Winship Street, Newsham

NORTH ELSWICK

Thomas Burtle
7 Derby Street, Newcastle on Tyne

NORTH SEATON

Robert Curtis
14 Institute Row, North Seaton

NORTH WALBOTTLE

W. Hendry
8 Coley Hill Terrace, North Walbottle

NORTH WYLAM

F. Maddison
9 Algernon Terrace, Wylam on Tyne

PEGSWOOD

A. Patton
57 Cavendish Place, Pegswood

PERCY PIT

Robert Douglas
The Cottage, Bell's Close, Scotswood

PLASHETTS

James Hymers
Tile Row, Plashetts, North Tyne

PLENMELLOR — Nolan
10 Lorne Street, Haltwhistle

PRESTON — J. Atkinson
23 Lansdowne Terrace, North Shields

PRUDHOE — J. Kennedy
96 Castle Dene, Prudhoe Station

RISING SUN, Wallsend — W. Rivett
33 Gibson Street, Willington Quay

SEATON BURN — W. Dunbar
19 Low Cross Row, Seaton Burn

SEATON DELAVAL — J. Fenwick
2 Camp Terrace, Seaton Delaval

SEGHILL — A. Maddison
Station Road, Seghill

SHANKHOUSE — J. Kerr
9 Stephen Street, Hartford

SHILBOTTLE — G. W. Bartram
7 The Crescent, Shilbottle

SLEEKBURN — James Routledge
37 South Row, Bedlington Colliery

SOUTH ELSWICK — J. Metcalfe
37 Elm Street, Benwell

SOUTH TYNE — A. Makepeace
6 Ashcroft Terace, Haltwhistle

STOBSWOOD — J. Parks
14 Edith Street, Widdrington Stn.

THROCKLEY	Thomas Kearman 23 Pine Street, Throckley
WALLSEND	W. Grayson 31 Jubliee Street, Wallsend on Tyne
WEST CRAMLINGTON	A. E. Bell 19 Cross Row, West Cramlington
WEST SLEEKBURN	R. Norris 29 North Row, West Sleekburn
WEST WYLAM	Henry Dunn 2 Clive Street, West Wylam
WHITECHAPEL	Charles Ingledew 5 Hawthorne Terrace, Bardon Mill
WHITTLE	E. Dowling High Street, Felton
WOODHORN	William Ross 43 Juliet Street, Ashington

Note that there were 68 collieries still operating in Northumberland in 1929.

The number dropped dramatically, according to the NCB map of 1956.

Now (1999) there is only one deep-shaft mine left in the north of England, Ellington Colliery.

15

HORDEN COLLIERIES LTD
1929 Publicity Booklet

A perusal of the following will demonstrate to the reader the continuous efforts made by the Horden Collieries Ltd to keep abreast of modern demands for a uniform quality of fuel.

For many years the London Gas Companies have regularly taken large quantities of Horden Gas Coal. This same quality also finds a ready market in Berlin, Paris and other Continental Cities.

The Screened Steam Coal is used extensively by Railways at home and on the Continent.

The Manufacturing and Bunker Coal both rank as First Class Durham quality and a large business in being built up with Coaling Stations in various parts of the world.

Skilled Chemists are constantly employed sampling and analysing the various products with a view to improving the quality still further.

The Company's four Collieries, Horden, Blackhall, Shotton and Castle Eden, are designed to win an area of about 28 square miles of coal in the South East of Durham County.

The important industrial shipping districts of the Tyne, Wear and Tees all lie within a radius of 25 miles; the nearest port, Hartlepool, is within 10 miles.

Facts and figures

Coal raised per day	12,000 tons
Employees	8,750
Tubs in use underground	9,000
Underground haulage roads	48 miles
Private railway sidings	19 miles
Ponies	830
Houses built by Company	3,361

The coal is drawn from the Main, Low Main and Hutton seams and is specially prepared for Gas and Coke-making and Steam-raising.

The coke is of excellent quality for Blast Furnace purposes and Nut Coke is cut to sizes suitable for central heating etc.

Horden Colliery

This is the largest Colliery in the group and the output has reached over 6,000 tons in one day, probably the largest quantity drawn at any colliery in the British Isles.

There are three shafts, two 20 feet each and one 17 feet in diameter, sunk to a depth of about 200 fathoms from the surface, all utilised for coal drawing.

The Seams at present being worked are the Main, Low Main and Hutton, and vary in thickness from 3 feet to 5 feet 6 inches.

Steam, Gas and Coking Coal is produced.

This Colliery has been laid out on a large scale in view of the vast area of Coal to be worked. Consequently all main ways are of permanent structure and of large dimensions to admit of ample ventilation to distant workings.

Special facilities for riding the men to the Coal Face are provided in the Hutton Seam. These enable the men to start fresh and save travelling time.

An aerial ropeway delivers the refuse into the sea.

Blackhall Colliery

Coal drawing was commenced in 1914 and the output now exceeds 3,350 tons per day. The two shafts are each 22 feet in diameter and 193 fathoms in depth from the surface.

There is a large well-equipped Coal Depot about half a mile South of the Colliery on the main road from which various grades of Household Coal are supplied by motor lorries direct to the residents in the neighbouring towns.

An aerial ropeway, as at Horden, delivers refuse into the sea.

Shotton Colliery

Ths Colliery was sunk in 1840 and after working for 36 years was abandoned. It was re-opened by this Company in 1900 as their first venture. The output now reaches 2,600 tons per day.

There are two shafts each 15 feet 6 inches in diameter, sunk to a depth of about 200 fathoms from the surface.

Brickworks situated about half a mile south of the Colliery produce 120,000 wire-cut common bricks per week.

Castle Eden Colliery

Castle Eden Coal was noted for its quality at a time when only exceptionally good Coal was worked. The Colliery was drowned out in 1892 and acquired by the Horden Company in 1900. The flooded workings are being unwatered and re-equipped. The 2,000,000 gallons of water at present being pumped to waste daily will be harnessed at the source and shortly delivered in a clean state to the local Water Company for domestic consumption. When the pit is so relieved Coal development will commence.

It is expected eventually to draw 1,500 tons of Coal per day. All the Plant, including winders, is electrically driven.

Housing

When operations were commenced at Horden in the year 1900 there were neither railways, main roads nor houses; even water for steam-raising had to be carted. Today there is an up-to-date township of 14,000 inhabitants.

Altogether the Company has built more than 3,000 houses and spent over £750,000 in this respect. In addition a considerable number have been built by the local Council and private builders.

Facilities have been provided by the Company to enable those men who wish to own their houses to purchase them on easy terms by weekly payments.

Streets, houses and business premises are all provided with electricity from the Colliery mains.

The domestic water supply for Horden and Blackhall is also provided by the Company from their own reservoirs.

16

MEMOIRS OF A MINING ENGINEER IN DURHAM

N. R. Smith

N. R. Smith, OBE was born near Manchester in 1911, one of a family of seven. He obtained a first-class Honours degree in mining engineering at Birmingham University. In 1983 he explained to the readers of the Nottingham University Mining Department Magazine *how he got involved in mining in the first place:*

I became a mining engineer almost by chance, mainly because I found Latin an impossible language to learn. I came up the school on the Modern side, finishing with three years in Maths VI, and here I obtained a Higher School Certificate with a distinction in Maths. My family expected that I would win a scholarship to Cambridge (where my two brothers had gone). But then came a big snag. In those days, to get into Cambridge at all, one had to pass a fairly simple exam in Latin, called 'Little-go'. This dead language was all double dutch to me, and I began to despair that I should ever learn enough to pass.

But then, just before the Easter holidays, a man from the Mining Association (which then represented the mineowners) came to the school to talk to the senior boys about the prospects, for public school boys, of a career in the mining industry. I managed to get permission to spend two weeks of the holiday at Pendleton Colliery, not far from where I lived. This contact set me off.

I accepted with alacrity the offer of a scholarship of £60 per year to enable me to read mining engineering at Birmingham. My professor there had recently written a book called *Gases, Dust, and Heat in the Mines*. Undergraduates being the same everywhere, this book was soon known as *Lasses, Lust, and Heat in the Mines*. I still have my copy.

After getting my degree, Professor Moss, who had a good many contacts in the mining industry, arranged for me to go to County Durham to complete the three years' underground experience I needed before I could sit my Colliery Manager's Certificate. So I went to Horden Colliery, which was the biggest in Britain at the time (1933). The output was 6,000 tons a day, which never varied by more than 20 tons per day, thanks to a clever 'borrowing' scheme which was operated successfully, but clandestinely, by the colliery manager. But 6,000 men and boys were employed, and the mining village was far from salubrious. It comprised row after row of rather mean houses, and streets were known as numbers instead of names. I remember that the furthest from the pit was 38th Street.

Here, although a University undergraduate, I was paid what I thought was a very meagre wage of £3 a week. Out of this, 30 shillings had to go on digs, all found, at no. 2, Pit Row, and I had to keep myself on the rest. After two years at Horden, I was 'taken over' by Lambton, Hetton and Joicey Collieries, who sent me for my last year to Silksworth Colliery, now closed. But I had a princely increase in salary, to £4 a week!

I had a feeling of great trepidation when the chairman at Lambton, Hetton and Joicey told me that, assuming I got my Ticket at the forthcoming examinations in November, there would be an undermanager's job for me at one of their pits. After an agonising suspense, the exam results were what I had hoped for. I was now the possessor of a First-Class Ticket of Competency and, provided I was over the age of 25, I was qualified to be a colliery manager anywhere in Britain.

On January 1st, 1937, I was appointed undermanager at Lambton D pit, probably one of the youngest undermanagers here. The salary was £7 a week, paid weekly in cash. I moved to new digs, nearer the pit, the address of which, appropriately enough, was no. 15, Success Cottages, Philadelphia, County Durham.

I stayed for two years, and in 18 months I had saved up £100, on the strength of which I married a girl from Lancashire I had first met many years earlier and fallen in love with at first sight. She is still my wife. During these years I had seen little of her because of the distance, my impecuniosity, pressure of work and paucity of leave. We set up house, more or less on orange boxes, in a free colliery house, with free coal and a full-time gardener. On £7 a week we even ran a car: an old Morris Cowley two-seater, given to us by a friend as a wedding present, which he had bought for £5. Our house was at the end of a row occupied by other colliery officials, and looked out over green fields to Lambton Castle. Our neighbours were very kind to the newly-married couple, giving us presents of fish they had caught and other 'goodies' from their gardens. So we started married life happily, and felt we were reasonably well off.

Late in 1938, I applied successfully for my first manager's job, and at the age of only twenty-seven became manager of Mosely Common Colliery, near Manchester, responsible for 2,000 men. I had two years there, then, following an explosion which killed several senior officials, I was moved to Astley Green Colliery to supervise recovery work.

In 1943, Pease and Partners, of Darlington, appointed me as the agent of their Fishburn and Thrislington pits. So I missed by a narrow margin my ambition of earning a four-figure salary by the time I was 30. Later, following the sudden death of the previous agent, the firm sent me as an agent to their East Hetton Collieries. My letter of appointment said, quite simply. 'A suitable house is available for your occupation—The Grange, at Trimdon Grange.' The word 'suitable' was just about the biggest understatement of all time. When I first saw it, the property seemed vast. There were ten bedrooms, four bathrooms, a corridor upstairs 25 yards long, two staircases, and the hall was panelled with polished oak timber which had come from the *Aquitania*. There were two full-time gardeners to look after about six acres of garden, a stable-block with stalls and loose boxes, a mechanic to look after and service my car whenever I wanted it, and the sole shooting-rights over about 2,000 acres of farmland. Decorations, inside or out, could be done, free of charge, whenever we wanted it, and if anything went wrong in the house one just rang up the pit, and a man came immediately to put it right. We were almost 'titled gentry' in the locality, and I admit to being spoiled for ever after. Our official address was simply Trimdon Grange, Co. Durham—surely one of the shortest in the country. Perquisites, in those day, were so extensive that they were often worth as much as the salary.

So far as our many full-time gardeners were concerned (and this was confirmed by my own experience in the pits) the working people in county Durham seemed to speak a foreign language, of which, at first, I comprehended very little, though they always seemed to understand me when I spoke to them in English. In relation to one of our gardeners, my wife swears to this day that the only thing she ever understood of his speech was 'Good Morning' and 'Good Night'.

I had a rather similar experience down the pit, initially at Horden. Everybody was talking about chummins: there was no chummins; they were waiting for chummins; or the chummins were off the way. Finally I asked a small boy what the word chummin meant. He gave me a pitying smile and said 'Divven't ye knaa what a chummin is, Mister? It's an empty full'un.' What a splendid definition. Years later I happened to come across a word spelt teeum in a dictionary. It was defined as a word of Norwegian origin, meaning 'empty'. Then, daylight appeared, and I realised that this word, and its many variations, must relate back to the many hundreds of years of trading across the North Sea. This also explained the meaning of 'teeming', heard in relation to cargo ships on the Tyne and Wear. When ships were said to be teeming or lading, it merely meant that they were either unloading (emptying) or loading.

Early in 1947, soon after the nationalisation of the mines, the Coal Board moved me to Seaham Harbour to take charge of the former Londonderry Collieries. There were three pits: Seaham Colliery, an old pit known by the locals as The Knack; second,

Dawdon Colliery, sunk late in the last century, and now doing very well thanks to an extensive face-lift some years ago which involved getting rid of the old double-deck cages, and installing skip winding: third was Vane Tempest, a name which has connections with the Londonderry family. This was sunk early this century, right on the edge of the North Sea, about two miles north of Seaham. It was thought to have vast reserves of very good thick coal for many miles under the sea. But in recent years unexpected serious geological troubles have been encountered, and there are now [1983] doubts as to whether this pit has any real future.

I count myself fortunate that I was never involved in a major accident which caused loss of life, but there are other incidents, some amusing and some of interest, which are worth recording. Before I was married and was an undermanager in County Durham, the manager and his wife invited my fiancée to stay with them for a weekend. This pleased me greatly, because I seldom saw her, but soon after dinner the first night, the pit phone rang and would I go to the pit at once, as there had been a serious outburst of water. Note that, as I was away from my digs that evening, I had had to leave a phone number where I could be contacted.

When I got to the pit, I found that some colliers, working a small piece of thick coal left many years before by the 'old men', had thirled into some water-filled goaf, and the water was now gushing out in a torrent.

So I spent the rest of the weekend at the pit, organising the supply of 4in. pipes and supervising the installation of a pipeline, nearly a mile long, which would conduct the water to the pit sump. During the whole weekend I saw my fiancée for no more than two hours, but I learned a great lesson, of which every young mining engineer must take heed. No matter what your personal plans may be, in the event of an emergency, abandon all your arrangements at once, and remember that the job must come first and take absolute priority over everything else.

Some years later, one Saturday afternoon, I was on the field at Seaham, playing cricket, when someone came out to say that I was wanted immediately at Dawdon as there had been an incipient spontaneous heating. I left my innings unfinished, dashed home to change into pit-clothes (there were no pit-head baths in those days) and when I arrived at the pit I was greeted by my old friend Alf Coulshed, the local rescue-station manager. I had known Alf for many years because he had trained me as a rescue man when he was manager at Houghton-le-Spring rescue station, and I was serving my time at Silksworth.

We proceeded on foot for nearly two miles, and just as were turning off the intake road, we were surprised to find a birdcage, containing two lively canaries, hanging up in the fresh air. About 200 yards further on, in some bord and pillar workings, and well out of the fresh air, we found two colliery-rescue men digging out heated material and loading it into tubs.

'What's the idea leaving the canaries outbye?' asked Alf. 'Don't you know they are provided for your protection?'

'Oh, yes, Mr Coulshed,' said one of the men, 'but ye see we only bowt them a fortnight since and they cost thirty bob; we aren't ganna take the risk of anything nasty happening to them.'

Although I had been always known as 'agent' for the NCB, this word must have had some unacceptable private enterprise connotations and, as far as I know, the NCB has never used it since. So my new job, though still being the same as an agent, now carried the cumbersome title of sub-area production manager. We had to live in Seaham in a large but ugly red-brick semi-detached house, and this seemed an awful come-down after The Grange at Trimdon. Seaham was a mixture of very old pit houses and a lot of new stuff. All the old has now gone but, even so, I don't think Seaham is a place anyone would choose to live in voluntarily. My office was right on the sea-front, and bitter winds always seemed to be blowing in over the North Sea. It was often said that the climate was healthy—if you could stay alive.

Mr Smith moved from the North-East in 1951 and later became Area General Manager for No. 6 Area, in the Midlands, retiring in 1972; he is also a past president of the Mining Society.

17

SPENNYMOOR SETTLEMENT, 1931

Modern Spennymoor was built on mining. It had its origins with the sinking of the Whitworth Pit in 1839 and was later linked with the Dean and Chapter Colliery. The first inhabitants of Spennymoor, like those in most pit villages, had to endure squalid living conditions, as detailed in this Local Government Board report of 1874:

Nothing could well exceed the nuisance attendant on the disposal of excrement and refuse in Spennymoor, There are entire streets without any closet accommodation whatever and in its stead open boxes are placed opposite nearly every door-way for the reception of excrement, ashes and other refuse; an arrangement which, besides being revolting to every sense of decency, is stated to be offensive in the extreme, especially in hot weather. It is impossible to walk between the rows of cottages without being convinced that the surface of the ground is to a large extent composed of the overflowing contents of these midden boxes. The back streets stand in filth and mud.

In 1931 the famous 'Spennymoor Settlement' was set up to provide a recreational centre with drama and art groups, and a wide range of other educational facilities. Tisa Hess, a German artist, was invited to teach at the Settlement. Here are a few extracts from her diary of 1936:

December 1936, County Durham. Rows and rows of men were standing in the drizzle. They stood there with drawn shoulders rather like birds perched on a bough on a wet day. So they stood, crouched, squatted, hundreds of them. Unemployed miners. Quite a number of them had nowhere to go. They had rented a bed which they used in shifts. The pubs weren't open all the time. The 'asylum' for the homeless, which was overcrowded, was closed from ten in the morning until five in the afternoon. They waited in the cold for hours on end.

A social worker had invited me to the Durham coalfield to give lectures on art and wood-carving lessons in the miners' clubs. Up to 200,000 miners had been out of work. They were on the dole—too little to live, too much to die.   Some of these men had been unemployed since the great miners' strike of 1926.   A number of mines, which were antiquated anyway, had been flooded, some had never re-opened.   The mines were small, most of them in private ownership.

There were retraining courses as early as 1936. There were vacancies in the south, but the men refused to go. A man got £1 6s. a week, his wife 12 shillings, and there was 7 shillings for each child. To put up a dog in London cost more than the 12 shillings for the miner's wife. The men did not seem in the least bitter; they were good-humoured and relaxed. You could count the communists on the fingers of one hand.

In 1936 I was put up in a hostel where several social workers were living. Or, to be correct, people doing social work on a voluntary basis. One was a well-known Himalayan climber, two were girl students. In 1937–38 I was invited to stay with Bill and Betty Farrell (the first Warden and his wife) in their Settlement in Spennymoor.

The Settlement was like a small 'pit university'. Supported by a £500-per-annum grant from the Pilgrim Trust, the Farrells had rented a small house with an adjoining shop, an empty place with a joiner's bench, a pine table and chairs. Volunteers helped by teaching art and drama and by giving lectures.   Bill had been an actor; he succeeded in starting a good amateur dramatic group. It was a place glowing with intense inner life, something quite outstanding in these drab and dreary surroundings.

The houses in the village had been built wall-to-wall. They ran uphill, downhill. Neither shrub nor bush was to be seen. Slums. The plan of these miners' cottages: no porch, one living-room downstairs with the hearth and open fire, a small scullery behind, and stairs leading up to two tiny bedrooms. Mattresses damp all the year round.

One talented man who benefited from the activities at the Settlement was the late Sid Chaplin, one of the North-East's finest writers, while another was Norman Cornish, one of the few miners who went on the paint professionally. Here are some of Norman's thoughts:

Many Durham towns owe their beginnings to the fact that a pit happened to be sunk in that place. Spennymoor was such a town, but the pits sunk in the area about 1839 did not last long. A huge ironworks was also started, but it too did not last. Eventually what had been a boom town of 20,000 people had very little work for its population. Many of its workforce were obliged to find work at collieries in neighbouring areas, which fortunately were developing.

Spennymoor was then, like today, a working-man's town with its long main street cutting through its centre, and its terraces of two-up, two-down houses built on either side. Perhaps the most imposing building is the centrally-placed Town Hall, which boasts a tall clock-tower. Immediately in front of this clock was Oxford Street, and in this street, almost in the shadow of the tower, I was born on 18 November 1919.

Oxford Street, along with many others, has long since been demolished. The housing conditions in those days were very primitive. Generally speaking, the houses had no bathrooms, gardens or indoor toilets. An earth closet or nettie, as it was locally called, sufficed for a toilet. There were several epidemics of diphtheria, smallpox, scarlet fever, etc, which was not surprising— indeed at the age of seven years I myself contracted diphtheria.

Some of my early years, from about three to five, were spent with my maternal grandmother, who lived a short distance away. In those days houses were lit mostly by gaslight and a penny gas-meter stood in the corner. I remember playing with marbles in front of the fire on a home-made clippy mat. On the mat was a complicated pattern, and in my mind the pattern was imagined as rivers, roads, mountains, etc. as I deployed my marbles—imaginary soldiers—across it. In the winter when it began to get dark in the afternoon my grandma would have a nap on the couch, leaving me to play in the gloom. The fire would flicker and cause the shadows of the velvet tassels of the mantel-cover to jump about on the ceiling, and I would lie on the mat fascinated by this ballet dance. I was too young to realise it then, but the afternoon nap cut down on gas bills.

When I was eight years old the Arcadia cinema at the end of our street was burnt down. It was discovered in flames early one morning. My brothers and I hurriedly got out of bed and rushed our clothes on to watch the high flames from the top of the slagheap.

Although I was doing quite well with my studies at school, it was difficult for my parents to find the 'wherewithal' to supply me with school uniform, satchel, woodwork overall, etc. Father was now out of work, and by the time I reached fourteen I began to realise that my chances of a college or university career were very remote indeed (even though my father had just managed to get employment at a nearby colliery). It was 1933, and the Depression years were well upon us. I was the oldest in an ever-growing family, and there were no Local Education Grants in those days. In short, I realised that I had to start work. My father reluctantly took me to his colliery to try to get me set on.

The pit, called the Dean and Chapter Colliery, was nicknamed locally as the 'Butcher's Shop', owing to the number of workers' accidents there. I was offered a job as an underground datal lad, and when I signed on the dotted line the official said in his deep voice: 'You've just signed your death warrant, son'— quite a happy start to working life! I spent Christmas 1933 as a schoolboy with the rest of the family, but in the early hours of the following morning I was destined for a dramatic change.

On Boxing Day 1933, at 14 years of age, I became a working

man. I set off to walk the two miles to the pit at two in the morning. It was pitch dark, and I felt very apprehensive as I walked through the tunnel under the railway embankment at the street end. I remember being relieved when it snowed, and everything became lighter.

The above is taken from A Slice of Life, *published by Mallaber Contemporary Arts; what follows is Norman Cornish's contribution to* Homespun, *published by Northern Voices in 1992.*

I was a boy of ten when the Settlement started, and I was 14 when I joined. I'd seen a poster in a shop window, a nice poster, and it informed me of the Spennymoor Settlement Sketching Club. At the time they were having their annual exhibition so I made a point of going down. It was November, cold and dark. I went into the Settlement, to a little room where they'd taken the lampshades off for more light. It was a very interesting exhibition. I was transformed. I was delighted and I was in and out of like a yo-yo every night.

I asked 'Could I join?' and the oldest member, who was quite an accomplished watercolour painter, asked 'How old are you?' and I said 'Fourteen, mister.' 'Oh,' he said, 'you're a bit young. Come back when you're fifteen.'

It was pretty obvious to me that he thought being a kid I'd be a bloody nuisance because all the other members were grown-up men. I was very disappointed. A year went by and the next exhibition came along. And in I bobbed and said 'Can I join now, mister, I'm fifteen?'

This time the Warden, Bill Farrell, was present. He told me years later that he was quite intrigued by this little black-haired boy full of enthusiasm. No way was I not going to be a member! However, I became a member and I'm pretty sure I wasn't any trouble to them. I was very keen to learn. It was joining the Settlement that sustained my interest. At school you did drawings, but when you start work you get cut off from things like that—you forget about it.

I was a member for years, very enthusiastic, putting pictures in the annual exhibition. And to my surprise it created a lot of interest, because I drew people of my own family: my father getting washed in the bath from work; my brothers pulling their socks on; and my mother toasting in front of the fire. It seems that people were interested in that.

The newspapers began to cover these exhibitions, and they dubbed it 'The Pitmen's Academy', which was a bit silly. It was a nice headline for them, but it wasn't strictly accurate. Bill Farrell wasn't a miner, although, as Warden, he was an active member of the Sketching Club; Bert Dees was a painter and decorator and the oldest and most experienced member of the Club, though he'd never been a miner. Jack Roche wasn't a miner—he was a blacksmith. Then, during the war years, we had people who came to Spennymoor to work in factories, and some of them joined the Sketching Club; one was Mitchell McKenzie, a commercial artist from Edinburgh.

I, of course, was a miner, together with John Heslop and George Warren. It would hardly be 50–50—a bit of a misnomer being called 'The Pitmen's Academy', but the name stuck. It was a kind of university. It wasn't what you were taught, it was the experience, the little bits of conversations you got into, the way you learned how to be self-sufficient, the way you somehow got to know yourself and became more self-confident in your thinking process.

Most of us used to go down and draw actors on stage during rehearsals. In a strange way, all this homed in on us without our realising it. All these various influences, from O'Casey to Bernard Shaw to Shakespeare, rubbed off on me—a kind of university education!

18

GROWING UP IN A COLLIERY VILLAGE
Sir John Hall

Sir John Hall's ancestors were Dunelmians. They crossed the Durham border in the middle of the 19th century plying their dangerous trade of shaft-sinkers. Their first Northumbrian stop was at West Sleekburn, and from there they began sinking the first pit shaft at North Seaton in 1859. His grandfather and father worked at the same pit and, had he not shown a degree of intelligence in gaining a scholarship, young John might have followed them into the oblivion of that particular mine.

But John Hall avoided the fate of many of his peers who were destined to become hewers of coal or bangers of metal. Although he was unaware of it at the time, his destiny was to be shaped in the red-brick Grammar School built alongside the railway track near Bedlington Station.

It was an apprehensive, grey-flannelled, 11-year-old who jumped aboard the 8.45 a.m. two-carriage Dilly at North Seaton Railway Station in September 1944. Behind him, the regimented rows of colliery houses lay huddled together for warmth on the doorstep of the raw North Sea. Ahead of him lay a ten-minute train ride that was to carry the pitman's son on a journey into the world of high finance, culminating with the glittering prize of a knighthood and control of one of Britain's leading soccer teams, Newcastle United.

But in the 1930s, when John was in his formative years, prizes were as difficult to win as low seams of coal, and obstacles had presented themselves to the Halls of North Seaton from the beginning. Sir John observed:

When you've never known anything else, you grow into your environment, and that is what I did at North Seaton, a little colliery village on the outskirts of the main town, Ashington.

My father owed a lot to Methodism for his way of thinking, as I do myself. There were two Methodist chapels in North Seaton; one was Wesleyan, which I went to, and the other was Primitive. On a Sunday evening it was 'The Glory of the Lord' from all sides. They were both competing for business, and in their eyes they were both right, until economics forced them to amalgamate.

Methodism is fairness, and I've never forgotten that. We have a chapel here at Wynyard Hall, and I've never really forgotten my Methodist roots. I'm an entrepreneur, worth a lot of money now, but I never forgot my roots. The friends I had then are the friends I have today; they stand by you in good times and bad times. I try to put over capitalism with a social conscience, enterprise with responsibility, and that's the Methodist background. You need people. You can't do without each other, no matter how much you think you can.

My father never used to have any money to speak of, same as the rest, but he liked a game of cards. And there would always be a card school going at the Welfare, with the room filled with baccy smoke. My mother would say: 'Gan an' get yor father for his dinner!' So I would go in and shout: 'Is Geordie Haall in here?' 'Waat do ye want?' he would grumble, and so on. My father was always in foreshift, he would never change—it suited him. He came in at eleven o'clock in the morning, had his dinner, went to bed, and he was up and out of the house at six. He never took my mother out— the night was his. She did her proggy mat while my dad was at the Welfare.

I went in there one night as a young lad when a card game was going. Now, gambling was illegal, and when this policeman came in they had to play cards with one hand over the money so that he couldn't see it. He knew all right, and just stood there and laughed. But they never got into trouble.

A lot of my spare time was spent at North Seaton Miners' Welfare Hall with its dancing and billiards. We've always played billiards and snooker there—everyone was a great player. I learned to play with my dad. There were some brilliant players, far better than what you get on the telly now, and no one taught them how to play. Men like John Jacques were tremendous players.

North Seaton was a lovely place. Yet, as you try to make your way in life materially, you look down on where you've come from, and you think you're so much better than them. But when you get older you realise that that is a load of nonsense.

There is always someone in a village who runs the place. The colliery manager was at the top; the headmaster was second; then the doctor; then the trade union man who organised everything. That man was Jimmy Wealleans, a councillor, and he ran just about everything, including the Flower and Garden Show. That was an annual event held in Armstrong's Field, beside the cemetery. It was always a lovely day, and we walked up what we called 'the Line', which was a mineral line coming in from North Seaton. We had to walk everywhere from the village until the buses started, but we never thought anything of it. Life was to be enjoyed, and it was great.

As a North Seaton laddie you could go flatty stabbing, and if you wanted a boat someone would give you one. I would go up the Wansbeck with the tide and then come back again. We had marvellous regattas every year; folks came from all over. It was great! I fished and went crab-hunting; there was a little island in the middle of the river—there's a dam there now—and when the tide dropped you could put your hand in, catch a crab and use it for bait. And then you went down to the links; watched the pit tubs come in; went to the pit pond; nature walks; collecting various things in the pit yard. There was a glorious freedom about the place.

I went to the infant school, which was in Office Row, where the pit officials' offices were based. Then I went to the junior school at the bottom of Railway Row where we lived. It was brick-built with inhospitable classrooms and old-fashioned heavy desks.

The senior school was at the other end of Railway Row which had

34 houses, and I can still remember everyone who lived in each house. That was a more modern school: a very good school. The headmaster was Mr Rhodes, and I passed the scholarship, which was my entrance to Bedlington Grammar School, under the tuition of a chap from Ashington, called Syd Nixon. He did so much for us and we didn't realise it at the time. He was a hard, hard man, but fair, and he made us work. It was him who got me through that scholarship.

Mr Rhodes lived in Newbiggin, and he was responsible for getting me my first job when I left Bedlington Grammar and couldn't find a position as a civil engineer, which is what I wanted to be. Rhodes told me that he knew someone who might give me a start in mine surveying. He rang Jed Brown, chief surveyor at Newbiggin Colliery, and that is how I got the job. I have happy memories of that school, and Bedlington Grammar had an enormous influence on my life, too.

The Grammar opened my eyes to what was happening outside our pit village. When I first started we didn't have flush toilets, we just had the earth closets over the road. And when I was invited to friends' houses, even though they were council-owned, the standards were way above what we had in North Seaton. That gave me a bit of a complex. But I got over it, and was introduced to all kinds of sport: tennis, soccer. I was a good footballer, captaining the juniors and seniors. I played for East Northumberland, but I never had the fine edge of, say, a Jackie Milburn.

At that time the school had a lot of very good footballers: the finest junior team in the area. And we took that complete team and played as West Sleekburn Juniors. The Tubbys were running it then. That was a fabulous team, and we won everything that was going.

Then there were the barn dances at the school, and all that social side of life which I didn't know existed. It was a revelation! It took me out of myself, and I still have very good connections with the school.

I was in the 'B' stream, never the 'A', always middle-of-the-road. I'm glad in some ways, because I think if you are too intellectual you are never a practical man, you're an academic, which is fair comment. In the second stream I found common sense and intelligence. I could still do things, and this is how I am what I am: an entrepreneur.

I made lots of friends: John Hewison whose father was a licensee of a pub at Choppington; Tommy Burns sat behind me at school, and he ended up as Ashington Colliery's last manager when the pit closed in 1988; other lads in the football team like Jackie Hogg, who later played for Ashington, Jeff Clarke, Pat Patterson, who also played for Ashington and was at Derby County; Micky Reed was a good centre-forward; Alec Tait was a year behind us and, of course, he played for England Youth and Newcastle United; Skinty Bowden was in goal, but the poor lad died during a game at the Larkies (Hirst Welfare). We all used to play two games on a Saturday: for the school in the morning and West Sleekburn in the afternoon.

Eventually, studying and courting changes everything—I went out with my future wife from Newcastle, so I couldn't play in the afternoon. But they were great days: playing tennis at the Larkies and up at the Recreation Ground at Ashington. The Rec was where the real tennis buffs played. George Browell and Eric Wallace were great players, much better than me. Then there was dancing at the Arcade; going to any one of the town's 20 workingmen's clubs. Great! It took me out of myself at North Seaton. There was nothing there. It was a closed environment.

Ashington was the big town, with its main street. You went there with your mother on a Saturday afternoon and while she went shopping you would go to watch Ashington FC play at Portland Park. People don't realise this, but the Metro Centre is built around that philosophy. The Metro Centre is Ashington main street under cover, and the Leisure Park is the Spanish City at Whitley Bay. There is never anything new in life. I kept telling people when we were putting the Metro Centre together that Ashington main street is where you met people. Your mother would meet Mary or Maggie, and the conversation would go something like: 'How are ye gannin' on? Have ye hord aboot Annie? She's expectin' again, ye knaa.' 'Never! And hor husband's left her!' It was the Coronation Street of Ashington. And then, when you went over the road from the Grand

Corner and stood in the queue for the Wallaw Cinema, the conversation carried on.

We used to go to the different picture houses; the Piv, where they showed all the adventure films which I wasn't supposed to see; then on Sunday nights you went to the Regal (when you got away from your parents). That was where you met the girls. You would let it drop: 'I'm going to the Regal on Sunday—will you be there?'

The area was stark. I remember Ashington's long colliery rows and its pit-heaps, which were huge and smelled awful. There were unpretty things to be seen, no doubt about it, but it still had a great influence on my life. That was because there was always a great joy about the town even when times were hard and there were shortages during the war, when you had to queue at different shops like Donkins for bread and cakes. There was Arrowsmith's; Chrisp's the newsagents; Keith Cazaly; and Jimmy Main's shop, where I got a bike at Christmas. And people used to think that these shopkeepers were oh, so rich. They were the hierarchy in Ashington. These was even a hierarchy in the managers and business people.

My mother used to take me to the Co-op Wholesalers, and she chose all my clothes then paid for them weekly at the Store. She bought me a long mac one day and a black and white scarf, because I often went through to St James's to support Newcastle United. One Saturday afternoon me and two mates went to Tilleys Restaurant in Newcastle before the match, wearing our long macs and scarves. But they wouldn't let us in! I could see through the door that inside was the 'Gosforth Set', dressed in the fashion. We had these long macs and scarves, but apart from that we were clean and tidy—we were canny lads! When I was building the Metro Centre I said I was going to get my own back. I was going to build a 'Tilleys' and I was only going to let my friends in from Ashington! But that taught me a lesson—being kept out of Tilleys—you had to learn your place, and your place was firmly set for you.

There was a nice dance-hall behind the White Elephant—the Parish Hall—and we had some great times there. Oh, the ham and pease pudding sandwiches that they used to put on! Delicious! That was where the Bedlington Grammar School lads used to congregate.

And then we graduated to the dances at Ashington. I remember Joe Dalkin thumping away on the keys with half of his fingers missing. There was the Arcade with singers Eric Nichol and Connie Allsopp; the Harmonic Hall; and then the Roxy in Blyth. The Clayton in Bedlington was out! We never went there—that was very rough. I met my wife at the Oxford Galleries. It was where everybody met their future wives.

The Grammar School made me, and I wish now that I had gone to University, but my mother never understood the implications, and neither did I. When I first went to the Grammar in 1944, it was still fee-paying, and it was like that until the Labour Party changed it a couple of years later. So my parents let me make my choice. I said I would just leave school and start work. What they should have done was force me to stay on, and then I could have gone on to University. My exam passes were good. I passed seven subjects, all with credit.

When I came out of Grammar School I couldn't get a job—I wanted to be a civil engineer. I tried council after council. They talk about getting on your bike now: that is what I did, pedalling all over the place. But I was always pipped; the jobs were always spoken for. Then my old headmaster, Mr Rhodes, rang up and told me to go and speak to Jed Brown, chief surveyor at Newbiggin Colliery, and he set me on.

I didn't want to go to the colliery. I had a tremendous argument with my father. I told him straight that I wasn't going down the pit. He said: 'Take the job—any job. Get into work, or you will grow lazy and not want to work at all. It's better to get a job if you've been employed.' And that is a maxim which stands in life today. That is what I keep telling students when I give a talk. I tell them: 'If you are a good artist then go away and be an artist; if you are a second-rate cricketer go and play cricket, so long as that is what you want to do.'

I am an entrepreneur, and what I do best is 'real estate'. We tried as a company to get involved in other things, but it didn't work out. So now I keep to what I know I can do. [*This latter comment was made prior to Sir John taking over as chairman of Newcastle United in January 1992.*]

Whole generations of my family were in mining. They worked at North Seaton pit, which was owned by the Cowpen Coal Company. My grandfather helped to sink the shaft. My father worked as a filler, having gone through all the tasks of being a datal hand and putter laddie. In the end—and this is what made me disillusioned with the pits—he was moved from North Seaton when it closed to Woodhorn, to Newbiggin, and eventually Ellington. Like the other miners, he was told by Alf Robens, NCB chairman then, to keep moving to where the jobs were. Father died on £12 pounds a week and £1 a week pension. My mother had his certificate for 50 years' service, and I have it now. And I wonder 'What was it all for?' Their generation definitely missed out.

Our parents never had anything; they were a section of the society who never had the good times—they always had the bad times. They had a few decent years under the Labour government after the war, and then, when the pits got into trouble, they were the first to suffer. So they didn't have anything, and the wages they did have were poor. They got a week's holiday then a fortnight's holiday —so what! They didn't have any money, perhaps a few quid in the Store bank, but they had no chance to save. They couldn't save, not like today when people have surplus income.

My father taught me the work ethic. He said: 'No matter how bad your employer is, you've got to work for him, but if you don't like him—get out!' I used to think that he wasn't wise, but full of wisdom. And it wasn't until many years later that I knew what he meant.

I went to the the pits, and the funny thing is that I enjoyed the work. That's where I met Jackie Milburn's pal, Raymond Poxon. I was fifteen and a half years of age, and Raymond was my boss. We had a great time, although going into a pit cage for the first time was frightening. On my first drop, as the keps were pulled away, we seemed to drop like a stone. Then, when we were halfway down, a joker piped up: 'Aye, this is the exact spot where the rope snapped a year ago to the day.'

Going into Newbiggin pit was a nightmare. Most of the seams were under the sea, and there would only be about 80 feet of rock between you and the North Sea. The water poured in through the cracks and crevices, and you could hear the boats chugg, chugging away just above your head. One day a joker brought some seaweed down the pit and threw it up so that it hung from the roof.

One day we were measuring up in a house in Ashington, and it transpired that there was a different family living in each room. To get up the stairs we had to climb over dozens of shoes on every step.

Those years working for the NCB were among the happiest in my life. We sank the Drift at Lynemouth, went down Woodhorn Colliery and Ellington. The pits were booming, money was there to be spent, and it was just a tremendous time. And there was a marvellous camaraderie and spirit in the office. Raymond had this portable telly, and if England were playing football on a Wednesday afternoon we would make sure that we were out of the pit for two o'clock. Then we would sit in the office with our cans of beer and enjoy the match.

We went to lots of NCB dances at the Rex Hotel in Whitley Bay —bussed ourselves there and back. And we thought we were so grand, sitting in this posh hotel, sipping glasses of Mateus Rosé. I wouldn't have a glass of that now if I was paid.

If Ashington appeared never to have changed in the 1940s and 1950s, it was because it had a static business when the pits were going strong, and there was no need to change. Had they looked ahead they would have seen that there should have been changes long before the pits started to close. Ashington never had a lot of private housing. Whether they were wanting to keep political control I don't know. But all the new housing was based at Stakeford. That was where I bought my first house, on Leeches Estate. That was the first mass exodus; the houses were sold up overnight with people queuing up to buy. The whole area was static for a long time and change was forced upon them in the end. You have got to know where you are going, and unless you have strong leadership you will fall behind until change is forced upon you.

I think that Ashington as a town should be telling the world about its successes. If they stand up and moan that the area has 20 per cent unemployment, that will do no good at all. Businessmen don't want to hear about a town's failures, they need to be told of all the good points.

The town has done well with its industrial estates, Riverside Park, and other leisure amenities like the Woodhorn Colliery Museum, but there is still a lot to do if they want to prosper even more. At Wynyard we intend to spend £1,000,000 on marketing all that this huge estate has to offer. We are in direct competition with Ashington and other former pit villages, attempting to bring new enterprise to this part of the M1/A19, which I believe is ripe for investment. Ashington is on the tip of this branch of investment potential in the North East, and it must work all that much harder if it is to succeed.

I know it won't make them popular with the poll-tax payers, but they have to say: 'We know that road needs resurfacing, and we are aware that building needs repairing, but we are not going to do it this year; we are going to spend the money on publicising the town, looking to the long-term prosperity that such a move will bring.'

I think Ashington and the district around it spawned so much talent because there was a great deal of commitment by the individuals concerned. There weren't just the footballers, there were artists, musicians, singers. Lots of gifted people. And the thing they had in common was a burning desire to succeed in spite of their environment. You could liken it to the hungry fighter who wanted to get on at any cost. For Jackie Milburn there was only the pits or football; he had no other choice. There was once a saying that if you shouted down any pitshaft in the North-East for a centre-forward to play for Newcastle United you would get half-a-dozen coming up. I wish we could do that today!

Every generation throws up its own crop of talent. There are still opportunities for people from former mining communities to attain a high degree of excellence—probably far more now than there ever was. But they must have the kind of will power and dedication that served the pitmen of the past so well.

I have lots of happy memories of North Seaton, Ashington and the people. Very happy memories. I am pleased that someone is putting pen to paper and preserving the history through the memories of the local people before it is all forgotten and lost forever.

19

MINING MILESTONES IN THE 19th AND 20th CENTURIES

1815 An engine called the 'Iron Horse' exploded at Newbottle, killing or wounding 57 bystanders.

1818 Netherton Colliery sunk.

1831 Shaft sinking began in South Hetton, County Durham.

1834 Sinking for coal began at Thornley, 9 January.

1835 Coal taken to Seaham Harbour by private railway.

1838 Murton Colliery sunk, 18 February.

1857 Six men killed at Seaton, nicknamed 'Nicky-Nack Colliery'.

1863 Northumberland miners vote to split with Durham and form their own union.

1865 Thomas Burt becomes first full-time Agent for the Northumberland miners' union, based in his own house in Blyth.

1866 Northumberland miners hold first 'Picnic' on 11 June in a field between Bog Houses and Shankhouse, near a pub, the Albion, owned by Paul Jamieson, known forever after as Pauly's (Polly's) Folly.

1870 Colliery sunk by Trimdon Coal Co. at Deaf Hill.

1872 The total output of coals in Great Britain was 123,386,758 tons, and the industry employed nearly 400,000 men and boys. Average production for each person worked out at about 314 tons. Smallpox rampant at Easington Colliery.

1880 After the great explosion at Seaham, rescue operations took place through the High Pit at Seaton.

1882 27 May, *Morpeth Herald* advertisement for the Morpeth Quarry Colliery gives prices of Best Screened Coal at 6s. 6d. [32½p.] per ton, orders left at Joseph Walton's, Rutherford's Yard, Bridge Street, Morpeth. Another advertisement on the same page asks colliery owners to bring all their dead pit horses to Licensed Slaughterer John Bell, Staiths Quay, Bedlington Furnace.

1885 John Wilson, of county Durham, prominent member of early Durham Miners' Association, was elected MP for Houghton.

1892 Strike in County Durham sees Peter Lee elected as check-weighman at Wingate Colliery.

1895 Northumberland miners' union now based in Northumberland Road, Newcastle; new headquarters named Burt Hall. Inscribed on foundations stone: 'Erected in 1895 by the Northumberland Miners in recognition of the valuable services rendered by Thomas Burt MP, as their General Secretary for 27 years.'

1900 Northumberland Aged Miners' Homes Assocation formed. Within the next 21 years the Association built 218 cottages; 20 groups of ten houses were built at Longhirst, Ashington, Newbiggin, Woodhorn, Chevington Drift, Bedlington, Cramlington, Newsham,

New Hartley, East Holywell, Walkergate, Backworth, Denton Burn, Dinnington, Prudhoe, Throckley, Annitsford, Gosforth, Cambois, and Westerhope; two groups of eight were built at Haltwhistle and Choppington.

1913 Electricity used for the first time at Murton Colliery.

1919 Deaf Hill Colliery closed for six months owing to water feeders breaking in. Peter Lee elected Chairman of Thornley Council. Sankey Royal Commission Report in favour of nationalisation, but ignored by Lloyd George.

1920 Under the Mines Industry Act, provision was made for the establishment of a fund for the improvement of social conditions for miners and their families. Many NE colliery villages opened new welfare halls and built parks, sports grounds and other amenities.

1924 First pit-head baths opened in Northumberland at Ellington Colliery, 15 March. Cubicles were provided for boys and officials, with two separate bathrooms for visitors. Total cost £12,000.

1926 Miners' Welfare Hall opened at Thornley, County Durham, as did those at North Seaton and Dudley in Northumberland.

1926 The year of the Great Strike. with miners out for six months. On May 6th, 1,000 adults and 400 children were fed at a soup kitchen by the Royal Antediluvian Order of Buffaloes at Ashington; by the third week of the strike, the Ashington Comrades of the Great War Social Club (the Comrades) had fed 6,000 women and children. Five hundred children were given soup and bread daily at Amble and West Moor.

1927 South Hetton village spends £4,240 of welfare scheme funds on an amusement park. First formal ballot for President of the Northumberland miners' union resulted in a win for William Golightly of Seghill, but there were 7,334 spoilt papers owing to some men putting crosses instead of numbers next to candidates' names.

1928 Klondyke Group of ten miners' cottages built with the 'Footballers' Group' money; raised by a committee sponsoring an Aged Miners' Homes Cup football competition. A foundation stone bore the name of the legendary Hughie Gallacher of Newcastle United.

1934 James Bowman, of Ashington, voted in as General Secretary of the Northumberland miners' union.

1936 Northumberland Miners' Picnic held for the one and only time at Newbiggin by the Sea; speakers: Ebby Edwards, Clement Attlee, MP, the Rt Hon. Arthur Greenwood, MP, and George Lansbury, MP. The Newbiggin Colliery band also won their section, with Cowpen and Crofton second, and Backworth third.

A total of 313 miners were provided with full travel allowance to visit convalescent homes at Gilsland, Whitley Bay, and Silloth

1942 In March, Blackhall Colliery miners went on unofficial strike, under strong attacks from the wartime press for being 'unpatriotic'.

1947 Vesting Day, 1 January, when collieries were nationalised.

20

EASINGTON DISASTER REPORT, 1951

Extracts from the report by H. C. W. Roberts, H. M. Chief Inspector of Mines, on the causes of, and circumstances attending, the explosion which occurred at Easington Colliery, County Durham, on 29 May 1951.

Narrative of the explosion

The explosion happened at 4.35 a.m. on Tuesday, 29th May. By a tragic trick of fate this was a time when there were two shifts of men in the district, 38 belonging to the stone-shift and 43 the fore-shift. Only one of these men was rescued alive, and he died of injuries a few hours later. According to the medical evidence, all the others, mercifully, died almost immediately. Two members of the rescue teams lost their lives in the recovery operation and so in all 83 persons were killed in the disaster. None of the 895 men at work in other parts of the mine was seriously affected. . . .

Cause and development of explosion

In the light of the evidence it was agreed by all parties concerned in the Inquiry that the point of origin of the explosion was at the retreating longwall face. There were other places, such as the junction at No. 22 Duckbill heading with the return, at which the lines of force indicated a possible origin, but in none of these, in fact in no place other than the longwall face, was any possible igniting source found.

Although electricity was so widely used, the evidence showed that it was not the means of ignition. Though some damage and defects were discovered in the electrical plant, it was shown either that they had been caused by the explosion itself, or that they were in such a position that they could not have given rise to the explosion.

In a careful examination no contraband was found. . . .

The evidence is that coal-cutter picks were moving at the time of the explosion, that they were cutting through pyrites, and that sparks from these pyrites proved, under test by the Safety in Mines Research Establishment, readily capable of igniting mixtures of firedamp and air. . . .

I have no hesitation, therefore, in finding that ignition was due to sparks caused by the cutter striking pyrites—a conclusion that was accepted by all parties at the Inquiry.

Easington Colliery Disaster, 1951

From Church of the Ascension Magazine

My Dear People,

It is difficult to write this letter at this time for no words can express our feelings for all that has happened. . . .

How wonderful people have been. I don't think any of us will ever forget the magnificent courage and dignity of the wives and mothers and fathers and relatives of the men we lost. They will know that our hearts go out to them, and here I am only trying to put into words what all of us feel towards them. They have shown us how men and women can endure in the most terrible trial that life brings us. . . .

The Church itself with its brightness helped everyone who came to it. We have to thank William Strike & Son of Sunderland for the beautiful flower arrangements in the sanctuary which they provided as a tribute to the men we lost. Our altar cross of miners' picks seemed more fitting than ever before, and paid its own silent respect to the bereaved and the men they lost. The use of the Welfare Hall for overflow services relayed from the Church and the admirable arrangements made by the Union leaders was of the greatest possible help. . . .The Miners' Banner looked magnificent above the altar at the Memorial Service. . . .

The collection in the the Halls raised £25 and this was sent to the Disaster Fund. In Church a collection was taken, and, as this came from the near relatives of our men, we are using it to buy a new silver chalice for use at the altar. It will be inscribed with the symbol of the crossed picks, together with the date and a short sentence....

Letters came from all parts of the country, from town parishes and mining villages in South Wales. Many people who knew Easington Colliery from our broadcasts sent their love and sympathy. . . .

Many of you have asked for extra copies of this magazine, and an extra 600 have been ordered and will be available after the normal distribution at the Vicarage. You will notice that the price of this double number is sixpence . . . all other parish enquiries should be made to Mr Robertson at 22 Seaside Lane. . . .

signed R. A. Beddoes (Vicar)

Letter of condolence

In June 1951, following the deaths of 83 men, letters were sent to all the bereaved families from E. H. D. Skinner, Chairman of the Durham Division of the NCB. This particular one was to Mrs Irene Jones, 1 Attlee Crescent, Easington Colliery, whose husband, Laurence, a filler, age 36, was killed in the disaster :

Dear Mrs Jones,
During the past few weeks you will not have been able to take much interest in happenings outside your family circle, and thus you may not have known how great is the sympathy expressed for you in many messages received by representative people in Durham.

Many such messages have been sent to me for you by people at home and abroad. I have written to thank them, and their names I have passed on to Mr Reynolds in order that he might inform the Miners' Lodge. But I think the time has come when I must tell you of two messages in particular of which in the circumstances you may not have heard.

One was received from His Majesty the King; the other came from the Flag Officer Commanding the Submarine Service. The original telegrams will be presented to the Miners' Lodge for safe keeping, but feeling that in days to come you may be proud to refer to these messages, I have had copies printed and am sending you one with this letter. . . .

I would very much have liked to see you to tell you all this, and to say how deeply I and other Members of the Durham Board feel for you in your bereavement. But, not wishing to intrude upon your privacy at this painful time, I can but write this letter.

Our sympathy with you, and with the other sufferers from this terrible disaster, is, I would ask you to believe, deep and sincere. I trust the knowledge of this and of world-wide commiseration will prove some consolation to you now, just as I hope that the achievements and successes of your sons will bring happiness in the future. They have our very best wishes.

With expression of condolence, I am,

Yours sincerely, E. H. D. Skinner.

21

A PITMAN'S DERBY
Mike Kirkup

It's the end of another shift. The end of another week's graft, and you are riding outbye on the main belt stretched full-length on your belly, travelling out from under the ploughed fields of Ashington Home Farm.

Near the shaft bottom, free ride over, you hurl yourself from the rubber belt, scattering pieces of small coal on to the rocky ground of the narrow drift. Inside the cage, the eyes focus on the thrupenny diddler of daylight at the top of the shaft, increasing in value as your precarious transport nears the surface.

You stumble out into the sunshine, guarding eyes from the unaccustomed fierceness of the light, and fumble in an inside-jacket pocket for a watch encased for safety in a round metal tin. It's five minutes to twelve noon, and you glance around to see other miners of like mind hurrying towards the lamp cabin. Pulling the hard black pit-hat from your head, you tug the cap-lamp from its slot. Off comes the leather belt, from which slides the heavy battery, left to clatter upon the shiny cobbles as you struggle to keep fustian trousers up with one free hand.

Now you join the queue at the lamp cabin, hobnailed boots shuffling impatiently all around. Your turn, and you place the lamp on a long wooden bench and hand over a small metal tally: your own private identity tag; proof that you are no longer down the pit; proof that you're safe . . . at least for another day.

The Ashington pit-head baths hadn't been built all that long. The mines were five years into a nationalisation which had promised so much but achieved so little. No privacy in the communal showers, with a naked marra (mate) entering the cubicle to wash away the coal dust from your back. Some miners were superstitious and thought that washing the back too often was strength-sapping. They were the original unwashed.

Getting ready in the clean-end is another mad scrush and there is jostling on either side from men throwing on their clothes in a frantic dash to be rid of the pit and all its trappings. But they can't—no one can—for even as they mingle with the rest of the population of the biggest mining village in the world on that fine Saturday morning, pitmen are betrayed by the dark rings of coal dust clinging to their eyelashes.

Then the bike-ride home, pretending you're Charlie Smirke on the Aga Khan's Tulyar, and the bloke 50 yards ahead of you is your kid brother on a cart-horse. You nail him with your one good eye, and just get up to beat him by a whisker as you flash past the winning line, which bisects Woolworths and the Linton and Woodhorn Miners' Union Hall. Hordes of Saturday-morning shoppers stop and turn at the sound of screeching brakes as you negotiate the Grand Hotel corner at breakneck speed. Dinner is consumed at the same crazy speed as your eyes wolf down Corsair's Nap selection gleaned from a floppy Newcastle Journal, propped up against the ubiquitous bottle of tomato sauce.

And now the foot-race to the bus stop. You are the top pro, Spence of Blyth, and that owld chep halfway up the colliery raa is Jack the Coalman, without a hope in Hell of beating you to the top of the street. And you breast the imaginary tape stretched between backyard gate and netty door, three yards inside even-time to record the fastest time in the world that year, just as the bus pulls around the Pavilion corner.

'Pass along the bus please', and the hard-faced conductress packs another twelve sardines into a tin that is already turning faces blue from lack of oxygen. Cigarette smoke billows around the bus, and you feel such an outcast because the one and only time you dragged on a tab it had made you retch.

'Anybody for the White Elephant?' and 40 pairs of eyes peer out of the single-decker bus windows to get a last glimpse of Ashington disappearing into the sooty blue-yonder. From now on it's foreign ground. A vile smell permeates the bus, and people stare into space, avoiding each other's eyes. They needn't have worried: the bus is just passing a rancid Choppington pit-heap, smouldering like a grumbling volcano.

'Hartford Hall anyone?' and a miner lucky enough to have a seat lifts his eyes from the Sporting Life. He surveys the stately building perched on the hillside and remembers the time he spent almost a year at the Hall, used as a rehabilitation centre for those injured down the pit. He had almost forgotten . . . but his gammy leg wouldn't let him.

Countryside now, completely alien to the pitmen. On the left is the old Cramlington aerodrome, and someone remarks about the airship that used to be housed there. Old heads nod in agreement: it's proving to be a good day out already. Two more pits in quick succession: Seaton Burn and Hazelrigg. Men stub tabs out underheel and squash racing papers into jacket pockets: almost there.

'Gosforth Park, anyone?' Need she have asked? 'Mind the step.' And we all jump off the bus, casting envious eyes through the windows of passing banana-coloured trolley-buses at the townies sitting inside. For the lads from Ashington there was still an uphill two furlongs to negotiate, shadowed by massive rhododendron bushes on either side.

It's the last Saturday in June 1952, and with pitmen being true men of the soil, they can appreciate the pink and purple blooms with their glossy leaves sporting 40 shades of green.

Nearly at the top of the hill now, and the adrenalin begins to flow as you hear the strains of brass-band music floating down to greet you. It is the same disabled soldiers troupe which had entertained the crowds since the end of the second war. Suddenly you see them, strung right across the road like barbed wire blocking your path.

Now you are in no man's land and the same old fella with the one leg is shaking his collection box in your face as you brush past. You feel you have to contribute or bad luck will pursue you all afternoon, just as it would dog these poor fellas for the rest of their lives. So your tanner goes flying into the box, and you are convinced that token gesture will keep you in credit with the Almighty.

It is the turn now of a dapper bowler-hatted gentleman to harangue the milling crowd: 'Get the Card—have a Gamble! Gamble till the Cows come Home!'

You recognise him as Kiwi, the same bloke who stands outside Portland Park dog-track, trying to flog his tips to rookie punters. A fresh-faced youth who cannot possibly be a pitman digs deep into his pocket and gives 'bowler-hat' a couple of bob in return for a small square piece of white card. 'Fresh-face' glances at the writing on it and thrusts it into his pocket lest anyone benefits from his meagre outlay. Passing the Border Minstrel pub you suddenly remember that it is named after the horse that won the Plate in 1927, for hadn't you just read it in Corsair's column? Corsair—a man you could have faith in, except when he was tipping horses.

There are more men now, this time waving official race-cards at you: 'One pound a card. Genuine information. Money-back guarantee if not completely satisfied.' And again some fool rushes in where angels and pitmen fear to tread.

Joining the queue for entrance to the course you jingle your pockets to make sure you can comply with the sign: 'Have correct money—no change given'.

Now you are at the turnstile and you hand your three-and-a-tanner over the counter before squeezing through the metal bars.

Yet another queue, this time for a programme. No need for a programme: you'll never get near enough to spot the colours, even if you did know whose they were. 'Beware of pickpockets' says the sign, and a hundred hands caress their britchy-arse pockets . . . just in case.

Another look at the watch spots the time at a quarter to two. Still a while before the first race, so you decide to mingle. You haven't a choice really, because the crowd here is so dense that moving singly is almost impossible.

A deeper than ever crush is grouped around a small table, behind which a man manipulates three cards in his hands, shuffling them around before placing them face down on the table. It is yet another con: 'Find the Lady'. A plant in the crowd shoves a pound note on top of one of the cards and the dealer simulates an aggrieved look as he turns up the card to reveal a red queen. 'Everyone a Winner,. folks,' shouts poker-face, paying a couple of quid to his sidekick. In step the dupes with their hard-earned cash, and another swindler starts off the afternoon on the right side.

Now you push a path through to the iron rails which bar the way into the Silver Ring. You squeeze your face against an opening, looking in envy at your more prosperous compatriots who have just that little bit more elbow-room. They also have access to the stone steps of the ramshackle stand which provides a better view and shelter from the prevalent north-east wind.

Beyond the Silver Ring is Tattersalls and, if you could have afforded binoculars, you may just have caught a glimpse of the flamboyant Phil Bull in his distinctive white panama hat, ambling around the Club enclosure. But here, at the popular end, that's your place, just as surely as if it had been reserved for you from birth.

As a Geordie lad who has worked down the pit since you left school at fifteen, you're a died-in-the-wool socialist—you can't afford to be owt else—yet you wonder who coined the magic phrase 'The Pitmen's Derby'. It is the year 1952, and probably nearer to belonging to the pitmen of Northumberland and Durham this year than it had ever done before.

For the previous 120 years the Northumberland Plate had been run on a Wednesday. Which was fine for the landed gentry, for whom each day was pretty much the same as any other. And it was OK for the tradesmen of Newcastle, as Wednesdays were traditionally early-closing. And it was great for the factory and shipyard workers who were given Raceweek off as an annual holiday. But the only chance the poor north-east miner had had to get involved with what was supposed to be his race was when he put his tanner-each-way bet on with the bookie's runner, all greasy cap and shifty eyes, who could be found in any one of the 20 workingmen's clubs that made Ashington the Las Vegas of the north-east.

Maybe the pit-townie got Race Wednesday off, but many a pitman never had the chance to attend any of the mid-week runnings of the Plate. How could he? If he was in the backshift he would be at work; if he was in the nightshift he would be getting ready for work; and if he'd been in the foreshift he'd be too knackered to get out of bed.

Almost time for the first race, and you rush across to the triple line of bookies shouting the odds. The tick-tack man in the white gloves is almost tying himself in a knot in an attempt to relay the prices from the Silver Ring. And the unwary punter standing out on the course suffers yet again, as he is forced to accept a price about his horse which is at least half a point less than in the other enclosures. But, as Esther Rantzen says, that's life. And you stick a ten-bob note into Honest John's flabby hand, point your finger in the direction of his board, and the bet is struck. Now it's a mad gallop to try to get some kind of vantage point, but you settle for a place near the rails, almost two furlongs from the finish.

'They're Off!' And you strain your ears to listen to the race commentary but it's a wasted effort: you can follow your next-door neighbour's sex-life far easier. A minute later the horses flash past you in a blur, but you catch sight of the number 9 on the saddlecloth of the clear leader, and that puts a few more revs on your pulse-rate. You've backed a winner—you're sure of that, and you float on a number 9 cloud across to the man who out of sheer generosity is about to quadruple your half a quid. For a moment your eyes fail to spot him and you fear the worst: he's done a runner.

But no! There he is, scowling into the faces of other successful punters as he dips into his bulging satchel, producing wads of green and white currency. At last you are face-to-face and almost apologetically you hand across what you're convinced is a winning ticket. The bookie tears it in half and in a bored voice enquires from his clerk 'Ticket Three Oh One?' The studious fellow with long sheets of paper held together by a bulldog clip scans his book.

'That's not a winner!' he exclaims. 'That bugger wasn't even shopped. I wish it had been.'

'What's your game, sonny?' asks the bookie, his fat red face growing more apoplectic by the minute. 'Trying to pull a flanker, eh? Now away with ye afore I skelp your arse.'

'But . . . I . . .' You skulk away, sure that everyone at Gosforth Park is privy to your wretched mistake. 'Wasn't even shopped', your voice echoes in a state of disbelieving shock.

In your wandering numbness you stumble across a couple of bookies who are laying bets on the Northumberland Plate — the third race on the card. Shrugging off your embarrassment, you scan the odds. With only six runners, it's the smallest Plate for 27 years.

Really, you have only come to the races to back one horse in the Plate: Souepi. Granted it's a stupid name for a horse, but, as Corsair had pointed out, even with a 12lb. penalty for winning the Ascot Gold Vase under 8st. 8lb. the previous week, it was still thrown in here.

It was what every pitman dreams about: a handicap certainty. The layers both had 4/5 chalked up next to Souepi. Oh no, not an odds-on shot! Another look at the Journal. Flush Royal was another to attract some attention; you could never disregard Captain Fawcus's selected. Maybe you should wait until the next race was over before you plunged on to Souepi. Perhaps you'd get evens for your money.

You make sure no one is watching before pulling out your wallet to check on the cash situation: you've still got ten one-pound notes, three half-crowns and a smattering of small change. More than enough to make a killing. The ten quid is earmarked for the Plate: that is sacred, whatever happens. But what if you could make the ten into 20? How quickly indecision turns to rashness.

So you thrash around the bookies prior to the second race: a two-year-old event for maidens at starting. You scan the boards. But what is this? You are distracted by a gaggle of noise and movement among the lines of bookies: there is a run on a horse, you know that because you've seen it all before.

A swirl of men clutching crisp white fivers ebbs and flows from one line to another, bobbing up and down for the best prices. But a price about what? You find yourself picked up and thrown around like sea-coal on the tide, and shout across to a fellow traveller 'Which horse is it?' And the reply comes drifting back to you, borne on a wave of misplaced optimism 'The favourite—it canna get beat.'

Then you are ungraciously beached in front of a flashy man in a check suit. He beckons to you with his hand: 'Well, what is it?' And you wave your ten pounds at him as if to say 'A pitman's money is as good as anybody else's.' But all you can manage is 'Favourite!' And he grabs your hard-earned cash and throws it contemptuously into his bag, grinning to his clerk: 'An even tenner, ticket number Fife-fife-seven.' And you suddenly realise you haven't been waving but drowning.

The loose change in your pocket rattles like Jacob Marley's chains as you stumble down to the rails to cheer on your ill-conceived wager. You wait impatiently. The horses could very well be donkeys taking part in the previous night's Donkey Derby at Brough Park for all you know of them. You listen for titbits of information from a chap who stands nearby, neck craning, his huge hands dwarfing the opera glasses glued to piggy eyes.

'It's got no chance,' he grunts at a neighbour. 'Not a bloody snowball's chance in Hell.'

What hasn't? you mouth silently. For God's sake, man, what hasn't?

'Information! That's your bluddy information for you!' And an angry man stuffs the glasses into his pocket and stomps off.

There is no need to try to pick out the horses as they stream past you, Indian fashion. And there is little need for the silent recrimination you heap upon your bowed head, trudging back to bury yourself in the animated crowd. With such an unexpected result, you wonder why the bookmakers are still scowling, but then . . . they complain whatever wins.

You have little appetite for racing now and, as the crowds descend upon the lines of bookies to place their bets on the Plate, you join the few dozen others who have already had enough for one day, sidling anonymously through a small wooden gate out on to the path that takes you back to the bus and then eventually to the pit.

The musical ex-servicemen have thrown down their instruments and crutches, and loll about on the grass drinking ale from large pint glasses. As you pass, your eyes meet those of the man with one leg and, for an instant, it is doubtful who bears the most pain. But you delve into your pocket and, setting two shillings aside for the bus fare, cascade the rest of your silver coins into the empty collection box.

That'll do for next year.

22

NATIONALISATION, TEN YEARS ON

Emanuel Shinwell, MP for Easington

from *National Coal Board—the First Ten Years* (1957)

The history of the coal-mining industry is not without its depressing features. The squalid conditions in the villages and townships of our coalfields, the blight of intermittent employment, the long and arduous hours of labour, the low wage rates, all conditioned by the economic power of individual coalowners, and the inability of miners to find employment in other industries; the victimisation of men who expressed themselves freely, and played a prominent part in trade union activities, together with the indifferent attitudes of successive governments in promoting beneficial legislation: all this created an atmosphere of crisis and bitterness which is not easily eradicated. Yet to dwell unduly upon the past can only serve to release embittered feelings, obscuring the many improvements that have accrued through national ownership.

However much the opponents of the new dispensation regret it the change was bound to come; the task of all who are associated with the industry is to remove as rapidly as possible the remaining defects; to create conditions beneficial to the mineworkers and of service to the nation.

It was my privilege to pilot the Nationalisation Bill through the House of Commons. If anybody imagines that was an easy task they are gravely mistaken. It is a remarkable fact, of which few people are aware, that although nationalisation was advocated for many years, when the time arrived to prepare the legislation there was precious little material to rely upon. So far as I am aware no blueprints were either in the possession of the Government, the Labour Party or the miners' trade unions. Previous surveys and investigations were confined to the production of a few pamphlets, reports of speeches and resolutions. It is true a private Member's Bill was debated in the House of Commons during the term of office of the first Labour Government. But its terms were unacceptable. As Secretary of Mines I had to say something in its support, confined to the basic principle of State ownership. The remaining provisions contained a mixture of Post Office administration and syndicalism. It failed to serve as a guide to the legislative proposals of 1946. Nor was the Sankey Report, which had strongly fortified the demand for State ownership, more than a bare outline of a scheme. A fresh appraisal was essential.

My choice as Minister of Fuel and Power lay between two broad ideas: ownership by the State with administration by the Post Office, or to vest the administration in an independent authority, leaving certain powers of direction in the control of the Minister. After prolonged discussion we decided in favour of the latter method.

Thus the National Coal Board was appointed and charged with the control of all assets, together with responsibility for Central and Area administration.

In retrospect it would seem that this decision was right, but in light of subsequent events it might have been wiser to have appointed a Board less functional in character. . . .

Naturally teething difficulties were inevitable; in the technical and other spheres they still exist, they are inseparable from coal production. But those problems were less troublesome than the disputes among members of the Board, which finally led to resignations.

'I should have appointed a small number of capable men to govern the industry and decide questions of policy, leaving the various functions to be carried on by mining engineers, the marketing, scientific, labour and financial experts. It should be placed on record that the wise diplomacy exercised by Lord

Hyndley, the Board's first chairman, prevented wholesale resignations and the complete collapse of the Board. . . .

Even the most bitter opponents of the nationalisation principle recognised that a drastic change in the structure and organisation of the industry was inevitable. The coalowners' representatives on the Sankey Commission of 1919 did not demur from the statement that 'The present system of ownership and the working of the coal industry stands condemned and some other system must be substituted for it, either nationalisation or a measure of unification by national purchase and/or by joint control.' It is true that the owners refused to accept that part of the report which advocated outright nationalisation; they preferred a modified scheme, in which private ownership played its part. . . .

Despite much ill-informed talk of a crisis in the coal industry, there is no demand for a return to private ownership. But is there a crisis in the coal industry? Of course, without the importation of coal the industry has failed to meet the demands of our industrial and domestic consumers. Nevertheless the NCB can claim to have increased annual output by no less than 25 million tons since the vesting date, which considering the difficulties which have beset the industry is no mean claim.

Is there a crisis because coal prices are too high? Percentage increases in coal prices are not higher on the average than the increase in other commodities, nor are prices higher than they are in any other coal-producing country.

Is the situation critical because mineworkers' wages are excessive? The average wages paid to mineworkers before the beginning of the war were about £3 weekly, they have now reached a level of £12. These are of course averages; some miners frequently earn much higher rates while day workers are receiving about £8 weekly. Compared with earnings in other trades the miners are not better off. It says much for the restraint that exists in the coalfields that miners do not exert their full economic power to force wages up to higher levels.

Are strikes too frequent? This is a familiar criticism both in Parliament and in the Press. No doubt there are too many petty and unofficial strikes, some unfortunately through failure to deal expeditiously with disputes at pit level. Yet they are no more frequent or devastating than are to be found in other key industries.

Critics of the NCB sometimes complain that far too much capital investment is available to the industry. The net capital investment since vesting date appears to be in the neighbourhood of £100 million . . . the amount spent by the NCB is far too little if the industry is to produce the coal required in the next decade. It is deplorable that we should be forced to import coal and cut down our exports. The loss entailed is substantial, but until the waste of years of neglect are overcome, and a large measure of reorganisation is brought about, it seems essential to import coal which can be injected into the manufacture of goods to be exported to our overseas markets.

No scheme of national ownership can succeed without the willing co-operation of all partners in the industry. Those include the Minister of Fuel and Power, the NCB with its functional directors, the Area Boards, the mine managers and their junior officials, and of course the mineworkers. Nor can we exclude the trade unions catering for the general body of the workers in the industry. . . . All the efforts in the direction of reorganisation, of mechanisation and expansion and of improvements in labour conditions will prove fruitless as long as the industry is based on the principle of 'Boss' and 'Worker'. It is in this sphere that progress has so far been impeded. . . .

No doubt in time all such problems will be resolved. The excellent efforts of the Board in the higher training of mines officials in technical studies and of personnel management, together with opportunities for the young miner to train for the higher posts in the industry, with tradesmen's courses and the like, will gradually eradicate the social differences, thus making for a real partnership.

The mineworker of the future will be more than a hewer of coal or a filler of tubs, he will be an engineer and a technician. Increased mechanisation, and perhaps the advent of automation in those pits suitable for the application of modern devices, will call for a higher measure of skill. . . .

There is no need for despondency regarding the availability of abundant coal supplies. It is estimated that about 43,000 million tons of coal remain for exploitation. Naturally seams will become deeper and thinner involving additional expense in working. But the resources of our scientists and mining engineers are far from exhausted. We may expect in future years a vast range of new devices for easier and more speedy production. . . .

Provided the basic conditions are satisfied, the coal industry can now enter upon an era far more satisfactory than in the past. For many long years to come coal supplies in abundance will be required to serve the nation's industrial needs. Increased power, the bulk of which can be derived from coal, is the essence of industrial and social advancement. The advent of atomic energy for peaceful purposes will not, as far ahead as we can see, replace coal as the principle source of our power supply, although it can undoubtedly serve an important ancillary purpose. Coal is still our native fuel supply, which not even all the oil discoveries have replaced. Indeed, it may well happen that excessive consumption of oil and the gradual exhaustion of oil resources may restore coal to its former supremacy.

23

EASINGTON RURAL DISTRICT, 1969
W. A. Moyes, from his book *Mostly Mining*

The economy of the area is still largely influenced by the mines, and employment for men and boys other than with the National Coal Board is not easy to obtain. Engineering and chemical apprenticeships can be obtained on Teesside and in Sunderland, and the presence of Peterlee with its two industrial sites has introduced a further element of variety, but still insufficient to meet the needs. The employment situation for women and girls has eased considerably and there are opportunities in factories, multiple stores and supermarkets -mainly at Peterlee. . . .

Although this present position [1969] represents a considerable improvement, the future of the area will include still more new and diversified industry and any industrial approach to Peterlee or to the villages must be welcome.

During the last few years some of the older collieries have closed because of exhaustion of economic reserves. Wingate ceased drawing coal in 1962 after being an important employer of labour for 125 years. Within a space of six years the closure of Deaf Hill and Wheatley Hill collieries has meant that one of the largest parishes of the Rural District has no working mine. In each case the pattern was the same, rumours were closely followed by Coal Board statements of phased closure. Many miners left the area, taking their families with them to find long-life collieries elsewhere. Transfer of a proportion of the workers to existing collieries within the area has meant increased travelling time and expense, often to jobs of reduced responsibility. Early retirement, salvage work and unemployment accounted for the rest.

The impact on the villages has not been so devasting as closures in the last century would have been. The increased mobility of labour meant that the villages without their mines can still remain residential with slightly smaller populations. Nevertheless, the occupation of industrial sites by other firms could do much to inspire confidence for the future. The age of many of the collieries within the Rural District is a matter for concern, and doubts have been cast upon the continuation of the pits at Thornley and at Blackhall.

The effect of industry on the landscape has always been fairly obvious because of spoil tips or pit-heaps, and this is a feature which has been much exaggerated outside the area. A large part of the land is distinctly rural in character, and as old tips become grassed over or planted with trees thisproportion will decrease. . . .

Unfortunately, the whole stretch [of the coastline] has been spoiled for the general public during the last few decades by the pollution of the foreshore with waste from Easington, Horden and Blackhall collieries. Tipping of waste is by aerial flight or directly into shallow water with resultant backwash of small coal, bits of wire, wood, metal and rubber belt. The washed-up coal has a commercial value and is collected in lorries for sale in nearby settlements. Collection on a casual basis has gone on for many years, but large-scale operation is a recent feature involving a number of firms bringing their lorries to the beaches at different points.

The nature of this commercial activity attracted the attention of the Crown Commissioners, who own the foreshore, and they decided that a royalty should be charged upon the coal. The Easington Rural District, as leaseholders, decided to sublet the collection rights at first to several firms and then to a single firm which constructed a road to the beach to minimise the damage.The firms which previously collected the coal took legal action 'to try to establish both their right to collect the washed-up coal and to continue to use Castle Eden Dene' (which Peterlee Development Corporation hoped to prevent). In the Durham Chancery Court a decision was given in favour of these coal traders but this was reversed on appeal. The access rights across Castle Eden Dene were to be the subject of action by certain individuals, but they withdrew their action and had to pay the costs to the Corporation.

24

NORTHUMBERLAND COLLIERY MANAGER
George Hetherington

The following is taken from a 1980 Presidential Address to the North of England Branch of the Institute of Mining Engineers:

I was a fourth-generation employee of Bedlington Coal Company, who were very conservative in their attitude to further education. I think it was a fortunate twist of fate which sent me to Ashington Mining School, sponsored by Mr J. Pumphrey, the newly-appointed Group Manager of the Bedlington pits, a few years after nationalisation. Mr Pumphrey was an Ashington man who had been undermanager of the Duke Pit, and whose father had been a prominent board member of the Ashington Coal Company.

It was an even stranger twist of fate which led me to spend the latter part of my career as manager of Woodhorn Colliery, then Ashington. I went to Woodhorn as manager in 1969. Unfortunately the colliery was a strong candidate for closure due to the thinness of its seams and the prevailing weakness of coal in relation to other fuels. However, it has survived a further eleven years by continuing to extract the very thin Lower Plessey seam, using Gleithobel ploughs with a high degree of skill and dedication, though with heavy financial loss. The pit will definitely close down in February 1981.

In December 1971 I was appointed Manager of Ashington Colliery. This was just before the National Strike. My first impressions of the Ashington miners were somewhat distorted because they were in the process of demonstrating to the NCB the seriousness of their militant threats by overtime bans and go-slows. I was particularly impressed by their expertise in operating a go-slow, in that there was neither rancour nor expression of ill-feeling towards management, but just a methodical and good natured grinding down to almost—but not quite—a standstill.

Like Woodhorn, the colliery was obviously well past its peak as a producer of coal and employer of men. It was largely a problem of how far to cut back in order to stretch out the reserves for as long as possible, at an acceptable level of financial loss. Some nine years later the colliery is employing 400 less men, losing a lot of money, and, as such, is a target for those who seek to strengthen the nation's economy by closing down uneconomic activities.

On the other hand, because of the social implications of job loss in a high unemployment area, it has the potential of becoming a cause to those who think economics are secondary to ideals. The main factor which swings the balance from one to the other is the prevailing national and international energy market. When alternative fuel is cheap and plentiful, as it was in the 1960s, it is difficult to justify keeping going an old mine with poor reserves.

At mines like Ashington and Woodhorn, which have been struggling for years under the threat of closure, the average workman gradually closes his mind to the possiblity and adopts a 'don't think about it' attitude. The most common response when the subject of closure is broached is: 'They have been going to close us for years, but we're still here.'

The prospect of job loss does not motivate men as it did some years ago. Attractive severance compensation and reasonable retirement pensions, together with transfer inducements, give a fair degree of comfort to the thinking of those with short-term ambitions.

The greatest resistance to closure comes from individuals and groups with deep local loyalties who see the erosion of jobs as a growing threat to the very existence of their town or village. These men are usually the active and inspirational components of the various unions, with a firmly established belief in the power of unified action. The task of maintaining unity within a mine and between miners has recently become much more difficult by the introduction of local incentive schemes. Men at long-life units, with higher earning potential, turn a less sympathetic ear to pleas for support from less fortunate and threatened neighbours. A manager's job in this situation becomes one of trying to avoid despair and keeping alive the spark of hope that the future holds some promise. Any success in overcoming old problems and thereby making possible what previously was thought impossible, has far-reaching effects on general morale and stimulates pride and confidence.

I thought it would be interesting to study the life cycle of Ashington Colliery, and attempt to separate the inevitable process of decay by extraction from the factors which are controlled by human decision and desire. As the colliery and the town were the creation of a single group of businessmen, the key to what was originally intended must lie with them; and since they were controlled largely by Quakers, whose lives were declared as being dedicated to the service of mankind, it is hard to imagine them contemplating a Klondyke-type society based on short-term exhaustible resources. The Milburns and Priestmans [major shareholders] were noted for the diversity of their involvements and long-term perception. On the other hand, they were not idealistic socialists; profitablility was their main objective and they would see no point in placing investment in any activity which was not likely to give them a good return.

A fair test of this assumption is to study the pattern of working available resources. ACC soon identified the best and most profitable seams and worked these almost exclusively from 1870 until shortly before the second world war. Inferior seams with shaft access, like the Middle Main, Bottom Main, Top Yard, and Maudlin, were ignored until very late in the colliery's life span. There was a short-lived attempt to work the Hutton seam in 1913 from a cross-measure drift in the south-east corner near the Stakeford Dyke. It was abandoned after two years and the seam was not reopened until the late 1930s. Similarly the Maudlin or Bensham seam was worked for a few years between 1905 and 1913, but again was abandoned until 1936. From this it is obvious that they had no great interest or intention to work the inferior seams.

Investment was concentrated on the development of new collieries to work the High Main, Yard, Low Main, and Brass Thill. Ashington Colliery seemed to have been designated as the administrative and main servicing centre of the expanding group, by the building of comprehensive workshop facilities, central stores, and new brickyard, shortly after the first world war. The future production was destined to come from new high capacity pits like Lynemouth, which was opened in 1931.

A paper published in *Colliery Engineering* in March 1951, under the title 'Modernisation in North Northumberland', describes the strategy of the Ashington Coal Company with regard to its own pits, pre-vesting date and the subsequent broadening of these plans to embrace other collieries such as Newbiggin. Briefly, the plan was as follows: No. 3 Area of the Northern Division of the NCB would have three main types of colliery. The smallest would produce 8,000 tons per week from locations near the outcrops. Next would be existing collieries enlarged to produce 15,000 tons per week until their reserves in the upper measures were exhausted—Ellington and Linton were quoted as examples of this category.

The main resources of the Area would be worked by three super-collieries producing a collective output of 80,000 tons per week. A typical example of the latter was Lynemouth Colliery. There was no mention of the role Ashington Colliery was expected to play. Newbiggin Colliery was to be closed and its reserves transferred to Lynemouth, as were those in the Low Main (5/4) of Woodhorn Colliery.

This rational approach to planning, without the constraints of company or colliery boundaries, was completely in accord with one of the main arguments for nationalisation as put forward by miners' leaders after the 1914–18 war. Unfortunately, Newbiggin miners put up strong resistance to the plan and their colliery was kept going, eventuallly closing in 1968. I mention this because I think it was one of the first examples of successful opposition by the Miners' Union to a policy decision which traditionally had been the unchallengeable right of the owners.

Nationalisation was looked upon by most Northumbrian miners as being a victory over tyrannical owners. Closing collieries for the purpose of improving efficiency, with consequent job loss, did not fit in with their expectations. Their influence in the corridors of power grew rapidly; unpopular owner figures disappeared from the scene and were replaced by men such as James Bowman, an ex-Ashington face worker, who had moved through the ranks to become general secretary of the Northumberland Miners' Federation in 1936. In 1950 he was made chairman of the Northern Division, and became chairman of the National Coal Board in 1956. He retired in 1961 after putting up a tremendous fight to retain miners' jobs in the face of overwhelming economic and political forces wanting to dismantle the coal industry because of the availablity of cheap oil.

It was natural that such leaders were somewhat inhibited by their special relationship with the men from whose ranks they had risen. If they made decisions which hinted at disregard for the full employment ethic, the co-operation of the unions, on which they depended so much to exercise their particular brand of leadership, would have been jeopardised.

This change of emphasis on the thinking of the men in control of the coal industry had a profound effect on Ashington Colliery. Instead of being cut back quickly to a size commensurate with its remaining reserves in the better seams, it was decided to maintain a large labour force for as long as possible. Face room was opened out in the Middle Main, Bottom Main, Top Yard, Maudlin, Hutton, and Plessey seams. During this period there were 60 hand-filled longwall faces being operated simultaneously.

The day-to-day management of a colliery of this complexity must have been extremely difficult, to say the least. Much credit goes to the management teams of that time, led by Joe Jones, Bill Riches, and Isaac Smeaton, who somehow kept the output around the million tons per year level until 1965. By then considerable reorganisation had taken place. All coal-drawing at shafts had been discontinued in 1962 and the output was delivered direct into a reconstructed coal preparation plant. The Woodhorn output was gathered into the same system in 1965.

The manpower had been reduced to 2,500 and the reserves in the upper measure were exhausted. The future of the colliery depended on its ability to work the Tilley and the Three Quarter seams. Results from the Tilley were poor, and when the Three Quarter was found to be over four feet thick at the southern section of the take, in contradiction to previous borehole information, there was a scramble to stop the Tilley and concentrate on the Three Quarter.

In 1972 manpower was cut to 1,200 and would probably have been reduced further had not social considerations, combined with a national shortage of coking coal, made it expedient to go into the Victoria Seam, using the difficult south access. There was misgiving when the coking market collapsed soon after the first Victoria face opened.

A series of successful retreat faces in the north Three Quarter, with seam sections between 40 and 60 inches, gave the colliery a boost between 1973 and 1977. However, the future looked bleak as each successive face in the north-east Three Quarter showed a thinning down to 30 inches, with a sandstone roof. Survival depended on the development of a method of work to cope with the new conditions. It so happened that at this time a relatively unknown shearer was available, manufactured by Eickhoff, and designed on the in-web double-ended ranging-arm principle. The first installation in 1975 using this machine was average in terms of work, but it did show the potential of this method of work, and a second face, modified from the experience of the first, proved a very consistent and productive unit.

Subsequent faces at Ashington and other collieries in the Area have confirmed the soundness of the system, which will probably be used to extract the remaining reserves. However, recent experience with a face at Woodhorn must bring ploughing back into consideration.

So there it is, Ashington past and present. From Milburn, Priestman and partners, with their ambitious enterprise, thrusting into what must have seemed an endless future, to the present socially well-equipped community choked with unemployment and uncertain of what lies ahead.

Since it started in 1867, Ashington Colliery has produced 92 million tons of saleable coal, of which 65 million were got from the High Main, Main, Yard, Five Quarter, and Low Main seams—the big five whose exhaustion has so often coincided with the closure of Northumbrian pits. I would like to think that the latter part of Ashington Colliery's life, whilst relatively unprofitable, has contributed, in its efforts to survive in the other seams, to the fund of mining engineering knowledge and technical experience which will be of value to others faced with the same inevitable problems which come to every pit.

25

THE PIT HEAP
Fred Reed

Ashington's own dialect pitman poet came out of the Duke Pit, where he worked as a drawer in 1930, to become a writer with the Ashington Colliery Magazine. Here Fred remembers the mountains of pit waste which surrounded every pit village in the north-east, but especially the one on the northern outskirts of Ashington, removed in the 1970s.

The Pit Heap

Horray! They've teun the blot away! The pooers that be are funny 'ns.
Us thowt its stench wuz heor t' stay. Phew! Rotten eggs and onions!
But noo the canny folks that dwell in collory raa abodes
At last can let thor lung-box swell, for noo blokes mekin' roads
Need dort t' feed thor speedway lust, and wor reed ash and clinkers
That med' the hairt-ache wesh-day dust frum such sulphuric stinkers.
He's gyen in screamin' trucks aall day that thunderin' doon wor lane
Hev' made y'ung parents waatch and pray and mebbies wax profane.
Yon heap filled hyems wi' dust and stink and tarnished paints and brasses

A plague, a fiendish corse, Aa think, on aal wor hooseprood lasses.
At neit the manmade mountain glowed and reeked and spat and
     twinkled,
And when the westorn air-stream flowed offended noses crinkled.
Aw! whaat a day of temper strain when claes weshed with high
     hairt
Should aal be tyekin' in again . . . the wind had changed its airt!
And while the wives wad sniff and froon, then t' thor claeslines
     horry,
A swarm of specks wad settle doon on clean weshed tarritory.
Abeun the heap the pit pond lay . . . a foul subsidence pool
Wheor with wor jamjars bairns wad play when on the wag frum
     scheul,
Plodgin' roond wi' soaken beuts, the education-haters,
For tadpoles, frogs and little newts us thowt war alligators.
Aa mind when jist an impish pup, a smaall playmate and me
Once pulled an oval bathtin up the steep-sloped pitheap scree.
We both got in and slid away, and cheered and yelled and
     chortled,
And nivvor war two bairns mair gay as doon the slope wuh hortled.
But, aw dear me, when halfway doon, the bath-tin cowped its
     creels.
Two imps spilled oot upon thor croon aall scratches, scrapes and
     squeels!
The big wheels and the pithead geor, the wagons 'nd the sidin's,
Us viewed each day withoot a feor the morn wad bring dark
     tidin's,
And aall wor labours heor wad cease King Coal wad abdicate,
His subjects findin' sad release, a lang dole queue thor fate.
Aa knaa the blot hes gyen at last, green fields cum inta view,
Strange silence broods wheor once the blast of despot buzzors blew.
But if them wheels could torn agyen wor joy me tungue could tell.
We'd put up wi' the blot and stain and dust and reek and
     smell.

26

NORTH-EAST AREA PITS AND PERSONNEL, 1973

SOURCE: *Colliery Guardian*

Northumberland collieries

Colliery	No. of workers down pit	No. of workers on surface	Manager(s)	Undermanager(s)
Ashington	1,062	210	G. A. Hetherington*	H. Swinburne J. Knox
Bardon Mill	237	33	D. Partiser	J. Scott
Bates, Blyth	1,573	307	Jack Spence† W. E. Hindmarsh‡	J. S. Brady G. Devine C. A. Bird J. E. Kenny
Brenkley Drift Mine, Seaton Burn	548	118	E. Thomas	W. Kidd
Burrandon	312	71	J. King	J. G. Lavendar
Dudley	493	82	J. Thompson	I. H. Gurnie
Eccles, Backworth			J. R. Stafford	J. Flanighan
Ellington	1,329	160	T. E. L. (Tot) Smith† A. Spratt‡	G. W. Allison T. F. Burns R. Ashurst
Fenwick, Backworth	485	124	W. Swanson	T. Wilkinson
Havannah Drift	727	84	G. Proctor	F. J. Richley

* Agent/Manager
† Colliery General Manager
‡ Deputy Manager

Colliery	No.of workers down pit	No. of workers on surface	Manager(s)	Undermanager(s)
Lynemouth	1,608	217	M. Widdas† J. E. Tubby‡ E. Dunbar‡	S. B. Burke R. Lillico A. E. Potts . A. C. Cessford A. Baggaley
Netherton	505	121	Tom Spence	P. N. Laird
Shilbottle, near Alnwick	637	142	R. Liddell	W.E.S.Blenkinsop W. T. Wayman
Whittle	537	119	C. Miller	J. H. C. Brown
Woodhorn	552	103	C. R. Fenwick	C. Kenny, J.Errington

North Durham collieries

Colliery	No. of workers down pit	No. of workers on surface	Manager(s)	Undermanager(s)
Blackburn Fell Drift	144	32	A. Button	D. Brackenbury
Boldon	755	185	T. S. Snowdon* W. Dumms‡	W. A. Heckles W. R. Nattrass
Eden, Leadgate	271	30	A. Hawthornthwaite	T. P. Watson
Herrington	915	214	S. Bainbridge† T. D. Hardy‡	I. Watson C. Dickinson
Houghton	293	91	T. A. Whitwell	J. Wilson
Hylton	542	159	P. J. Harris	P. R. Carling
Kibblesworth	785	106	A. Robson*	J. P. West W. Carr A. Gilfillan
Marley Hill (including Clockburn Drift)	681	126	A. Button	J. Devlin, J. H. Carr
Morrison Busty, Anfield Plain	480	68	A. M. Pollock	T. Beadling, A. Stephenson

* Agent/Manager
† Colliery General Manager
‡ Deputy Manager

Colliery	No. of workers down pit	No. of workers on surface	Manager(s)	Undermanager(s)
Nettlesworth Drift, Chester-le-Street	96	17	J. Robson	
Rainton, Leamside	87	19	S. B. Rochester	
Ravensworth, Birtley	261	27	W. Boggon	J. W. Hunter
Sacriston	222	36	J. C. Hughes	G. Richardson
Usworth, Washington	716	123	H. M. Sheil	W. Rutherford A. H. Smith
Wearmouth, Sunderland	1,883	370	T. Harbottle† J. A. Braidford‡ W. Day‡	R. Ramsey J. Melvin W. Mason F. Kerswell, T. Harrison, J. Slater
Westoe, South Shields	1,935	268	W. Williams† N. Box‡ R. S. Bunker‡ G. H. Rolfe§	G. C. Cullen C. F. Davis T. Gray T. Dalziel G. Maughan R. Foley

South Durham collieries

Colliery	No. of workers down pit	No. of workers on surface	Manager(s)	Undermanager(s)
Bearpark	451	50	R. Blance	vacant
Blackhall	1,244	321	J. K. Martin J. W. Dorrington‡	R Sanderson, R. Greenwell, R . Boulton
Dawdon	1,819	457	W. Carr† N. Revell‡ T. Selby§	J. G. Hough J. Carrick

* Agent/Manager
† Colliery General Manager
‡ Deputy Manager

Colliery	No. of workers down pit	No. of workers on surface	Manager(s)	Undermanager(s)
Easington	1,967	460	W. Bradford† J. R. Wood‡ N. Coates‡ H. M. Ridley§	J. S. Crocket I. Smith H. Senior
East Hetton	689	163	S. Charlton W. Iceton§	G. Smailes
Elemore, Hetton Le Hole	329	55	W. Hutton	G. Bruce
Eppleton	1,143	140	R. M. Scarr J. Lormer‡	H. W. Flannigan H. G. Watson J. Straughan
Fishburn	645	107	vacant	R. W. Bignall, G. Smailes
Hawthorn	38	90	vacant	vacant
Horden	1,414	413	J. D. Hesler† E. Young‡ E. T. Taylor§ J. R. Napier§	W. Wilson M. Cessford G. Fullard G. Heydon
Langley Park	462	70	T. L. J. Chiverton	E. T. Smith J. C. Sutton
Metal Bridge Drift, Ferryhill	198	14	J. Porter	D. Watson
Murton	1,168	200	F. G. Swan	J. Hughes A. W. Walker W. N. Owen E. Nelson
Seaham	753	275	W. R. Donaghue	B T Haswell, R. Reay, K. Liddle
South Hetton	455	135	J. Downes	S. Poulson
Vane Tempest, Seaham	1,232	312	K. Henderson E P Farrage‡	J. Readman D. Murray, T. A. Robson J. Parkins
Whitworth Park, Spennymoor	216	24	J. Porter	S. Pearson

* Agent/Manager
† Colliery General Manager
‡ Deputy Manager
§ Assistant Manager

27

A YEAR OF WINTER
Denise Robertson

Denise Robertson set her novel in the Durham coalfield during the 1984–85 miners' strike. The action takes place in the fictitious village of Belgate. Here are a few diary extracts from her book, as related by Fran, a young widow on a teacher-training course:

Wednesday, 22 February 1984
In summer the car-park would be a sea of cars, red, blue and yellow, disgorging families eager to enjoy the beach. Today it was empty, except for a man wheeling a bicycle in through the gate. Fran looked toward the sea. There was a tiny blob on the horizon, a cargo ship or oil rig drilling for coal. She felt a glow of pleasure. It was nice to stand here, warm in her sheepskin coat, and look at the grey North Sea.

The pit stood above the cliff, its wheel and headstock almost dwarfed by a mountain of stockpiled coal. Each day the papers were full of an impending strike, but everyone knew you couldn't strike with so much coal already on the ground. She had come late to the life of a pit village, but even she knew that.

Thursday, 15 March 1984
It was still dark in the bedroom but Fran could hear the clamour from the pit-head. The shift must be changing, tub-loading over, back-shift going down. The Durham coalfield had been officially on

strike for three days, but still the Belgate men were going doggedly to work. Yesterday there had been Yorkshire pickets waiting. A car had been overturned and stones thrown. A few Belgate men had turned back but the majority had gone through with Fenwick as their leader. Thinking of Fenwick she turned on her side, trying not to remember. It was useless. She would never be able to forget! Even now, three weeks later, the memory made her cringe.

Bethel had brought the news. 'It's Fenwick's pigeons. Gone, every one of them. Necks wrung, feathers all over the place. He's just sitting there holding the cock bird. It's dead as a dodo, but he won't admit it.'

Fran had gone round to offer her condolences. 'It was too late when I saw them, Mr Fenwick. Even if I'd dialled 999, it was all over by then.' The birds were laid out in rows in front of the cree, limp bundles that had once flown free, heads dangling from wrung necks. It was windy, and the fine breast feathers stirred. Impossible to believe they would never soar and circle and head for home.

Fenwick had not moved or spoken, and it frightened her. She had wanted to provoke him to some emotion, even grief. 'I'm so sorry, I know how much you loved them. People are saying it's because you were demanding a ballot before you would come out on strike—but you can't believe anyone would do such a thing. Not for such a trivial reason.'

Wednesday, 21 March 1984

'Well, they've done it!'

The smell of new bread was filling the kitchen but Bethel was flushed more with the light of gossip than the exertion of baking. So it had happened: after ten days of conflict the die was cast and Belgate was on strike!

Fran dropped her books on to the table and sank into a chair. 'When did they decide?'

Bethel was filling the kettle, words spilling faster than the flowing tap. 'The Union men came from Durham this morning. . . . 'Come out or else,' they said, and the daft buggers just downed tools and walked out.'

'Even Mr Malone?'

Bethel's satisfaction rose in the air like steam. 'Oh, yes ... "Our Jerry won't come out," she says this morning. "not without a national ballot," . . . an' the next minute he's slinging his pit-boots in the back passage and off down the club. She'll feel it now! Debt? They're up to their eyes . . . three wage-packets coming in and it's tick this, tick that. Her back garden'll be full of clubmen next week, they'll think she's growing them.' . . .

'Has Fenwick come out too?'

Bethel nodded. 'Him as well. They've cut their throats, throwing the rule book out of the window. They'll pay for that.'

Monday, 2 April 1984

As she half-listened to the dissertation on the teaching methods of Montessori, Fran thought about the strike. Belgate seemed quiet now that all the men had come out. There was only a token picket and apart from the odd rumble about Fenwick everyone seemed to be bearing up. But there was a strain beneath the surface. Yesterday she had waited in the bank as man after man queued to cancel his standing orders. Cars and mortgages and finance-company loans were all suspended, pending a return to work. As each one finished his business and turned away she had seen bewilderment in his eyes, and anger, and the beginnings of fear. . . .

There was a group of miners outside the pit as she drove home, huddled in a gateway, woollen-hatted and mufflered against the cold, but still shivering. A tattered banner proclaimed Coal not Dole and someone had sprayed Maggie Out on the left-hand gatepost. It was a relief to leave them behind and drive into the back street. Here, at least, normality reigned.

28

BRENKLEY MINERS' WIVES SUPPORT GROUP

'A Weekend to Remember'
Sheila Graham

Seaton Burn Colliery and its offspring, Brenkley Drift, existed for 147 years, between 1838 and 1985. The Drift made history by being the last to close in the Newcastle upon Tyne area. During the bitter dispute in 1984–85, miner's wife Sheila Graham and some of her friends decided to form a support group. This is how Sheila described one eventful weekend in Their Lesson Our Inspiration, *a book she later wrote:*

A march and rally was to be held in London on Saturday August 11th, 1984. We were women, we were against pit closures, and we didn't see any reason why we should not support the march and rally. It was to be held on the Saturday; our bazaar was on the Sunday. What a weekend in prospect!

On the Wednesday evening I had a coffee evening for Support Group members. We were excited at the prospect of our trip to London, even if we were a little apprehensive. However, as our arrangements were being finalised, we decided something was missing—we needed a banner! An old, washed-out bolster case, a black marking pen and a bit of floor space was all we needed. Doreen Telford outlined 'Brenkley Miners' Wives' on one side, and

'Howay the Lasses' on the other. Clare and Ruth, my nieces, and Alison, my daughter, carefully penned in the letters, and our banner was born. It was to accompany us wherever we went, whether it be fund-raising events or rallies. It was part of us; we were proud of it. It was a symbol of our unity.

Fourteen of us set off at around 4 a.m. on the Saturday, bound for the big city. Jimmy Anderson, our picket-van driver, volunteered for the job, not knowing what he had let himself in for. The journey to London was to be a build-up for what was to come during the rest of the day. We met up with other Northumberland miners' wives and their supporters at Doncaster service station. Because the picket van was full, we were asked by Ashington women to fill empty seats on their 'luxury' coach. We declined the offer as we wanted to stick together as Brenkley miners' wives. It was just as well, as we learned later in the day that their 'luxury' coach had broken down and the march had already started by the time they arrived in London.

As we travelled south we passed busloads of women on the motorway who were going to London for the march and rally. They were easily recognisable as miners' wives and their supporters by their home-made banners which, like ours, were adorning the bus windows. We waved to each other in acknowledgement.

We arrived in London around 10 a.m., remarkably fresh after our journey. The march wasn't due to start for at least a couple of hours, but already thousands of women were gathering. There were ever so many fringe political parties present, pushing leaflets and pamphlets on to us. I don't think any of us realised there were so many political organisations about. We were certainly politically naïve.

Jimmy left us and set off for Burgess Park, where the rally was to take place.

After the inevitable trip to the loo, we were stopped by a road sweeper. He encouraged us to have a good day and asked where our collecting-box was. When we explained that we hadn't brought one, he threw a crumpled pound note into Margaret Elliot's shopping basket and wished us the best of luck in our struggle. After thanking him we promptly organised a box for collecting.

While we were waiting for the procession to form, vanloads of placards were delivered. Their message read: Support the Miners and Victory to the Miners. We were also given Women against Pit Closure balloons, two of which we attached to our banner.

Earlier in the day, officials from the organisation had handed in a petition to Buckingham Palace. It was hoped to bring to the attention of the Queen the injustices and plight of the miners and their families.

Considering the massive crowds that were gathering, the organisation was remarkable and the atmosphere warm and friendly. We were eventually ushered into some sort of processional order. Northumberland and Durham women had the honour of leading the march. We, as Brenkley miners' wives, were at the end of the area grouping, just in front of the women representing the Scottish coalfield. Shortly before the march started, officials from the Women against Pit Closures organisation asked us to tear the top off the placards we had been given. This bore the name of a fringe political party, and we were all reminded that the march was not political but a measure of our solidarity with the NUM in their struggle. However, this reminder was soon forgotten.

After what seemed like an age, tension and excitement growing every second, the march set off, the main chant of the march being: Maggie, Maggie, Maggie—Out, Out, Out. You couldn't get anything more political than that! Here We Go and We Will Win were some of the kinder chants, and anyone paying attention knew exactly what to do with Margaret Thatcher or Ian MacGregor, 'Early in the Mornin'. And for us, being from Tyneside, 'Blaydon Races' featured at least half a dozen times.

They say the people from the North East are a friendly lot; well, the people on the streets of London that day were magnificent. They clapped us, they cheered us, and they encouraged us by telling us we were the best thing that had ever happened to their city. 'You are Magic' their posters read, and we felt like magic. What a way to see London; we marched 5½ miles through the capital, passing Big Ben, the Houses of Parliament, Westminster Bridge, and Downing Street (we weren't invited in for tea and sandwiches!). We passed by the Elephant and Castle and on to Burgess Park where the rally was to be held. The police, of course, were also out in force. We didn't want trouble of any sort, we only wanted to show our support and solidarity with the NUM. Some of the police were very nice but others lived up to their image and they certainly didn't allow us to collect during the march. Alison, along with our collecting box, was pushed off the pavement and into the roadway.

Nothing, but nothing, marred our day, not even the weather, The sun shone brilliantly all day. We marched, we chanted, we sang, we waved our banners, we laughed and then we cried with emotion. History was truly made that day as 22,000 working-class women converged on the capital with a genuine, massive show of solidarity, and although there were only 14 of us in the gigantic crowd, we felt part of a huge family, There was a great bond of unity between us all.